SAARC
Origin, Growth and Future

SAARC
Origin, Growth and Future

E. Sudhakar

GYAN

GYAN PUBLISHING HOUSE

NEW DELHI-110 002

SAARC : Origin, Growth and Future
(International Relation, Politics Current Affairs, Development Issues)

ISBN : 81-212- 0459-3
Library of Congress Card No. 93-900320

Published in 2009 in India by
Gyan Publishing House
23, Main Ansari Road, Daryaganj,
New Delhi - 110002
Phone : 23282060, 23261060
Fax : (011) 23285914
e-mail : books@gyanbooks.com
website : gyanbooks.com

Laser Typesetting at : Spectrum Media
Printed at : G Print Process, Delhi

PREFACE

Regional cooperation has gained new significance in the context of the increased competition among the developed countries, rising protectionism and growing crisis in the international economic system. The dilution of the North-South dialogue and the increasing emphasis on South-South cooperation also prompted the growth of regional cooperation in the recent times. One of such ventures of collective self-reliance and development is attempted by the states of South Asia which took the form of SAARC (South Asian Association for Regional Cooperation).

South Asia is a complex region with striking similarities in social, cultural and ethnic matters among its component states while there are sharp differences in their political systems, economies and political and strategic perceptions. While diversities divide these states, the similarities bring out their common heritage, common problems and common goals. This very complexity of this region witnessed a late and slow growth of the regional cooperation. SAARC, thus, has an unenviable task of achieving its objectives in a region this is never free from internal conflicts and tensions.

Against this background, the present study tries to probe into the evolution and growth of SAARC, the various factors that influence its functioning and its future prospects in the given political situation of South Asia and the world. This book also tries to throw light on the structure of SAARC, various areas of cooperation undertaken and the progress achieved so far.

The present study, which is an adaptation of my doctoral thesis, is mainly intended to be an inquiry into the whole gamut of international and intra-regional relations that have a direct bearing on the evolution, growth and the future prospects of regional cooperation in South Asia. It, therefore, concentrates on the political factors that influence SAARC rather than going into the details of various areas of cooperation undertaken by it. The main thrust of the study, thus, is that SAARC is primarily an offshoot of political compulsions of South Asia and as such regional cooperation could not take roots to a deeper level because there are still doubts about the political will and commitment towards regional cooperation on the part of the member states.

This book is intended to generate opinions of academics, policy makers and persons interested in the politics of the region about the role intended for and played by SAARC in bringing about a change in the political, social and economic conditions of South Asia and its people.

I am deeply indebted to Prof. B. Venkateshwarlu of Kakatiya University for the inspiration, encouragement and guidance given by him in doing this project, without which this work would not have seen the light of the day. I also owe a debt of gratitude to my friends Srinivas, Murthy and Sharth for their invaluable help. I have taken the help of a number of institutions and individuals and it becomes a long list to name all of them. I owe each one of them my sincere gratitude. Finally I thank my wife who has helped me in many ways right from the conceptualization of this work till its completion.

While I value the contribution made by many people in giving a shape and finality to this work, I accept the responsibility for any omissions and commissions that might have crept into it.

Kakatiya University
Warangal

E. SUDHAKAR

ACKNOWLEDGEMENTS

The basic inspiration, encouragement, guidance and assistance came from Prof. B. Venkateshwarlu, my supervisor. The largest contribution for the successful execution and completion of my work came from him. I have to thank his family members for bearing with my intrusion at their place at odd times also. I cannot thank Prof. Venkateshwarlu enough for his kind cooperation. I am ever so grateful to him.

I express my sincere thanks to the Department of Political Science, Kakatiya University, Warangal for admitting me as a research scholar and providing me an opportunity to do this study.

Prof. M. Kishtaiah, Department of Public Administration has inspired and encouraged me like a father-figure right from the beginning till the end of my work. I am immensely thankful to him. Prof. V. Bhaskar Rao, Prof. G. Srinivas Reddy and Prof. A. Amruth Rao have evinced keen interest in my work. I am thankful to them. Dr. K. Raghuram Reddy, Dr. K. Bhaskaramma, Dr. P. Hussain Khan and Mr. Krishna Kant of the Department of Political Science have been kind enough to encourage and assist me at various stages of my research work. I am particularly thankful to all of them.

Dr. K. Srinivasulu, Reader in Political Science, Osmania University, Dr. C.S.R. Murthy, IPO, Dr. H.S. Prabhakara, CEAS, and Mr. M.M. Kunzu, CEAS, School of International Studies, Jawaharlal Nehru University, New Delhi, Mr. Ashok Tankasala, Journalist based in New Delhi and Mr. Ch. Sharath Babu, of W.H.O. New Delhi have helped me in securing rare books and documents relating to my research topic. I owe them all a deby of gratitude.

Many people at various stages have contributed for the successful completion of this study. If I name them it will become a long list. But I am very much thankful to each one of them.

My sincere thanks are due to various Institutes, Centres and Universities which I have visited to gather information on my research topic.

I thank my wife and children who have many times during this study relieved me of my family obligations and cooperated with me in completing this work successfully.

Last but not the least, Mr. N. Komura Reddy has given a reasonably good and neat final-shape to this work. My thanks are due to him.

CONTENTS

CONTENTS

CHAPTER I
INTRODUCTION

South Asian Association for Regional Cooperation (SAARC) is a late comer on the international scene.[1] Its evolution in the mid 1980s has evoked a lot of interest among the political observers and academics the world over. Its progress is watched, analysed and compared with other regional organizations. It has also raised a lot of expectations among the people of South Asia.

In fact, regionalism in international relations has become a widespread phenomenon in the post-war era. Apart from the consideration of collective security, the desire for a collective approach in solving economic and social problems and achieving collective progress has served as the motoring force for the growth of regionalism. It has become a vehicle for mutual cooperation and social and economic progress for the States forming parts of well-defined regions. The study of regionalism and its theoretical aspects has therefore witnessed a spurt in 1960s and 1970s. It has also assumed more importance as the world was divided into rival power blocs on political and ideological lines.

While rest of the world witnessed a remarkable growth of regional organizations, South Asia with a sizeable chunk of land area and about one-fifth of the global population remained aloof from such developments. The States of South Asia were all the time entangled with either the problems of internal political stability or the disputes with their neighbours. the South Asian States inherited poverty, unemployment and underdevelopment as well as political instability from their former colonial masters. Naturally, removal of poverty and achieving social and economic development occupied a place of priority in these States. They have started looking up to the developed countries of the west to assist them in achieving their national goals. In the process the potential of regional cooperation has suffered a neglect.

The evolution of South Asia as a region is invariably connected with the decolonization of the Indian sub-continent and the consequent birth of newly independent States of India, Pakistan, Sri Lanka and Bangladesh at a later date. Particularly, the partition of India by the British when they left India caused a trail of bizarre developments in the Indian sub-continent. The history of the Indian sub-continent, forming the bulk of South Asia, in the post-war period is nothing but a tale of a divided house.

The other States of South Asia, viz., Nepal, Bhutan and Maldives have a relatively independent evolution. Their smaller size, weak economic and military strength made them either dependent on India, the core State of the region or recede into isolation.

Thus, in spite of being poor, underdeveloped and weak the States of South Asia did not have any serious inclinations to come together and make a collective endeavour to tackle their common, economic and political problems.

Another major reason that kept the States of South Asia away from thinking on the lines of regional cooperation was the subordination of the region to the international political system. Though India preached and practiced a policy of keeping away from the power blocs, most of the other States of the region did not really adhere to this principle. Pakistan, in particular, willingly joined the American dominated western military alliance. Sri Lanka also was a keen supporter of the western power bloc. The international power rivalries thus widened the cleavage between

India and Pakistan. Therefore any thought of regional cooperation was forestalled with Pakistan aggressively pursuing its hostile postures against India with the political and material support of the West.

The smaller States of South Asia, i.e. Nepal, Bhutan and Maldives did not have much of external relations until 1970s. Their political leadership was seriously engaged in grappling with their domestic problems. They lacked the political clout or confidence to come out with any proposals of far reaching importance in the region.

All these factors and many more others had their influence on the non-evolution of any regional organization in South Asia. Whereas the States of South Asia with their racial, social, cultural and ethnic homogeneity and common historical background had all the necessary conditions for the growth and success of a regional organization.

As is well known by now, the roots of the present regional organization of South Asia namely SAARC could be traced to early 1980s. By 1983 the precursor of the present organization South Asian Regional Cooperation (SARC) came into existence. Finally, in December 1985 at the Dhaka summit of the Heads of State or Government of the States of South Asia, the South Asian Association for Regional Cooperation (SAARC) was launched formally.

The Problem

The evolution of SAARC has generated a lot of interest both among the scholars and the politicians of South Asia. In fact it has generated a lot of interest in the West also. It is natural because South Asia occupied an important place in the global balance of power equations and the concomitant strategic formulations.

SAARC has generally been accepted as a necessary and desirable mechanism for the countries of the region to achieve self-reliance and progress in social and economic matters. The fact that South Asia is a complex region full of contradictions cutting across the social, ethnic, cultural, economic and political issues makes SAARC an offspring of strange bed-fellows. The circumstances under which SAARC came into being and how far these circumstances i.e. the intra-regional relations of South Asian States and their internal political conditions helped the evolution of SAARC makes it an interesting study.

However, from the very beginning SAARC faced a hostile and sceptic political environment. It has witnessed a lot of vicissitudes in its short existence. Obviously, since its evolution several doubts were raised about its survival and success. On the other hand its launching was lauded as a new land-mark in South Asian relations. The past few years of the existence of SAARC sometimes belied the expectations and sometimes raised hopes of a bright future. Still it is an enigma defying any definite formulations.

In a nutshell, the importance of South Asia in the global political system, i.e. its strategic importance for the major powers, its political composition and inter-relationships within the regions, its intricate political and social systems etc. makes the SAARC a very complex phenomenon to understand.

A reasonable understanding of SAARC makes a thorough inquiry into the whole gamut of political, social, cultural and ethnic dynamics of South Asia an imperative. The success or failure of SAARC cannot be simplistically measured on the basis of the utterances made by representatives of the member countries in various forums. Nor can it be gauged by the institutional framework, its efficacy and financial position of the organization. Only a thorough examination of the factors that influence the inter-relationships of the regional actors, the nature and functioning of their political systems and their actual interest and commitment for regional co-operation will bring out a clear picture of the problems and prospects of this nascent regional organization. Thus the study of SAARC involves an inquiry into the contemporary history of South Asia, including an analysis of political influences both internal and external on the South Asian politics.

SAARC is seen as a reflection of the political realities of the South Asian region. Therefore, the problem we have chosen involves a study of the political, social, ethnic and cultural relations of the States of South Asia in a historical perspective. In the course of the study many issues of importance both internal and external to the region may also be discussed. Thus the study of SAARC not only involves an inquiry into the political and related problems of the region but also the inter-relationships of the South Asian sub-system with the dominant international system.

It may be observed that the existing literature on SAARC mainly deals with the evolution and the prospects of SAARC. It does not often touch the core of the regional cooperation. Wherever the core issues of regional cooperation are given due importance, it is generally done without a direct reference to SAARC and its actual performance or its future prospects in that light. The studies which have focussed on SAARC and its actual functioning are either collection of essays or smaller articles. By their very content and nature they are brief and fragmentary incapable of giving a picture of totality.

Thus, it is a fact that a vast amount of literature has come into circulation on South Asia and its nascent regional organization. It is very useful in providing a thorough understanding of the entire range of issues related to SAARC. However, there is still a serious dearth of single author perspectives on SAARC covering comprehensively the entire gamut of issues related to it.

As it is a dynamic subject and a matter of contemporary relevance and importance, SAARC is still attracting the attention of scholars, particularly from South Asia. Thus, studies on SAARC will continue for quite some time and the point of saturation as far as the inquiries into the phenomenon of SAARC is concerned is certainly far away.

In spite of a huge amount of literature produced on SAARC there still have not appeared any full-length studies that could give a thorough insights into the various aspects of SAARC, i.e., the attitudes and policies of its members, the programmes and achievements of SAARC, the internal and external influences on SAARC, its successes and failures and future prospects. This gap in the existing literature on SAARC provides scope for more intensive studies. Studies of this nature are useful not only to highlight the problems and prospects of SAARC but they may also be useful in mobilising public opinion in favour of more meaningful regional cooperation.

The need for more comprehensive studies is justified not only on the ground that full-length studies are in dearth but also to provide different analyses and perspectives on the problem.

At different stages of its evolution and existence, SAARC has brought into focus many positive and negative aspects of regional cooperation in South Asia. In its initial stages of its evolution the basic and fundamental questions of whether South Asia could be called a region, or does it fulfil the necessary criteria or conditions for being a region etc. were raised. Then the question posed was whether the South Asian States will be successful in giving shape to a regional organization worth the name in this region. The emergence of SAARC has raised many hopes of brighter future for the South Asian region but the events that have followed have caused disappointment.

The very fact that the South Asian States in spite of their mutual differences have come together and agreed to strive for collective self-reliance under a regional organization is itself a welcome development. Interestingly, in spite of the frequent discordant notes, all the members of SAARC have time and again reiterated their faith and commitment in the regional organization. But the gap between the words and deeds is wide enough to create internal turmoils in the newly born regional organization.

SAARC has completed seven years of its existence, which may not be a period long-enough to judge the success or failure of the organization but which may be sufficient to identify trends in its progress. The progress of SAARC during the past few years has been zig-zag and rather unenviable. Different reasons are attributed to this by different individuals and different member States. But the undeniable fact is that SAARC is an organization representing a complex region which never ceased to be turbulent during the past four and a half decades. In spite of the coherent and contiguous nature of the region, South Asian intra-regional relations and the external postures of most of its constituent States has been intriguing. Against this complex background of the regional politics, it becomes difficult to gain a reasonable understanding of SAARC and its political dynamics without going into its basic under-currents.

This leads us to pose a few questions, the answers to which will hold the clue for the proper comprehension of the SAARC phenomenon :

1. What is a region and how far is South Asia a viable region? How far does SAARC fit into the general framework of the United Nations and the Non-Aligned Movement (NAM) ?

2. How committed are the members of SAARC to its avowed objectives of peace, cooperation, progress, prosperity and stability of the region?

3. Are there any mutual suspicions among the member States of SAARC and how far is India's much publicized hegemonism true? How does it affect the functioning and prospects of SAARC?

4. Do the members of SAARC have a clear perception of their role in the organization?

5. How far is there any direct or indirect influence of outside powers on South Asian region and SAARC and the extent of their nature and impact?

In order to find answers to the above questions and a comprehensive understanding of SAARC, its political dynamics, its successes and shortcomings and future prospects, a thorough inquiry is needed into SAARC. In the process an inquiry into the South Asian political systems and their connected issues, the nature and problems of intra-regional relations, external influences on the South Asian region and SAARC is also undertaken in the present study. It is thus aimed at achieving a clear picture of the whole gamut of issues surrounding SAARC and its future prospects on that basis.

Objectives of the Study

With this hypothesis as the basis the present study undertakes an inquiry into the phenomenon of SAARC with the following objectives in mind :

1. It intends to bring out a thorough analysis of the evolution, nature, structure, characteristics, objectives and performance of SAARC as the regional organization of South Asia;
2. It undertakes to analyse attitudes, postures and commitments of the member States of SAARC to its goals and objectives;
3. It aims to throw light on the political dynamics inside South Asia and the influence of external powers directly or indirectly on the growth and functioning of regional cooperation under SAARC;
4. It also intends to make an estimate of the problems and prospects of SAARC based on the above observations;
5. Finally, the study hopes to evaluate the achievements and future prospects of SAARC.

The study hopes to provide insights into the political undercurrents operating on the functioning of SAARC. At the least it is intended to partially fill the gap in the existing literature on the SAARC by providing a full-length study with a single and unified perspective.

Perspectives

Firstly a word about perspective. The present study views the international system as a community of States dominated by the developed countries and the major powers. The less influential and dominated States are the developing countries known as the Third World countries. Their destinies are sought to be influenced by the dominant powers of the international system. The underlying thrust of this study is that a cooperative endeavour and collective approach by the developing countries towards their developmental problems is desirable and necessary. It is more so in view of the increasing protectionist tendencies among the developed countries and the increasing barriers raised by them particularly against the developing countries. Thus it is considered that regional cooperation as a part of the South-South cooperation could be a viable alternative in reducing the developing countries dependence on the developed world. With this background a distinct Third World approach to the problems of social, political and economic development of the developing countries in general and South Asia in particular is envisaged by the present study.

It is also considered that in the complex areas of international relations power games are played by nations which are dominated by reactionary forces like religious parochialism, national and racial chauvinism or other narrow-minded tendencies. It is, therefore, observed that the concept of 'power' plays a definite role in international relations both for political and economic considerations, under the garb of national-interest spelt in terms of race, religion, language etc. Thus, a just international system or sub-system requires the constituent political systems to conform to the values of democracy, freedom, equality and justice.

The study is mainly intended to deal with the political dynamics of SAARC, its existence and problems. It is envisaged to be a dispassionate study of the phenomenon of SAARC and hence it does not boast of being normative except making certain observations on the basis of understanding obtained in the process of the study.

References

1. Bimal Prasad, Regional *Cooperation in South Asia : Problems and Prospects*, Vikas, New Delhi, 1987, p.5.

CHAPTER II

SAARC—GENESIS OF THE ORGANIZATION

Like human beings, the States also have to exist and progress in association with other nations[1]. They may also further divide into groups. The groups of nations are generally formed with the objectives of gaining security, economic development and social progress. At any point of time in the history of mankind, the relations among States were characterized by formation of groups with different motives and interests.

In modern times, when the whole gamut of inter-relationships between States is viewed as international system at the global level, there are regional groups at the secondary level which are termed as international sub-systems. Generally, scholars of international relations, as well as the actors in the international system, perceive the global system as a cluster of various sub-systems mainly identified on the basis of geopolitical criteria. These sub-systems, which are also called 'regions', are considered important not only in balancing the power equations at the global level but are considered important also in shaping the socio-economic and political destinies of the constituent nations.

The Concept of Region

What constitutes a region or regional sub-system and what

are the criteria for the identification of a 'region' or a regional sub-system in the context of international relations, has been a widely discussed topic. Many a scholar have developed theories, offered different definitions and prescribed criteria for a 'region' (sub-system).[2]

One of the earliest contributions in the development of the theory of regions is that of Boutros Ghali.[3] Ghali defines a region or a regional system or what he calls *(ententes)* as "organisms of a permanent character, grouping in a geographically determined region of more than two States which by reason of their proximity, their communities of interests or their affinities.... (establish) an association for the maintenance of peace and security in their region and for the development of their economic, social and cultural cooperation with the final purpose of forming a distinct political entity".[4]

According to Cantori and Spiegel, "a subordinate (regional) system consists of two or more proximate and interacting States which have some common ethinic, linguistic, cultural, social, and historical bonds and whose sense of identity is sometimes increased by the actions and attitudes of States external to the system."[5]

Besides defining and conceptualizing regional system, many scholars have tried to determine the criteria or conditions that are necessary to identify a region. In fact, it is this exercise which is useful in giving a clear definition to the concept of region, which is both viable and coherent. Let us, therefore, consider some of the prescriptions given by various scholars in this regard.

Michael Brecher advocates that identification of a regional sub-system requires six conditions : (1) the scope of the group is delimited with a primary stress on a geographic region, (2) there are at least three actors, (3) taken together they are objectively recognized by other actors as constituting a distinctive community, region, or segment of the global system, (4) the members identify themselves as such, (5) units of power are relatively inferior to the units in the Dominant system, (6) changes in the dominant and system have a greater effect than the reverse.[6]

Russet, another scholar of regional sub-system offered a

different set of countries of five conditionalities viz., (1) social and cultural homogeneity among the members of the region, (2) similar political behaviour and attitudes, (3) political interdependence, (4) economic interdependence and (5) geographical proximity among the members of the region.[7]

The variety of definitions offered and criteria presented are so vast that it is not possible to discuss all of them in the present study. Moreover, the contexts of the above referred theories and criteria are quite different from the realities of the global politics obtaining at the present moment. Because, these theories were conceived in a particular historical context of emergence of regional sub-systems for collective security in the interests of the Western powers. The main flaw in the theories of regionalism and the criteria of forming regional groups and organizations developed by most of the western scholars, in 1960s and 1970s, is that they are dominated by the mindset of the evolving post-war international political system. Essentially, all the regional organizations were conceived to be closely linked and affected by the international system dominated by certain powers i.e., they are supposed to be subordinate to it. Thus, these theories as they are developed in a specific historical context have a limited applicational value to understand the emerging trends in international political system.

Without any prejudice to the theoretical formulations propounded so far, we can come to an understanding of the basic features of necessary criteria of a regional organization in the present day world. Thus, we may say that a regional sub-system is a group of States with a reasonable and viable geographical proximity with a definite political commitment and desire to cooperate among themselves with the intention of achieving social and economic progress of their people. Social, cultural and ethnic homogeneity is helpful indeed in binding the region together. Even in the absence of such commonalities, friendly relations and close social and economic interaction among the people is desirable. Another desirable factor is that such group of States should be free from serious bilateral problems and deep-rooted political hostilities. This is because, political harmony forms the basis of any closeknitted association for alround cooperation. Whereas its absence will only lead to superficial conglomerates plagued with mutual suspicions and vulnerable to eventual disintegration.

Especially in the context of the North-South divide, a distinct approach needs to be considered in the case of the regional grouping belonging to the developing countries. This is particularly so because of the fact that the gulf between the rich and the poor countries is ever widening and the rising tide of protectionism coupled with the resource crunch is further threatening the future prospects of the developing countries. One may say that this makes it imperative for the developing countries to reduce their dependence levels and free themselves from the political and economic domination of the developed countries. In order to strengthen their position vis-a-vis the developed countries the developing countries have been striving to achieve collective self-reliance. In the case of the States seeking regional identity and trying to forge socio-economic cooperation the above suggested manner is considered to be the best way to realize their objectives. South-South cooperation which is considered a stepping stone for the collective self-reliance of the developing countries[8] has become the *raison d' etre* for the emergence of the regional groupings. A group in order to gain identity as a region should atleast try to exhibit a fair degree of political and economic autonomy from the dominant international system, or from the influence of the great powers.

On the basis of the foregoing discussion, we may now infer and conclude that a viable region, to be identified as such, shall at least fulfil the following basic conditions:

1. Presence of two or more actors;
2. Geographical contiguity or proximity among the units;
3. Historical, ethnic, social and cultural affinity among the people or a reasonable level of social and cultural interaction among the people of the region;
4. More or less common political perceptions or/and a semblance of cordial political relations among the countries of the region;

5. Economic and political inter-dependence; a stake in the regional cooperation;
6. A desire for forming as a group and recognition as such;
7. A reasonable degree of autonomy both politically and economically from the dominant powers at the global level.[9]

Is South Asia Region?

Having set the basic criteria for the identification of a region (for the purpose of regional cooperation), let us now examine whether South Asia fits into this conceptional framework.

It is a widely accepted fact that South Asian countries have a common historical background, cultural homogeneity and sociological affinities apart from a compact and coherent regional formation.[10] Geographically, more than three-fourths of the land mass, consisting of five countries of South Asia, is the Indian sub-continent. This itself speaks of the contiguity and proximity of the South Asian Region. Historically, the entire sub-continent was either under the colonial rule or under the political tutelege of the colonial masters until the close of World War II.

The cultural, ethnic and social affinity among the people of the South Asian countries is such that more or less the entire sub-continent was regarded as one nation through ages.[11]

However, the newly independent countries of South Asia alongwith those which remained independent throughout the 19th and 20th centuries have chosen diverse paths for political and economic development in the post-colonial period. Consequently, heterogenous political and economic systems have come into existence in the region, affecting the monolithic social and cultural fabric of the sub-continent. At the end of the colonial rule, the newly independent States of the region especially, India and Pakistan, which emerged as consequence of the partition of India, inherited mutual rivalries.

The divergence in the political systems, perceptions and postures of the constituent States of South Asia, which are by no means natural factors, appear to come in the way of their identifying as a cohesive group. How far these divergences are real and how they affect the regional identity of South Asia is a debatable issue though.

Despite the problems of intra-regional political compatibility and the heavy external interference and dependence, there is a general agreement on the historical, cultural, ethnic and geographical compatibility of the South Asian States.[12] Hence, without going further into the conceptual and theoretical complexities, it can be said that *prima facie* South Asia is a well defined and viable regional group (or sub-system).[13] Besides, some of the leading western scholars while making a division of the world into regional sub-systems, have distinctly identified South Asia as one of them[14].

However, the theoretical and conceptual prescriptions appear tenuous if the nations which are parts of definite geographic regions do not express willingness to come together as a group. Thus, whether any particular regional group or organization's viability or otherwise can hardly be perceived in terms of theoretical frameworks. For, it is mainly dependent on the wills, interests and attitudes of their component countries. This explains, the absence of regional organizations in some regions despite satisfying the other criteria and in some cases the regional organizations have faded away within short periods.

The launching of the South Asian Association for Regional Cooperation (SAARC), is the result of the explicit desire and efforts of the States of South Asia formalizing the status of the 'region'.[15]

Now, although there is little scope left for contention about South Asia as a regional entity, there is a bit of uncertainty about the composition and geographical delimitation of this region. Quite a few scholars have put the South Asian States and South East Asian States together and called it the Southern Asia.[16] Even those who separate South Asia, include Burma (Myanmar) and Afghanistan in it, taking the historical and geographical factors into consideration.

Afghanistan was also a part of Indian subcontinent historically and the British have also regarded it as such. They have called it the 'gateway of India.'[17] However, in the present context, it is regarded as an outsider of this region. Because of the recent developments arising out of the Soviet intervention, Afghanistan was left out of this region. Burma (Myanmar) too is excluded from this region because of its lack of communication and interaction with the other countries of South Asia. It is also in a state of self-imposed political isolation in the recent years. The matter rests settled, at least temporarily, with the formation of the SAARC with India, Pakistan, Nepal, Bangladesh, Bhutan, Sri Lanka and Maldives as member States. These seven countries are now regarded as the constituents of South Asian region.

This has not only legitimized the identity of South Asia as a region, but also demarcated its geographical limits. However, in case Myanmar and/or Afghanistan seek entry into SAARC, this question may have to be reopened.

In fact, on one occasion (during the Kathmandu Summit) Afghanistan expressed its desire to join SAARC but due to the objections raised by Pakistan, it was ruled out. This brought to the force the inherent drawback of the SAARC Charter its provisions and modalities regarding admission of new members into its fold.

It has to be mentioned here that most of the Western scholars have evolved theories and concepts on regionalism inspired by the security perceptions of the western bloc in the wake of cold war, the main objective being the containment of communism. But gradually divergent approaches to the study of the regionalism have come into existence, new concepts and categories. According to this the existing regional systems can be broadly categorized into the following three types:[18]

(i) regional systems which are essentially subordinates of the international system especially from the strategic, military and security points of view;

(ii) regional groups that have come together, for fulfilling some limited (economic) objectives;

(iii) comprehensive regional organizations with the objectives of achieving political harmony and economic and social development.

Needless to say that SAARC, based on the objectives listed in its Charter, falls into the third category of the above-mentioned regional systems.

SAARC : A Late Comer

Despite being one of the most coherent and viable regions, South Asia did not see any organizational development during the first four decades of the post-war period. In sharp contrast to this, during the same period, a number of regional organizations of different hues have emerged in various other geographical regions of the world.

The reasons for non-evolution of a regional organization in South Asia are many and varied. Some of them are inherent and structural whereas the others are political and psychological. According to Michael Brecher the main features of this region which contributed to non-evolution of any formal regional body are: (1) low intensity of communications and transport within the region, (2) conflicting ideologies and values, (3) diversity of political systems, and (4) internal instability within the member States.[19] While these can be taken as inherent drawbacks of the region the political and historical reasons for the non- or slow development of the organizational structure emanate from the colonial legacy inherited from the British which left a heritage of bitter feelings and distrust between the member States, particularly India and her neighbours.[20] Differences in the political and security perceptions are concomitants of mutual suspicions arising out of geographical limitations and conflicting value systems contributed to the apathy towards regional cooperation in South Asia. The most important factor, however, is political one. Everything in this regard hinges on the political intentions of the member States and hence there lies the key to the problem.

The policies and attitudes adopted by the governments of these States have developed mutual antagonism among the people of the States of the region, resulting in low interaction and hence low communication and transport facilities within the region. Hence there was little scope for generating interest for or against the evolution of a regional cooperative endeavour.

However, attempts were made to bring about a semblance of solidarity and integrative vision among the States of Asia in general and South Asia in particular. The Asian Relations Conference of 1947, the Conference on Indonesia in Delhi in 1949 and the Bandung Conference in 1955 are notable among them. Attempts were made in this direction especially, at Delhi in 1947 and at Bandung in 1955. But no tangible results emerged. The reasons accounted for this are: (1) the leadership rivalry between India and China, and (2) the fear among the smaller States that one or the other or both the giants might dominate them.[21] The climate of suspicion among the smaller States as well as the bigger ones was main hindrance.

In spite of the fact that no organization for regional cooperation emerged, the realisation of the need for cooperation among the States of South Asia as a historical and political necessity for attaining peace and economic progress was always present. Nehru is on record advocating for political integration of the region in various international forums. But he had a larger vision for Asia as a whole rather than South Asia.[22] Subsequently, the foreign policy of Janata Party during 1977-79, which is termed as "Beneficial Bilateralism" had the main objective of building an infrastructure for regional cooperation in this area. It was thought that such a policy would "tackle the common enemy of poverty and inherited degradation" and in addition it was also thought that the Indian sub-continent would remain free of tension and could command unique weight in the counsels of the world.[23]

The successful formation and continuous functioning of European Community and the ASEAN have also served as examples and inspired the policy-makers in South Asia for forming a cooperative structure in the region. In the words of the then External Affairs Minister of India, A.B. Vajpayee " if western Europe with all its criss-crossing national predilections and diversity could knit itself together in an integrated economic community there is no reason why we in the region of South Asia should not be able to do so. There is a great deal more that unites us.[24]

While India was thinking in terms of South Asian cooperation, some of her neighbours however were showing an interest in extra-regional affiliations. Shri Lanka in fact sought to become a member of ASEAN and Pakistan was always looking towards the Arab world. While Sri Lanka's request was turned down by ASEAN, Pakistan continued to forge political, economic and cultural links with West Asia.[25] Moreover, the differences in the political and strategic perceptions of the South Asian countries have kept them away from evolving a regional organization.

However, the need for forging regional cooperation on strategic lines was also encouraged by the then superpowers, in their own different ways. It is a common knowledge by now that the Soviet leader Leonid Brezhnev wanted to build an Asian Security System with India taking up a leading position. But India showed little interest in this idea. During the tenure of President Carter, USA too was keen to establish a cooperative regional security framework in South and Southeast Asia. For this purpose Carter sent emissaries to India and Pakistan. While India's response remained lukewarm, President Zia of Pakistan was favourably disposed towards the American idea.[26]

The Evolution of SAARC

The formal proposals for the setting up of a regional organization have come from President Zia-ur-Rahman of Bangladesh in 1980. President Zia mooted the idea of holding a summit of the heads of the seven South Asian States by India, Pakistan, Bangladesh, Bhutan, Nepal, Sri Lanka and Maldives. Though the idea itself was welcomed the summit was deferred till the discussions at the lower levels were completed. As a follow up to the proposal Bangladesh has circulated among the other six States of the region a Working Paper on South Asian Regional Cooperation in November 1980. The emphasis of the Bangladesh's Working Paper was on creation of an atmosphere of mutual confidence and political understanding among these seven States and to remove disparities and to adopt a gradual approach to the development of a regional cooperation. It also recommended for the setting up of an institutional mechanism towards this end.[27]

The formal discussions began with the first meeting of Foreign Secretaries of the seven States of South Asia at Colombo on the initiative taken by the Government of Sri Lanka. The meeting took place between 21-23 April 1981. The first meeting of the Foreign Secretaries was held with all the fanfare and rhetoric. But the approach of the participant States was cautious. No one was in a hurry to see the early evolution of an institutional framework for regional cooperation.

The cautious approach adopted by the major States at the first Foreign Secretaries Meeting at Colombo was typified by the Pakistani delegate's remarks: "Let us build the structure of cooperation brick by brick and on solid and secure foundation".[28] In conformity with this, the members have "agreed that decisions should be taken on the basis of unanimity" and that "bilateral and contentious issues should be excluded from their deliberations."[29]

The participants at the meeting were very much aware that the relations between most of the South Asian States were marred by the mutual suspicions and lack of understanding of each others problems. As such it was "agreed that regional cooperation should be based on and in turn contribute to mutual trust, understanding and sympathetic appreciation of the national aspirations of the countries of the region."[30]

Though the genre of the attitudes and deliberations at Colombo was rather cautious given the state of bilateral relations between the countries of the region at that time, it was more or less realistic. Nevertheless, significant advances were made in initiating cooperation among the countries of the region. The following five study groups have been set up with the country mentioned against each as the coordinator :

1. Agriculture — Bangladesh
2. Rural Development — Sri Lanka
3. Telecommunications — Pakistan
4. Meteorology — India

5. Health & Population Activities — Nepal

The Study Groups were to review the existing cooperative arrangements in the region to determine the potential and scope of the cooperation and to draw up a programme of establishing and strengthening regional cooperation.[31] A Committee of Whole comprising of the senior officials of the seven States of the region was also set up to identify other areas of possible cooperation. Thus, no doubt, foundations for the regional cooperation in South Asia were laid at the Colombo meeting of the Foreign Secretaries in April 1981.

It must be said that the regional cooperation sought to be established by the First Meeting of the Foreign Secretaries was on functional basis. The Meeting deliberately and conspicuously avoided any political issues to be discussed. Neither the economic and trade issues were discussed at the meeting. By and large, it was supposed to be a humble beginning with a pragmatic note that the potential for cooperation would be further explored, strengthened and expanded. The fact that to avoid bilateral and contentious issues clearly indicated that the parties to the meeting had certain bilateral and unresolved problems. In spite of this there was general willingness among the States of South Asia to bring about some sort of regional cooperative mechanism.

The Second Meeting of Foreign Secretaries was held at Kathmandu between 2-4 November 1981. This meeting also reiterated that the regional cooperation in South Asia was beneficial, desirable and necessary and reaffirmed the determination of the participant countries in evolving and accelerating the process of cooperation.[32] While endorsing the recommendations of the Study Groups established at the First Meeting, it was agreed to convert the Study Groups into Working Groups in the five areas of cooperation already identified. Further, it was agreed to set up three more Study Groups in the following areas and with the countries mentioned against them as coordinators :

1. Transport — Maldives
2. Postal Services — Bhutan

3. Scientific and Technological Cooperation — Pakistan

And the Working Groups were to draw up a comprehensive programme of action on both immediate and long term basis. They were also to report on the progress with regard to the implementation of the action programme.

Consultations on the modalities of the implementation of programmes of action etc. for promoting Regional Cooperation in South Asia continued with the same pattern of deliberations and decisions at the Third Meeting of Foreign Secretaries at Islamabad held during 7-9 August 1982. Apart from the normal euphoria on the necessity of furthering the cooperation in the South Asian region, the Islamabad meeting considered the need for stepping up the consultations to the level of Ministers and initiated preparations for a ministerial level meeting. At the Islamabad meeting, all the reports of the Working Groups were accepted and yet another Study Group on Sports, Arts and Culture was set up. It was also decided that another meeting of Foreign Secretaries would be held at Dhaka during February - March 1983 before the ministerial level meeting.

The Committee of Whole which was constituted under the chairmanship of Sri Lanka at the Islamabad Foreign Secretaries Meeting prepared an Integrated Programme of Action. The Dhaka meeting (the fourth one of the Foreign Secretaries held on 28-30 March 1983) endoresed the report of the Committee of Whole on the Integrated Programme of Action and decided to recommend its adoption by the ministerial level meeting. The emphasis is now shifted to the expeditious implementation of the Integrated Programme of Action. It was also decided that the meeting of the Foreign Ministers of the seven countries be held at New Delhi.

The New Delhi meeting of the Foreign Ministers of the seven States of the South Asian region held during 1-2 August 1983 is the watershed in the evolution of the South Asian regional organization under the banner of South Asian Association for Regional Cooperation (SAARC). The meeting was inaugurated by the then Indian Prime Minister Indira Gandhi. It was here that the South Asian Regional Cooperation (SARC) was formally launched amidst considerable hope and optimism about the promotion of cooperation for the welfare of the people of the region and for the economic and social growth of the States of the region.

Strangely, while the seven States of the South Asian region set out to hold deliberations at a series of meetings (though at Foreign Secretaries level) for evolving a mechanism and *modus operandi* for the cooperation among themselves, the political situation in the region has been simmering with tensions. The relations between India and almost all of her neighbours have steadily deteriorated. The Afghan crisis which started in late 1979 reached a level of blowing up into a bigger crisis. It has triggered an unprecedented arms race between India and Pakistan as USA armed Pakistan to its teeth with the ostensible of driving out the Soviets from Afghanistan. This, in turn, increased the tensions between the India and Pakistan.

Indo-Nepalese relations also reached a low ebb by then over the trade and transit treaty. Added to this, Nepal and Bangladesh have made a common cause over the river waters disputes with India. Bhutan too, which was hitherto guided by India in her external relations set out on the course of framing independent foreign policy. In Sri Lanka the movement of the Tamils for autonomy escalated into an armed struggle. The Tamils of Sri Lanka who had the natural sympathy of the Tamil people of Tamil Nadu State, expected India to support their cause. The Sri Lankan Government which had troubled relationship with India over the past three decades in connection with the repatriation of Tamils in Sri Lanka found naturally a scapegoat to blame India.

Obviously, by 1983 almost entire region of South Asia was reeling under tension and turmoil. Punjab and Assam crises in India have reached a boiling point. The movement for Restoration of Democracy was gaining momentum in Pakistan. The Sri Lankan situation was inflammatory. Bangladesh too faced political turbulence and tensions in the border regions. The situation in Nepal and Bhutan was also none too happy. Against this scenario the tendency in the relations between the States of South Asia could be nothing but mutual suspicion and distrust.

Thus, the South Asian Regional Cooperation (SARC) was

launched at the formal level in August 1983 which the South Asian States on the one hand were accusing each other of hegemony, aggression, interference in internal affairs and on the other affirming the lofty principles of sovereign equality, territorial integrity, political independence and non-interference in the internal affairs of the other States.[33]

Prime Minister Indira Gandhi while inaugurating the Foreign Ministers, meeting at New Delhi has, however, sounded a note of caution. She said, "ours is a troubled region. Most of our countries are multi-racial and multi-religious. It would be idle to pretend that we are not affected by what happens everywhere. Even as we meet here there are disturbing and tragic developments in our neighbourhood."[34] At the same time she stressed that regional cooperation was an important factor in bringing about economic and social progress.

The Declaration of SARC was adopted on 2 August 1983 was a note of pragmatism and hope at the end of the Foreign Ministers, meeting at New Delhi. The main objectives, *inter alia* laid down in the Declaration are :

(a) to promote the welfare of the people of South Asia and to improve their quality of life;

(b) to accelerate economic growth, social progress and the cultural development in the region, and

(c) to promote and strengthen collective self-reliance among the countries of South Asia.

The objectives also include the collective resolve to contribute mutual trust, promotion of active collaboration and mutual assistance in various fields to strengthen cooperation with other developing countries, to strengthen cooperation among themselves in international forums and to cooperate with international and regional organizations with similar aims and progress.[35]

As far as the institutional arrangements are concerned the SARC envisaged a 3-tier system of committees. The first and bottom tier consists of Technical Committees to be represented by all the seven States. They were supposed to be responsible for implementation and coordination of cooperation in each area identified. The Action Committees (second tier) were to comprise of the countries concerned in the case of specific projects in their implementation. At the third and higher level was the Standing Committee consisting of the Foreign Secretaries of the member States with the ultimate authority to control the Technical and Action Committees. The Standing Committee was also entrusted with the responsibility of coordination and monitoring the South Asian Regional Cooperation. Approval of the projects and programmes, deciding the modalities of financing, determination of priorities, mobilization of resources and identification of new areas of cooperation was also rested with the Standing Committee.

Financial arrangements were to be shared on mutually agreed basis and in the case of long term projects the technical committee concerned was to submit recommendations on the modalities of meeting the costs. It was also mentioned in the Declaration that in the case of projects and programmes for which financial resources cannot be mobilized within the region, recourse may be had to external assistance from the appropriate sources with the approval of the Standing Committee.

The note of caution and the apprehension of running into political controversies sounded by most of the participating countries is reflected in the general provision which ruled out the inclusion of bilateral and contentious issues in the deliberations. In the given circumstances, it was the only realistic course to avoid the areas where the differences persist and are likely to aggravate. It was always better to keep the hopes alive by pursuing the cooperation in non-controversial matters.[36]

The Foreign Ministers have agreed to meet once a year and they also decided to advise their respective heads of States to meet at their level. It was also agreed that the dates for the summit would be finalised at the next meeting of the Foreign Ministers.

Two more meetings at Foreign Ministers, level took place at Male in July 1984 and at Thimpu in May 1985, the latter one being a preparatory meeting for the summit of the heads of States of the South Asian region. Finally, the summit meeting of the Heads of States of South Asia was held at Dhaka in December

1985 culminating in the emergence of the South Asian Association for Regional Cooperation (SAARC).

Obviously, the States of the South Asian region were very slow in evolving the regional organization. This was indeed reflected in the remarks made by Mrs. Gandhi in her inaugural address at the First Foreign Ministers, Meeting at New Delhi on 2 August 1983.[37] Between August 1983 and the final evolution of the SAARC in December 1985 there was a considerable delay. This is attributed to the ambivalent attitude of the constituent States of the region. The way the deliberations were held and the approach adopted towards various problems that have arisen in the region and dichotomy between the expressed desire for strengthening mutual trust and the increasing tensions in bilateral relations has raised serious doubts about the viability and sustenance of the fledgling regional organization. To the outside observers and political analysts the members of the SAARC were the "cautious seven" or the "hesitant seven". In contrast to this the members of the ASEAN were termed collectively as the "Smiling Five".[38] As mentioned earlier the period of evolution of the SAARC was paradoxically marked by the intermittent tensions in the bilateral relations between the major powers of the region, viz., India and Pakistan[39] and also the deterioration of bilateral relations between India on the one hand and Nepal, Bangladesh and Sri Lanka on the other.[40]

The ambience of simulated goodwill and regional bondage coupled with the desire and willingness to institutionalise cooperation somehow overtook all hurdles and paved the way for the setting up of the South Asian Association for Regional Cooperation (SAARC) in December 1985 at the Summit of the Heads of States of South Asia. In fact, the Dhaka Summit of the seven States was the culmination of the efforts made for achieving a semblance of solidarity in the region over the past three decades. The adoption of the Charter of the SAARC was indeed institutionalization of the concept of South Asian Regional Cooperation which had gradually taken shape since the beginning of the 1980s.

The Charter of the SAARC is in fact the solemn reaffirmation of the basic principles of international law, international relations and cooperation. The objectives and the basic principles of the SAARC as laid down in the Charter are, to say the least, ambitious, optimistic, idealistic and unquestionably value-based. It is, undoubtedly, a laudable and lofty statement.

The basic driving force behind the establishment of the SAARC, according to the Charter, is the desire of the contracting parties for promoting peace, stability, amity and progress in the region through strict adherence to the principles of the UN Charter and non-alignment.[41] The document also enunciates that the States of South Asia are conscious that in an increasingly interdependent world the objectives of peace, freedom, social justice and economic prosperity are but achieved by fostering mutual understanding, good neighbourly relations and meaningful cooperation. Towards this end, the participant States are "convinced that regional cooperations is mutually beneficial, desirable and necessary".[42] With these convictions, desires, intentions and hopes the SAARC is brought into existence.

Article I of the Charter enumerated the objectives as given below :

(a) to promote the welfare of the people of South Asia and to improve their quality of life;

(b) to accelerate economic growth, social progress and cultural development in the region and to provide all individuals the opportunity to live in dignity and to realise their full potentials;

(c) to promote and strengthen collective self-reliance among the countries of South Asia;

(d) to contribute to mutual trust, understanding and appreciation of one another's problems;

(e) to promote active collaboration and mutual assistance in the economic, social, cultural, technical and scientific fields;

(f) to strengthen cooperation with other developing countries;

(g) to strengthen cooperation among themselves in international forums on matters of common interest; and

(h) to cooperate with international and regional organizations with similar aims and purposes.

These objectives were infact taken *in toto* from the earlier Declaration of the SARC at New Delhi on 2 August 1983 at the end of the First Foreign Ministers, meeting. The above mentioned objectives are so broad based that they encompass all conceivable fields of cooperation between the members of the organization. It kindles a hope, vision and necessary confidence among the people of the region for ushering in an era of peace, prosperity, democracy and development.

However, the past record of the existence of this fledgling organization and the conduct of mutual relations among the members of this regional outfit prove how hollow these high flown rhetoric and the idealistically proclaimed objectives are (The performance and achievements of SAARC are discussed in Chapter VI).

The Charter also reaffirms that the cooperation within this framework is based on respect for the principles of sovereign equality, territorial integrity, political independence, non-interference in internal affairs of other States and mutual benefit. It is further stated that such cooperation should not be a substitute for bilateral and multilateral cooperation and neither should it be inconsistent with bilateral and multilateral obligations.[43]

These principles, *per se*, might appear to be in order for such an arrangement but against the background of South Asia where most of the States have bilateral problems with the core State of the region, i.e., India, the affirmation of the said principles appears to be not only ironical but also symbolic and ominous.

The lofty principles and rosy objectives that embellished the Charter of SAARC appear to be hollow and unrealistic to a keen observer. The founder members and framers of the Charter were not unaware of pathetically realistic inherent weaknesses of the cooperative venture. Therefore, they had included a general provision that stated that bilateral and contentious issues should be excluded from the deliberations of the Association[44] which is tantamount to a total exclusion of political and economic issues from the general framework of cooperation.Thus, excluding the core areas that are crucial for tackling the problems of peace, stability, economic and social progress, the Charter leaves only peripheral areas to be covered under the jurisdiction of the Association. It is argued that avoiding the controversial areas and concentrating on non-contentious issues would pave way for mutual understanding and ultimately lead to the easing of tensions.[45] On the other hand, it is criticized as putting the cart before the horse, because without achieving political understading and mutual trust and confidence it becomes impossible to enter into any meaningful cooperation.[46] According to the functional approach advocated by David Mitrany and others it is not necessary to iron out political issues before entering into regional cooperation. However, going by the track record of the organization, it is more a reflection of the inherent weaknesses of the organization than a realistic approach to the problem. These problems invariably lead one to treat them as historical and structural, a discussion of which is built into the entire study.

SAARC — Its Structure

SAARC retained the institutional mechanism set up by the SARC in1983 with the addition of the Summit of the Heads of the States. The Charter of the SAARC clearly demarcate the functions and powers of each of the institutional part as well as laying down the principles of composition. It can be said that the institutional framework that was in force in 1983 was quite effective, in that it has given proper momentum in providing a final shape to the organization. Thus, no wonder that the same pattern of mechanism is continued for the SAARC.

The shape and structure of the institutional mechanism of any organization has to be formulated in accordance with the quantum of the operations involved and the intensity and seriousness of the political will of the parties concerned in realizing the objectives envisaged. However, where the desire and the will to achieve the goals set forth is followed by deep commitment, the magnitude of the institutional mechanism does not really cause any handicap. Given the limitations and initial inhibitions involved in SAARC the modest institutional framework that has been agreed upon was quite sufficient.

The SAARC Charter, thus, chalked out a four-tier institutional set up which is as follows :

(1) At the apex level there are Heads of States or Government Meetings which take place annually. The Thimpu Foreign Ministers, meeting in May 1985 which finalised the Draft Charter had, in fact, recommended to hold the summits of the heads of States or governments once in two years.[47] But the Charter that has finally approved at Dhaka went a step ahead and recommended to hold it once a year.

The Charter does not however, specify the modalities of the summit meetings. However, by implication and importance the summit meeting is the highest deliberative body of the SAARC and all decisions taken at the lower levels are formally endorsed there. The significance of the meetings of the Heads of States lies in the fact that they reinforce the bonds of friendship, mutual respect and trust among the member States and rejuvenates the cooperative endeavour. The chance of interpersonal contacts between the Heads of States or governments provided by such meetings give them an opportunity to remove misunderstanding if any and ease tensions in the relations among their respective countries. The Colombo summit of December 1991 stands as a clear testimony to show as to how misunderstandings can be cleared to keep the organization in tact and on the move.[48]

(2) The second tier of the institutional structure, the Council of Ministers, consisting of foreign ministers of the member States, is the most important organ of the SAARC from the functional point of view. It is endowed with a wide range of policy and decision making powers. Its functions include formulation of policies, review of the progress of cooperation, deciding on new areas of cooperation and to establish any additional mechanism if deemed

necessary. The Council of Ministers is supposed to meet as often as possible and if necessary extraordinary sessions may be held by agreement among the members.[49]

(3) The third one in the ladder of the institutional hierarchy of SAARC is the Standing Committee, comprising the foreign secretaries of the member States. This is entrusted with the responsibility of the overall monitoring and coordination of the programme of cooperation apart from the function of approval of projects and programmes and the modalities of their financing, determination of inter-sectoral priorities, mobilisation of resources and identification of new areas of cooperation. The Standing Committee is supposed to meet as often as necessary but at least once a year. It has to submit reports to the Council of Ministers periodically and refer to it as and when necessary for decisions on policy matters.[50]

(4) The Technical Committees, which are at the bottom of the structure, comprising representatives of all member States are responsible for the implementation, coordination and monitoring of the programmes in their respective areas of cooperation. Their functions are so broad-based that they include everything pertaining to the programme of cooperation, i.e. from determination of potential and scope of cooperation in the paticular area to the determination of the financial implications, and finally to the monitoring of the progress of implementation. The Technical Committees submit periodic reports to the Standing Committee and their chairmanship rotates among the member States in alphabetical order every two years. The Technical Committees are authorized to use different modalities and mechanisms as and when considered necessary.[51] Thus, the Technical Committees are the ground level institutions for implementing programmes of regional cooperation in various areas identified for that purpose.

Apart from the institutional framework detailed above, the SAARC Charter provided for a Secretariat to the Association to be set up at an appropriate time. The appropriate time came in November 1986 at the Bangalore Summit of the Heads of the States. The Bangalore Summit finalised the plan for the SAARC Secretariat and decided that Kathmandu would be its headquarters. Accordingly, the SAARC Secretariat was inaugurated on 16 February 1987 at Kathmandu with a Secretary-General and four Directors.

The Secretariat now consists of the Secretary-General and seven Directors, one each from the member States. The Secretary-General is to hold office for a non-renewable period of two years. He is appointed by the Council of Ministers on nomination by the member States on the basis of the principle of rotation in alphabetical order. Accordingly, a Bangladeshi diplomat, Abul Ahsan, on nomination by his government, was appointed as the first Secretary-General. The second Secretary-General, K.K. Bhargava, was from India. The present Secretary-General of SAARC is Ibrahim Hussein Zaki who was the Deputy Foreign Affairs Minister of Maldives before taking up this office.

In establishing a Secretariat the SAARC has acted swiftly in comparison to the ASEAN which took nine years to set up the Secretariat.[52] The SAARC Secretariat is also patterned on the lines of the ASEAN Secretariat.

The decision making process of SAARC may be considered as one of the fundamental drawbacks of this fledgling organization.

The Charter stipulates that (i) contentious and bilateral issues shall be avoided and (ii) all decisions at all levels shall be taken unanimously.[53] Obviously, this is considered as the only plausible course to avoid controversies and mutual apprehensions and hurdles in the implementation process.

Though, *prima facie,* the need for avoiding contentious and bilateral issues, appeared to be reasonable to avoid problems in the nascent organization but it is more like avoiding the hurdles rather than clearing them. Without solving bilateral problems, it may look naive to believe that any meaningful cooperation could be achieved among a group dominated by centrifugal forces.

The unanimity principle, however, is likely to create procedural problems in future. Because, the question generally confronted is, unanimity among whom? Among all the members or only among those present? Besides, this condition would preempt many crucial issues from being discussed at any joint forum.

Because of these inbuilt inertia, SAARC in spite of its ambitious objectives, lacks the necessary strength and commitment. It only gives the impression of being a subordinate to the dominant international political and economic system. Ironically, as the Charter clearly mentions it is based on the same laudable principles of United Nations and Non-alignment whose record has been rather discouraging either in changing the economic conditions of the people in the South (the poor countries of the world) or in keeping the world free from the dangers of wars and conflicts. Ostensibly, SAARC also talks of bringing about a change in the lives of the people of the region for better. If one goes by its practice it may be found that it is too small and inadequate for the tasks to be achieved. It is only presenting itself as a cosmetic decoration.

As mentioned above, the decision making process agreed upon and adopted by the SAARC is the most striking indication of the weakness of the organization. Following a "do not touch the controversies" approach, the members of SAARC adopted a vehicle of cooperation free from possible controversies. But while the desire for gaining an individual identity marked the main motive of the Smaller States in evolving SAARC as will be shown elsewhere in Chapter III, the fear of touching the problems by the major countries of the region, made it an organization based on status-quoism. In spite of that it could not however totally avoid the discordant notes that have been raising frequently. Naturally, it points to the dichotomy between the desire for a symbol of collective economic development and maintain one's own parochial national interests simultaneously.

The inherent weaknesses of the SAARC cannot be said to have crept into it inadvertently, but they are only a reflection of the crisis in the international system in general and in the regional system of South Asia in particular. An attempt is made to elaborate this in the ensuing chapters.

SAARC and Other Regional Organizations

Though comparisons are generally odious, everything is looked at, evaluated and judged on the basis of comparison with other similar entities and their performance. Right from the embryonic stages the SAARC (SARC before December 1985) had been more frequently than not compared to other regional organizations established and functioning elsewhere. Especially, SAARC has been looked at with an analogical vision taking the examples of the European Community, the ASEAN and GCC etc.

While comparisons do not always establish complete analogy with the organizations compared, they are helpful in bringing out the peculiarities of various organizations, their weaknesses and to draw some lessons from the others. One should also keep in mind that, the results or achievements or track records may not be similar, however similar or akin various entities may appear to be. That is to say, that every single organization or entity acts and functions under a unique set of influences and circumstances and its success or failure will be unique too.

The evolution of SAARC has been rather late and slow. The EEC, ASEAN, GCC etc. were created quite earlier than the SAARC and their evolution, though, also took place at different points of time. EEC is said to be a product of the post-war international political and economic system. It was necessitated by the devastation left behind by the World War II and it was also a part of the international system shaped by the politics of cold war.

The ASEAN also can be put in the same category, in as much as it is the off-shoot of the SEATO (South East Asia Treaty Organization), a part of the collective security system evolved by the western bloc under the leadership of the United States.[54] However, the membership of SEATO and the ASEAN differ. But the members of the ASEAN also subscribed to the same threat perceptions as the US and its allies. Hence, it is argued that ASEAN is imposed or to say it mildly established under the guidance of the USA. Thus, not only ASEAN but also the EEC and GCC also are the result of the convergence of political outlook, especially prompted by the security outlook.[55]

There are other regional organizations that have come up with their members with different political systems and divergent foreign policies. The ECOWAS, LAFTA, Nordic Council etc. are such organizations. Their achievements are also varied. Some have faded away, whereas others have proved to be successful. In a limited way, SAARC falls under this category. But it is too early to say anything about its success or failure.

While for the EEC and ASEAN the security concerns were one of the motivationg factors, for the GCC the cultural and religious factors were a strong uniting element. But all of them were guided by economic necessities primarily. In the case of SAARC, the above mentioned factors, viz., the security concerns, the economic motives are not strong. It is actually a product of the ingrained feeling of the ruling elites of the South Asian States that there was a need to have a regional organization. It was an assertion of national identity and independent status *vis-a-vis* other States of the region as well as the world. That is why the smaller States of the region were more enthusiastic in setting up the regional organizaton than the major ones. For them it was a means to find an alternative to the bilateral approach in dealing with their neighbours and the outside world.[56] Thus, SAARC is a product of the indigenous factors governing the political systems and the inter-relationships of the South Asian States.

While the democratic system was the more uniting factor for the European Community, convergence of foreign policy has been the common ground for both the EC and the ASEAN. South Asia on the other hand finds itself in a diametrically opposite situation compared to these organizations. For, its member States neither have a similarity in political systems nor have common approach in their foreign policy. Moreover, the South Asian States' security perceptions are directed more against each other than the outside powers unlike the ASEAN or EC States.[57]

As far as the organizational structure is concerned, the EEC has adopted an elaborate system, The ASEAN too has a larger organizational structure compared to SAARC. But the organizational or institutional framework does not really become a hurdle in the progress of the organization, because it is the political will of the members of the body which counts more in shaping the destiny of the organization.

Both the ASEAN and the EEC have initially taken some time to take off in their cooperative endeavours. The ASEAN had taken nine years to form a Secretariat whereas SARC/SAARC has taken just four years from its inception to establish its Secretariat.[58] However, the ASEAN and EEC have achieved remarkable progress in regional cooperation and formulated a common agenda for economic and social development for the people of their region. There has been tremendous progress in the cooperation among the member States of these regional organizations, especially in the fields of trade, commerce, science and technology, communications, transport, culture and education. Political homogeneity is cited as the cause of success of these regional bodies. Hence, it is said that SAARC cannot be judged by these standards. However, SAARC can gain by emulating them in evolving a common approach to the problems of poverty alleviation, economic development and cooperation in the fields of trade, commerce and industry.

One of the basic differences between the SAARC and ASEAN, EEC or GCC is that in the case of the latter there is a pivotal power which always stood by them and extended them the necessary help in achieving the desired progress. In the case of EEC, the USA, in the case of ASEAN, both the USA and Japan were there to support them. The GCC has its own core State viz., the Saudi Arabia which, of course, enjoyed the support of the USA. In the case of the SAARC, India can be regarded as the core power though which it is in fact the other members of the region have not been ready to regard it as such. On the contrary, they have been accusing it as the "Big Brother", the "Hegemonist power" etc. In fact, it was one of factors for the delay in evolution of the regional organization for South Asia.

The European Community and the ASEAN are poised for momentous changes in their cooperative framework. The recently held summit of the Heads of States of the EC at Maastricht in

December 1991 finalised plans for a United Europe by the turn of the century, including creation of the European Monetary Union by the beginning of 1999.[59] The Fourth Conference (Summit) of the Heads of States of the ASEAN held in January at Singapore also finalized plans for establishing an Asean Free Trade Area (AFTA). These developments offer SAARC great inspiration for achieving tangible progress in the fields of political, economic and scientific and technological cooperation for the benefit of the people of the region.

SAARC and the Non-Alignment

The Charter specifically mentions that the regional cooperation under SAARC was not inconsistent with multilateral cooperation or obligations. The basic desire as has already been mentioned earlier in establishing the SAARC is said to be the promotion of peace, stability, amity and progress in the region through strict adherence to the principles of the UN Charter and Non-Alignment. As such, SAARC is an organization fully compatible with the Non-Aligned Movement (NAM). The guiding principles of NAM and the SAARC are not merely identical but more or less one and the same.

There is however, a fundamental difference between SAARC and the NAM, in that the latter is an informal association of like minded States which has yet to establish an institutional mechanism to implement its programmes and achieve its objectives and goals. In fact, the NAM has originally evolved as a forum or a common platform of those countries which did not approve of the division of the world into two power blocs on political and ideological lines. It was a approach to look at the international relations based on the principles of equality, justice and amity. It also has an economic content in it, as it advocates promotion of peace, stability and amity in the world so that the poor and developing States of the world could concentrate on economic development and social progress instead of engaging in rivalries and resultant arms race. Of late (NAM) has been taking up the cause of the developing countries of the South in their bid to bring about a New International Economic Order. In a limited perspective, as far as South Asia is concerned, SAARC is in fact a step ahead from the NAM. It is not only aimed at achieving peace, stability in the region but also aims at accelerating economic growth, social progress and cultural development of the region. It, unlike NAM, has an institutional mechanism to work towards this end.

The NAM is a motley group of heterogenous States from different parts of the world.[60] The SAARC, inspite of being a coherent and compact region, also consists of States with different political systems and divergent political and ideological perceptions. It is a common knowledge that NAM has the dubious distinction of being many of its members trucked in military and political alliances with one or the other superpowers while advocating non-alignment as basic policy. This sort of ambivalence was not absent in some of the South Asian States at the beginning of the SARC/SAARC and to some extent it exists even now. In fact, this unity in diversity of sorts is one of the basic characteristics and in a way an inherent weakness of both the organizations.

Neither the NAM nor SAARC has been associated with one or other the superpowers formally from the very beginning. This is not however the case of ASEAN or EEC, as it has already been explained in the previous section of this chapter.

However, SAARC and the NAM have an identity of purpose in promoting peace, security, stability and economic development of its members. To some extent the NAM has functioned as a rallying point for the demands of the developing countries against the developed world in various international organizations, viz., the United Nations, the UNCTAD, etc. Thus, it could not only help easing tensions in the world but also help in achieving some sort of cooperation among the developing countries of the world which is now known as South-South Cooperation.

The SAARC, as an organization, having the ideals of non-alignment as its guiding philosophy is expected to gain in adopting a common and united approach towards the problems of the developing countries in general and South Asia in particular. This can be achieved by evolving consensus on the basis of issues in relation to the other regions or States outside the region. Notwithstanding the inherent weaknesses NAM can serve as a guiding force to the States of the SAARC. This is more so in the light of the incredible changes that have taken place in the global system in the recent past.

SAARC and the UN

Just as the NAM and SAARC are complementary to each other, SAARC and the UN are also perfectly compatible and complementary to each other. The objectives of SAARC and UN more or less coincide with each other. However, there are many differences between the two. First of all, the UN is an institution set up to manage the international relations in the post-war period as desired by the then superpowers, the USA and the Soviet Union. Secondly, the UN, though professes the sovereign equality of the member States, in actual practice, however gave more powers to a few members. The Permanent Members of the Security Council are considered more equal than the other members of the UN. In contrast the SAARC is a spontaneous outcome of the desire of the States of South Asian region and it functions strictly on basis of the principle of sovereign equality of the member States, irrespective of their size, population or military or economic power.

Thirdly, the UN is a worldwide organization and its activities encompass a wide range of social, economic, political, cultural and scientific areas. SAARC is also a comprehensive organization but its membership and *ipso facto*, its operations are limited to the South Asian region only. Fourthly, there is a lot of difference in the institutional framework of both the organizations. The UN has a wide and elaborate network of institutions whereas the SAARC has a limited institutional framework commensurate with its present stage of operation and financial resources. Lastly, the UN is dominated by the big powers of the world, particularly, the United States and its allies and by the erstwhile Soviet Union.

The SAARC is, therefore, different from the United Nations in its nature, structure, composition and powers. But as an organization it has the same responsibility to the people of the South Asia, as the UN has towards the humanity at large.

In this chapter we have given a theoretical framework of the concept of region and a working definition thereto and the suitability of identifying South Asia as a distinct region for the purpose of regional cooperation. We have also dealt with the evolution of the SAARC, its objectives, structure and functions and its comparison with other regional and global organizations. An attempt has also been made to analyse the structural features of the SAARC and its weaknesses, if any.

References

1. We will be using the terms States, nations and countries interchangeably throughtout the present study.

2. A few important contributions in the field of study are Richard A. Falk and Saul H. Mendlovitz (Eds.), *Regional Politics and World Order* (W.H. Freeman, San Fransisco 1973); Louis J. Cantori & Steven L. Spiegel *International Politics of Regions : A Comparative Approach* (Eaglewood Cliffs, N. Jercy, 1970), Ronald Y. Yalem, *Regionalism and World Order* (Washington D.C. 1965); and Bruce Russet, International Regions and International Systems (Chicago, 1967).

3. His much acclaimed work on this topic is in French Language, viz., *Contribution a L' Etude Des Ententes Regionales* (Paris, 1949). Boutros Ghali is the present Secretary - General of the only comprehensive global organization, the United Nations.

4. Quoted by Ronald Yalem in sub-article "Theories of Regionalism" in Richard A. Falk and S.H. Mendlovitz (Eds.), *op. cit*, p. 220.

5. L. Cantori and S. Spiegel, *op.cit.*, p. 341.

6. Michael Brecher, "International relations and Asian Studies : The Subordinate State System of Sourthern Asia", *World Politics*, Vol. 15, No. 2, p. 219.

7. Bruce M. Russet, *op. cit.*, pp. 1-7.

8. Bibek Debroy, "South-South Cooperation, *Foreign Trade Review*, Oct.-Dec. 1988, p. 262.

9. Some of these criteria, however were listed in Theodor A. Couloumbis & James H. Wolfe, *Introduction to International Relations : Power and Justice*, (Prentice-Hill India, N. Delhi, 1982), p. 284.

10. Salahuddin Ahmed, "The Identity of the *Sub continent*', *India International Centre Quarterly*, Summer 1987, p. 79.

11. Raj Kumar,'Regional Organizations and Third World Countries', *India Quarterly*, Vol. 47, Nos. 1-2, January-June 1991.

12. Mohammad Ayoob,"The Primacy of Political", *Asian Survey* 25 (4), April 1985, p. 443 ; P.K. Srivastava and Rajni Kothari "SAARC', *Seminar* (324), August 1986, p. 22.

13. R.V.R. Chandrasekhar Rao, 'Regional Cooperation in South Asia, *The Round Table* (293), 1985, p. 54.

14. See Cantori and Spiegel, *op. cit.*, pp. 338-40.

15. According to *Encyclopaedia of Social Sciences* (New York, 1968), one of the important pre-requisites of a region is a formal organization (Vol. 13, p. 378).

16. Craig Baxter, Y. Malik *et al*, *Government and Politics in South Asia* (Vanguard, Lahore, 1988), p. 269.

17. See Michael Brecher, in Falk and Mendlovitz, *op. cit*, p. 273.

18. Partha S. Ghosh, *Cooperation and Conflict in South Asia* (Manher, Delhi, 1989), p. 7.

19. Michael Brecher, *op. cit*, p. 230.

20. Pramod Kumar Misra, "Determinants of Intra-Regional Relations in South Asia", *India Quarterly*, 36 (1), Jan.-March 1980, p. 69.

21. Michael Brecher, *op. cit*, p. 224.

22. R.V.R. Chandrasekhar Rao, *op. cit.*, p. 56; and Upreti, "Regional Cooperation in South Asia : Nepal's Role and Attitude", in Dharmdasani (Ed.), *South Asian Regional Cooperation* (Shalimar, Varanasi 1985), p. 139.

23. S.D. Muni, "Beneficial Bilateralism in South Asia", *India Quarterly*, 35 (9), Oct.- Dec., 1979, p. 417.

24. A.B. Vajpayee, "India and the Changing International Order", *Indian and Foreign Review*, Vol. 15 (9), 15 Feb. 1978, p. 12.

25. R.V.R. Chandrasekhar Rao, *op. cit.*, p. 58, and Rehman Sobhan "The Economic background", in Bimal Prasad (Ed.), *Regional Cooperation in South Asia: Problems and Prospects* (Vikas, Delhi, 1989), p. 21.

26. S.D. Muni, "Building Regionalism from Below", *Asia Survey*, 25 (4), April 1985, p. 292.

27. P.K. Misra, "Towards a Framework of South Asian Regional Cooperation : Colombo to Kathmandu", *Foreign Affairs Reports*, 31 (12), December 1982.

28. Quoted in Imtiaz H. Bokhari, "South Asian Regional Cooperation: Progress, Problems, Potential and Prospects', *Asian Survey*, 25 (4), April 1985, p. 376.

29. Joint Communique issued after the First Meeting of Foreign Secretaries at Colombo, 21-23 April 1981, para 7.

30 *Ibid.*, para 8.

31. *Ibid.*, para 12.

32. Joint Communique of the Second Foreign Ministers' Meeting held at Kathmandu, 2-4 November 1981, para 5.

33. See SARC Declaration, 2 August 1983, Section I.

34. Reproduced in *India Quarterly*.

35. See SARC Declaration, *op. cit.*

36. Imtiaz H. Bokhari, *op. cit.*, p. 379.

37. Indira Gandhi, *op. cit.*

38. See *Far Eastern Economic Review*, Nov. 13, 1981 and Aug. 13, 1982 (At that time there were only five members in the ASEAN).

39. P.K. Srivastava & Rajni Kothari, *op. cit.*, p. 22.

40. P.K. Misra, "Regional Cooperation in South Asia: Constraints and Realities" in M.D. Dharmdasani, *op. cit.*, No. 19, pp. 188-191.

41 See the Charter of SAARC adopted at Dhaka, 8 December 1985.

42. *Ibid.*

43. *Ibid.*, Article II.

44. *Ibid.*, Article X, Clause 2.

45. Gammani Corea, "Regional Cooperation in South Asia: Perspective and Prospects", *South Asia Journal*, Vol. I, No. 3, July-Sept. 1987, p.1.

46. A. S. Abraham in the *Times of India*, February 15, 1985.

47. K.P. Saksena, Institutional Framework, in Bimal Prasad (Ed.), *Regional Cooperation. in South Asia, op. cit.*, p. 88.

48. See Gursharan Singh Dhanjal, "SAARC: A Sumit Fiasco", *Mainstream*, December 14, 1991, pp. 25-26.

49. SAARC Charter, Article IV.

50. Article V of the SAARC Charter.

51. *Ibid.*, Article VI.

52. K. P. Saksena, *op. cit.*, p. 89.

53. Article X of the SAARC Charter.

54. R.V.R. Chandrasekhar Rao, *op. cit.*, p. 55.

55. Mohammad Ayoob, "The Primacy of the Political", *Asian Survey*, 25 (4), April 1985, p. 447.

56. P.K. Srivastava and Rajni Kothari, *op. cit.*, p. 23.

57. Mohd. Ayoob, *op. cit.*, pp. 450-451.

58. K.P. Saksena, *op. cit.*, p. 89.

59. *Frontline*, p. 53.

60. Jivogan Jagic, "Non-alignment and Asia", *India Quarterly* Vol. 44, 1 & 2, Jan.-June 1988, p. 23.

CHAPTER III

A PROFILE OF THE REGION

The very process of evolution of the SAARC or the delay in its emergence, to say so, had given room to doubts about its viability and survival. The future of this nascent organization is said to be dependent on the attitudes and responses of its members and various other factors that affect the inter-relationships among its members. Behind the simple facade of this organization, there is a very complex group of States, which defy definition or clear characterization.

A clear understanding of the multi-faceted background of these States and the factors that govern their mutual relations will be a great advantage in understanding the process of its evolution, the ups and downs it faced in its short period of existence, the nature of its achievements or failures if any and the prospects that the future holds for it.

Hence, in this chapter, an attempt is made, to make a study of the historical background, political systems, economic background and foreign policy postures of the member States of the SAARC. As the linkage between domestic politics and the foreign policy postures are considered to be quite close in the case of nations and the members of SAARC are no exception. The domestic political problems, especially that of ethnic and religion related politics are also taken into consideration in presenting the profiles of the member States. The present analysis acquires crucial importance in our study because the final evaluation of the present, past and future of SAARC is directly related to it.

The Historical Background

A major portion of South Asia has the unique distinction of enjoying a common historical background. Almost all the member States of the SAARC were under the British rule or supremacy till the end of the World War II. The degree of subjugation, however, ranged between complete political subjugation to protectorates. But the sway of the British military, economic and political power in the region was unquestionable and complete.

The Indian sub-continent, which consists of present day States of India, Pakistan and Bangladesh, was under the direct rule of the British for about two centuries preceding their attaining independence. Thus, the historical roots of these countries are one and the same though their present ramifications are diverse and mutually antagonistic.

The fight to drive out the colonial masters and the struggle for freedom had revived the concept of nationalism in India. The nationalist movement has brought the people of different linguistic, religious and cultural groups together and bound them in a single and unified cause of freedom from the shackles of the British colonialism. India is the best and the most striking example of this kind of cultural, social and political revival of nationalist sentiments. In the struggle for freedom the Hindus, the Muslims, the Sikhs, the Christians and the other groups have come together under one banner, viz., the Indian National Congress[1] which at that time was the sole representative of the nationalist forces in India.

The influence of the nationalist movement was such that the Indian sub-continent, extending from the mighty Himalayas in the north to the Indian Ocean in the south and from Quetta in the west to the borders of the Burma in the east, was expressing in terms of one nation and one people. In spite of the geographical, linguistic, ethnic, religious and cultural divergences, the whole sub-continent remained in tact and moreover the social and cultural bonds got strengthened. The sub-continent was divided into many States politically and these States were ruled by Hindu, Muslim and Sikh rulers. Yet the pan-Indian feeling was the converging point for the people of the sub-continent.

This unity and sentiment was always present, during the past several centuries before the advent of the British colonialism in India. The British were successful in gradually making inroads into the imperceptible social cleavages of the diverse groups in the Indian society and thereby exploiting the situation to their own benefit. Until then the Indian sub-continent stood as one monolithic socio-cultural entity preserving itself against the vicissitudes of time. The British could gain entry and entrench itself into the Indian soil mainly on its political acumen coupled with military strength and the docile and tolerant nature of the Indian people came handy. The present States of India, Pakistan and Bangladesh together could be called the heirs of a common historical and cultural legacy.[2]

The tide of nationalist movement and patriotic fervour which rose against the British colonial domination transcended all ethnic, geographic, religious barriers in India. The diversities that exist today are only created deliberately for narrow political gains. The nationalist movement inspired all sections of the Indian society irrespective of its diversities. The Indian National Congress which is the major representative of the national movement in India consisted of all religous and linguistic groups of people.[3] The Indian nationalism of that day, which signified the unification of all sections of the society, was essentially a secular and democratic movement. It was a complex combination of the traditional Indian identity and the unity of the Indian people with the liberal democratic ideas of the west that have crept into the Indian sub-continent through the British policies. Later this very admixture of tradition and modernity was to form part of the Indian polity.[4] The essence of the Indian nationalism represented by Gopal Krishna Gokhale, B.G. Tilak, M.K. Gandhi, Sarojini Naidu etc. was built on the basic tenets of Hindu social and cultural ethos, namely, the universal brotherhood, tolerance, peace and justice (dharma), simplicity, kindness and hospitality at the same time encouraging the spirit and courage to fight evils with conviction. The colonial rule and the freedom movement have also contributed to reinforce the unity among various cultural, ethnic and linguistic groups. This has come to stay as the main characteristic of the Indian society. In fact, it has become its strength and its weakness.

The historical roots and the cultural heritage of other States of South Asia are more or less akin to India. Particularly, Pakistan and Bangladesh are the co-heirs of the historical, social and cultural legacy of India. As a matter of fact there was no separate Pakistani indentity or nationalism prior to the partition into two independent States of Pakistan and India.[5] Though, the people of India, Pakistan and Bangladesh were one and the same, inheriting the same historical and cultural legacy waging a struggle against the British colonialism along with each other to gain freedom, have become in the course of time bitter enemies. Once the common enemy, the British masters, retreated, they were divided on the basis of personality clashes and religious sentiments. The prospects of sharing power in the aftermath of the retreat of the British had given rise to 'two nation theory'. The people who have joined the newly formed State of Pakistan got their identity as Pakistanis mostly due to the fact of their being Muslims. Even within the newly formed State of Pakistan, the ethnic and cultural differences persisted. Thus, the new nation emerged out of the hitherto undivided India, shed its Indian identity and vigorously pursued a separate identity and Muslim nationhood, viz. the Pakistani. The hitherto shared social, cultural, ethnic and national heritage is totally and deliberately discarded in favour of the newly attained Pakistani nationhood.

Bangladesh had the unique distinction of being a heir to the Indian historical and cultural heritage as well as to the Islamic nationhood of Pakistan. During the freedom struggle against the British colonial rule, Bengal was a very prominent province in the Indian union and its contribution to the growth of freedom movement was by any standards very significant. It is observed that Bengali nationalism was one of the major threats to the British rule in India. Curzon had come out with the idea of the partition of Bengal only to assuage this growing force of Bengali nationalism.[6]

The emerging trends of Bengali nationalism among the Muslims of East Bengal were evident in their initial hesitant reaction towards the annulment of partition. A.K. Fazlul Haq , a prominent leader of the Bengali Muslims is on record to have opposed the general approval by the Muslim League of the annulment of partition of Bengal.[7]

After the formation of separate State of Pakistan, the Muslims of East Bengal were initially wholeheartedly accepted their newly developed Pakistani identity.They had quite high expectations under the new dispensation. But gradually there was a definite and steady erosion of their expectations. Within a short period, they got disillusioned with the Pakistani govenment (West) and have started to vent out their discontent. Imperceptibly the consciousness of deprivation and disillusionment paved way for an urge for separate identity. The lack of proper representation for the East Pakistanis in the army and bureaucracy and denial of official language status to Bengali and continuous domination of the Urdu speaking Muslims from the West Pakistan have given an impetus to the growing disenchantment with the West and also have given fillip to the subtle undercurrent of Bengali nationalism.[8] Thus, interestingly, the Bengali nationalism had its historical roots dating back to the Mughal period, freedom struggle of India, but it has reached its culmination under the domination of the West Pakistan, ultimately resulting in the emergence of a new State of Bangladesh.

Sri Lanka, like the sub-continent of India, too was under the British colonial rule. But its evolution has a different dimension. Her political and economic conditions under the colonial masters were different, rather better compared to India or for that matter any other non-white colony. Hence, the circumstances under which a unified struggle for freedom and the nationalist movement emerged in India were, more or less absent in Ceylon (as Sri Lanka was then called). There was in fact no freedom struggle worth the name.[9] As such, no nationalism worth mentioning was evident in the history of Ceylon. However, a faint idea of forming a united platform *vis-a-vis* the colonial administration was evident and consequently the Ceylon National Congress was formed with the coming together of both the dominant sections of the country, viz., the Sinhalese and the Tamils.[10] But, that was a shortlived unity. Within a short period of few years the Sinhala Maha Sabha was formed by S.W.R.D. Bandarnayake and a few other political outfits have come into existence to represent various hues of the island politics.[11] In the absence of a common ideology, political perception and a common enemy, the Ceylonese people were divided and their ethnic and religious diversity remained stable during the colonial period and it is in tact in the post-independent period as well.

Nepal and Bhutan were never colonies of any power and they have enjoyed independent status albeit subject to the British paramountcy and without prejudice to British interests in the Indian subcontinent.

The contemporary Nepal was established when King Prithvi Narayan Shah brought together various principalities of the Himalayan region under his control in 1769. Since then, till 1864, it was an absolute monarchy. In 1864, Jang Bahadur Rana, the Prime Minister emerged as the most powerful man, using his influence with the queen. Thus taking over the political power from the King and relegating him to the background, he succeeded in making the position of the Prime Minister hereditary.[12] The power of the Ranas superseded the institution of monarchy. This system continued till King Tribhuvan Bir Bikram Shah. Deva overturned it and established monarchy again in 1951. Since then some sort of a constitutional monarchy was evolved.

The changes that have taken place in the world at large during the 50s have raised the aspirations of the people of Nepal also. As a result a system of democracy in the shape of limited monarchy was introduced in 1959. But it was a shortlived one. The then Monarch, King Mahendra abolished it and re-established the monarchy with the system of partyless panchayat as a facade.

Broadly speaking, the people of Nepal are generally traditional minded more or less unaffected by the cultural onslaught of the western civilization. One of the reasons for this lies in Nepal being the only Hindu State in the world and the people of Nepal are proud of this fact. Secondly, the political system that existed in Nepal all these years did not permit any such liberty to the people. The political, social and cultural conservatism of Nepal is well reflected in the words of King Birendra to quote him "We must never expect that a country which has never been a colony cannot adopt a policy directly from outside.[13]

However, this is only a partial representation of the present state of the Nepalese system. But it can be said that the political system that functioned during the past four decades has exercised a definite influence on the political, cultural and social attitudes of the people of Nepal. Of course, Nepal could not withstand the tide of democratic movement and ultimately succumbed to it.

Bhutan, another Himalayan State, sandwiched, like Nepal, between the two giants of Asia, China and India, too is a monarchy. While the Indian sub-continent and the other Asian countries were reeling under the political turbulence, Bhutan was ruled by a combination of Buddhist Lamas and local headmen and tribal chiefs. In 1907 the monarchy of Bhutan was established under the rule of Ugyen Wangchuk who became the first Druke Gyalpo, the King. The British have also encouraged it and have entered into a treaty with Ugyen Wangchuk to thwart any Chinese designs on it.[14] Since then, till 1949 the British have controlled the external relations of Bhutan under this treaty. Like Nepal, Bhutan also did not witness any nationalist movement. It was not necessary for her as the circumstances did not warrant it. Bhutan is also a traditional society. However, of late, Bhutan is also gradually opening its eyes to the realities in the outside world and also started modernizing. Whatever little changes or progress taken or taking place is under the third and fourth Kings Dorji Wangchuk and Jigme Singye Wangchuk respectively. Like any nation transforming from tradition to modernity, Bhutan is also witnessing turmoil in its social, cultural, economic and political system.

Maldives which is an archipelago of over 1000 tiny islands (of which only about 200 are inhabited) in the central Indian Ocean, was a protectorate of the British empire during 1867 and 1966. It became independent in 1966 and a republic in 1968. There was no freedom movement as the British have left the native Sultan with adequate independence to deal with the internal affairs of his country.[15] Nor was there any necessity for any nationalist movement to unite the people as the people in its entirety, belonged to one religion and more or less one ethnic group. In Maldives 100% of the population adheres to the Islamic religion.[16] However, the Maldivian brand of Islamism it totally different from the Islam of the West Asian type.[17]

Obviously, while the major States of the South Asian region, namely India, Pakistan and Bangladesh, have an identical or evenly unified historical background, the smaller States on the other hand have another analogous pattern of historical antecedents. Again, the major States have emerged from a common land mass and out of a common set of circumstances and almost at the same time in the world history, i.e., the immediate aftermath of the World War II, The reason d'etre of the smaller ones is diverse but uneventful.

The emergence of the States of India and Pakistan as sovereign and independent States is preceded by a long drawn struggle for freedom. India's freedom struggle marks one of the epic stories in the annals of the world history. Its significance lies in the fact that it is also accompanied by a series of the administrative reforms introduced by the British rulers. The freedom movement and the administrative reforms had an indelible impact on the emerging new polity and political and socio-economic system in India. Both of them together brought about a composite system of Western based liberal democracy and a nation-State into a traditional society. But the reforms introduced beginning in the year 1909 (Minto-Morley reforms) have gradually caused a schism not only in the India nationalist movement but also in the social fabric which ultimately led to the partition of the sub-continent into India and Pakistan.

The emergence of Muslim League, claiming to represent the interests of the Muslim community can be traced to the concessions offered to them by the colonial government under various reforms. In all the successive reforms the Muslims got a good chunk of the political power. Thus, the Muslim League and the British have found friends in each other. The final shot in the arm to the cause of Pakistan was given by World War II and attitudes of the INC and the League as regards India joining the war. While the Congress opposed it vehemently, the League supported and the British were pleased with the League's stand.[18] Not surprisingly, after the end of the war the British have come out with a favourable deal to the Muslim League (August Declaration, Communal Plan and the Partition Plan). Thus, the two-nation theory made the British and Muslim League close allies which finally led to the evolution of Pakistan.

The evolution of India and Pakistan as two separate States is rooted in two different ideologies and also their divergent approaches. While India emerged out of a nationalist movement inspired by the ideals of freedom, democracy and secularism, the basis of the formation of Pakistan was religious identity. In other words, while India represented the aspirations of the people for a free, just and equitable society, Pakistan is the realisation of the 'two-nation theory' advocated by its main architects. Thus, as a climax to the saga of the turbulent freedom movement which assumed violent and tragic dimensions towards the final stages, a partition plan was offered by Mountbatten in 1947 which came into effect on 14-15 August 1947. Pakistan was carved out of the sub-continent and had two wings—one in the west and the other in the east—which in itself was another quirk of the shrewd policy of the colonial rulers.

Sri Lanka (Ceylon), as mentioned earlier, did not have to wage any struggle to win her freedom. On the contrary, the Ceylonese were so happy with the colonial rule that they regarded their land as a part of England.[19] The British rule in Ceylon was liberal and benevolent enough towards its subjects that right from the 1870s the Ceylonese were inducted into the civil service whereas the Indians had to wrest that right after a prolonged struggle. The Colebrook Commission, a couple of decades later, marked the beginning of the constitutional reforms in Ceylon with a fair share of power to the Ceylonese, far ahead of other colonies of the British empire.[20] A century later, the Donoughmore Commission gave 70% of independence with a State Council elected by universal adult franchise and a Board of seven ministers consisting of Ceylonese.[21] Finally on February 4, 1948 the sovereignty of Ceylon passed into the hands of the Ceylonese without much ado or flutter. Thus the road to freedom for Sri Lanka was smooth and uneventful. The euphoria of patriotic sentiments and nationalist fervour evident in the case of India was apparently missing in the case of Ceylon.

The birth of Bangladesh is a different story. She had to fight the internal colonialism and exploitation to emerge as an independent State. East Bengal, which was the eastern part of Pakistan, was never comfortable in Pakistan as it was always looked down by the West Pakistanis. Right from the beginning, the East Pakistanis were denied a fair deal in the recruitment to army and bureaucracy and also in the economic sphere. The denial of due place to the Bengali language was another blow to the sentiments of the East Pakistanis.[22] The disillusionment with the Pakistani government has reached a crescendo by 1960s. This has led to a demand for autonomy for East Pakistan which was articulated by the Awami League leader, Shaikh Mujibur Rahman's Six Point Programme.[23] The arrest of Mujibur Rahman in 1966 in connection with the alleged Agartala Conspiracy has further aggravated the estrangement with the West Pakistan and Mujib earned the sympathy of the people as a martyr.

After Ayub Khan's resignation as Pakistan's President, his successor, Yahya Khan, ordered elections to be held on 7 December 1970. The overall antipathy of the Pakistani government towards East Pakistan has reached a boiling point by 1970. The demand for autonomy had reached a point of no-return when the government failed to offer adequate help to the victims of severe cyclone that caused devastation in most parts of East Pakistan.[24] The results of the December 1970 elections reflected the feelings of the people with the Awami League winning 167 seats out of a total of 313 in the National Assembly thus confering the right to rule on its leader Shaikh Mujibur Rahman. The West Pakistani rulers could not swallow this bitter pill and prevaricated the convening of the National Assembly, which was also supposed to decide on the shape of the new Constitution. The National Assembly was convened to meet on 3 March 1971 but was postponed later to 25 March, 1971. The dealy in convening the

National Assembly meeting raised the tempers of East Pakistanis. But, once again the date of the National Assembly meeting was postponed. While these delaying tactics were going on, Zulfikar Ali Bhutto, leader of the Pakistani People's Party laid his claim to share power with the Awami League as his party has got majority in the West (Pakistan). This was not acceptable to the Awami League and the East Pakistanis. Deprived of their genuine right, the East Pakistanis have declared their intentions to separate from West Pakistan and form a new State called Bangladesh.[25] Yahya Khan, the then military ruler of Pakistan, instigated by Bhutto, decided to deal with the Bengali (East) recalcitrants with a firm hand and ordered a crackdown on 25 March 1971. Bangladesh declared independence unilaterally the same day and a civil war followed. The Bangladeshis, under the banner of Mukthi Bahini, a militant volunteer group, fought the Pakistani forces. This is followed by an unprecedented exodus of the Bengalis into India. This aggravated tensions in Indo-Pak relations which ultimately broke out into a full-scale war which ended with the surrendering of the Pakistani army in Bangladesh on 17 December 1971.

The historical background and the evolution of the member States of the (SAARC) has a peculiar and strange interconnection with one another. Especially, the most populous States of the region, viz., India, Bangladesh and Pakistan have a common history and common socio-economic and cultural heritage but the centrifugal forces that have precipitated their emergence have caused an instinctious apathy and even hatred towards one another. The Indian sub-continent have got the other neighbours, viz., Nepal, Bhutan, Sri Lanka and Maldives as *fait accompli* as they were already on the scene with a political and geographical coherence. By 1947 Nepal and Bhutan were already enjoying independent status and Sri Lanka and Maldives were on the threshold of gaining complete independence.

Political Institutions and Political Instability

This region has an unenviable composition of complex and diverse political systems. A majority of the population in South Asia is under democratic governments. India and Sri Lanka have consistently been maintaining some semblance of democratic systems while Pakistan and Bangladesh have, most of the time, been under the military dictatorships. Nepal and Bhutan, on the other hand, remained as monarchies. Maldives has also been under autocratic rule though it claims to be a republic with an elected President.

Right through the period of the freedom struggle and the constitutional reforms under the British rule, India has been experimenting with a democratic system. Soon after attaining independence India set out to forge a new Constitution for itself with the help of a Constituent Assembly. The new Constitution was completed and adopted on 26 November 1949 and it came into effect on 26 January 1950. The Constitution in content and spirit made India a Sovereign, Democratic Republic based on the West-minster model. Since then India retained its Constitution and democratic structure ensuring a reasonable degree of stability to its political system.

India adopted more or less a federal structure (it is in fact federal, but the Constitution makes the centre so strong that it appears like a unitary system with federal features at times) and parliamentary form of government. To reinforce the democratic system an independent judiciary is incorporated. The party system in India is still in a state of flux. Defections and intra-party dissidence and factionalism is the main source of threat to the stability of the political system. Illiteracy, poverty and the unequal socio-economic structure makes the party system mostly dominated by individuals rather than politics.

It is rather difficult to put the Indian political system in a straight jacket. It is, in fact, a combination of both modern and traditional elements. The modern element being the democratic values and traditionalism is characterised by the parochial caste system, personality cult verging on deification and the values like Dharma and toleration etc.[26] This very complex nature of the Indian polity is the source of its weakness as well as its strength and stability. That explains why in spite of the growing unemployment, poverty, misery and social unrest, India remained a democracy although. While the democratic institutions are subverted by the autocratic elements in the ruling elite and the concentration of power in a few hands and institutions continued the system could withstand this onslaught successfully. Though the participation in the democratic process by the people at large is minimal with the passage of time the consciousness of the people is growing to the level of asserting their rights and questioning the legitimacy of the government. This is reflected in the results of the elections in 1977, 1980, 1989 and 1991. The participation of the people in the electoral process has been quite impressive during the past two decades.[27] Notwithstanding the socio-political and economic challenges faced by her, India has developed an inherent strength of resilience to maintain the basic structure of the polity. The main problem with the Indian political system and its institutions today is the fusion of democracy, social justice, national integration and economic development into its national goals.

Shri Lanka, the other democratic State of the region, proved to be successful during the past four decades. However, she also faces the problems of economic development and national integration etc. Like India, Sri Lanka also enjoyed a near stability. The elections are held periodically and the power changed hands smoothly without any deviation from the democratic process.

However, the Sri Lankan polity is a heavily majority oriented one, with the least constitutional protection to the minority communities in the country. The Tamils, who are concentrated in the north and eastern parts of the island constitute the largest minority, aspired for a federal system for Sri Lanka so that their right could be protected properly. But the majority Sinhalese looked down Tamil ethnic minorities aspirations for a federal polity as an anti-social and anti-national concept threatening their own security.

Sri Lanka has changed Constitutions several times so far. The original one created by the Soulbury Commission was a copy of the Westminster system. The Sri Lankan government headed by the Sri Lankan Freedom Party (SLFP) changed the Constitution and adopted a new one in 1971 which was prepared by a Constitutional Convention consisting of members of parliament.

This Constitution gave a special place to Buddhism and Sinhala language and abolished the Senate.[28] The United National Party (UNP) government of J.R. Jayawardene in 1978 altered the Constitution and changed the structure of the government from parliamentary one to presidential one which is still in force as the UNP is enjoying an uninterrupted stint of power. Unfortunately, the Tamils were not associated with the formation of either the 1972 Constitution or the one that is in vogue since 1978. Therefore, they felt alienated and the recent developments in the Island country have totally estranged them with the mainstream (But more on this in the following section).

Pakistan and Bangladesh have so far had a none-too-favourable experience with democracy. In Pakistan the first Constitution took nine years to come out with a final shape. This was, of course, given a democratic facade more in deference to the wishes of the founder leader of Pakistan, Mohammad Ali Jinnah. It was promulgated on 26 March 1956 making Pakistan an Islamic Republic with federal structure and a parliamentary form of government which proved to be a dead letter as no elections could be conducted to the parliament.[29] Since then, Pakistan embarked on a series of military dictatorships. General Ayub Khan took over the reins of power as the martial law administrator but gave himself legitimacy by assuming power as President under the new Constitution promulgated by himself in 1962. The National Assembly i.e. the Pakistan Parliament were there only to accord legitimacy to the decisions taken by the President.

Ayub Khan continued to rule Pakistan till March 1969, after that General Yahya Khan continued the tradition of military dictatorship. The Bangladesh war and dismemberment of Pakistan saw Yahya Khan out of power and the first democratically elected government came to power in 1972 under the leadership of Zulfikar Ali Bhutto, the leader of the Pakistani People's Party (PPP). Bhutto was overthrown in a military coup and the then Army Chief, Gen. Zia-ul-Haq, who was made the Army Chief by Bhutto himself by superseding many of his seniors, came to power promising to hold elections to the National Assembly within 90 days. But Gen. Zia stayed in power for eleven years till August 1988 when he died in an air crash under mysterious circumstances.

From 1947—through 1988 while various experiments with Constitution and building of political institutions have invariably ended in a fiasco, the army in Pakistan systematically consolidated its position and today it is in a position to dictate terms to any government including democratically elected one.[30] This can be attributed to the higher level of politicisation of the military and lower level of consciousness of the people in general. The role of religion is another factor which invariably tried to weaken any democratic, secular or progressive thinking among the people and at the same time tried to strengthen autocratic rule in the name of God.

After the abrupt exit of Zia-ul-Haq from the political scene of Pakistan, elections to the parliament were held in an attempt to restore democracy. However, the military kept its option open to interfere if warranted and a trusted follower of Zia, Gulam Ishaq Khan occupied the post of President. Thus the democracy restored had these constraints on its functioning. Benazir Bhutto, the daughter of Z.A. Bhutto, the deposed and executed former Prime Minister, led her father's party (PPP) to power in late 1988. Though, initially Miss Bhutto talked about democratic values, within a short period she became a victim of political conspiracy hatched by the Islamic fundamentalists, the President and the army. After surviving the no-confidence motions twice in the National Assembly, she was finally dismissed by President Ishaq Khan in August 1990. Subsequently, elections were held to the National Assembly and amidst charges of rigging, the Islamic Jamhoori Ittehad (IJI) returned to power routing the Pakistan People's Party of Miss Bhutto. Nawaz Sharif, a Punjabi industrialist became the new Prime Minister of Pakistan in November 1990.

Today, the political clout in Pakistan lies still in the hands of the army, the President and the fundamentalist Islamic lobby. The parliamentary system is at the mercy of this trioka as the fledgling elected government is decimated into a fragile institution.[31]

Pakistan is a typical example of an Islamic country whose

political culture is dominated by theocratic and autocratic elements. The democratic institutions, however legitimate they may appear to be, do not carry much weight in this type of a political system. But Pakistan is not immune to the breath-taking changes that are taking place in many parts of the world. The struggle for democracy is still going on there. How far will it succeed is a big question which time only can answer.[32]

Bangladesh is also in a similar situation at the present juncture. The parliamentary system initially followed by the newly born State in 1971 was changed by its own leader Mujib-ur-Rahman into a presidential one in 1975. But Mujib maintained a semblance of democracy in Bangladesh as long as he was there at the helm of affairs. But the ouster and eventual murder of Mujib-ur-Rahman brought a new political culture in vogue in Bangladesh. The power was held by the army under Gen. Zia-ur-Rahman who tried to turn Bangladesh more into an Islamic State than a liberal democracy. However, he tried to legitimize his rule by changing the structure of the government and assuming as its President. He formed a political party of his own viz., the Bangladesh National Party (BNP) and gave a new twist to the military rule. But Zia was paid in his own coin as he was overthrown and assassinated and shortly a new military regime under the leadership of H.M. Ershad took the reins of power. In the face of serious public resentment against his authoritarian regime, which assumed alarming proportions over the past few years, Gen. Ershad submitted his resignation paving the way for restoration of democratic government.

Though military and religion play an important role in the political system of Bangladesh, the political groups led by the Bangladesh National Party (BNP) of Begum Khaleda Zia, the widow of late President Ziaur Rahman and the Awami League led by Shaikh Hasina Wajed, daughter of late Mujibur Rahman, the first Prime Minister of Bangladesh command considerable respect and support among the people. In fact, it is due to the relentless struggle waged by those political groups that a wave of popular opposition to the dictatorship of Gen. Ershad has been built up ultimately forcing him to relinquish power. Elections were held to the Jatiya Sangsad (Bangladesh Parliament) in March

1991 and the BNP of Begum Khaleda Zia came to power winning a comfortable majority. A few months later, Bangladesh switched over to a parliamentary form of government. This marked the end of military regime in another State of South Asian region after Pakistan turned to the democratic process in the last quarter of 1988. However, it cannot be said how secure the new found democracy in Bangladesh is. But given the changes in the political horizons of the world in general and South Asia in particular the changes that have taken place in Bangladesh in the past one year could be expected to consolidate a stable democratic system there. The pattern of voting and the enthusiasm shown by the people in the last elections symbolize the heralding of a promising future for Bangladesh, as a democratic State.[33]

Nepal remained a limited monarchy with the King actually enjoying a large share of power for nearly past four decades. The King was the main source of power in Nepal since 1951 and all other political institutions have been relegated to a secondary level. But the people's support and the political activity that helped the King in 1951 to regain his preeminence have raised the aspirations of the people. The first ever democratic experiment introduced by the King under a new Constitution in 1959 was a right step in this direction. The people of Nepal exercised their democratic rights in 1959 as a result of which a new government under the Primeministership of B.P. Koirala assumed power. But this experiment proved to be a shortlived one. The Prime Minister was arrested in December 1960, the parliament was dissolved and the monarchy assumed absolute powers since then.[34] A dubious democratic system under a Rashtriya Panchayat (the National Parliament) was constituted to be elected on a non-party basis. That system continued uninterrupted for two decades.

In May 1980 King Birendra held referendum giving a chance to the people to choose between a party system and a non-party system. The people exercised their choice in favour of the non-party system and thus it continued further.

But, since the beginning of the 1980s the movement for the restoration of party system and a popular democracy gathered momentum under the leadership of the banned Nepali Congress and the leftist parties. The movement reached its climax in 1990 and succeeded in overthrowing the partyless Panchayat system. Under pressure from the agitated people and various political groups on 16 April 1990 the King abolished the partyless panchayat which ruined the economy and the political aspirations of the people.[35] Political party system has been revived and elections to the Panchayat on a party basis took place in May 1991. Consequently, the Nepali Congress Party came to power with G.P. Koirala as the first elected Prime Minister of Nepal after more than three decades. However, even under the new Constitution the King retained considerable political power.

With Nepal transforming into a constitutional monarchy with a parliamentary form of government, the democratic wave has covered a major portion of South Asia, leaving only Bhutan and Maldives.

Bhutan is a limited monarchy. There is also a semblance of representative system, with a parliament, called Tshogdu, consisting of members partly elected by the people and partly nominated by the Druke Gyalpo (the King). There is a Council of Ministers and a Royal Advisory Council to assist the King. The political system of Bhutan is said to be a peculiar one suited to the hill kingdom as it allows proper representation and participation to the people.[36] However, the polity of Bhutan is vulnerable to imminent political turmoils as the predominantly Nepali population of the southern Bhutan is already witnessing the rumblings of political dissent.[37] Besides, in the past, there were a few attempted coups that have rocked the palace and the State.[38] As such, the dramatic changes that are sweeping the traditional and modern States of the world alike are likely to affect Bhutan too in the near future.

Maldives is also a traditional system, but it boasts of a democratic structure and a republican form of government. It has a presidential system. There is the Majlis (the legislature), elected for a period of five years. However, it enjoys little power as the *de facto* power rests with the President of the Republic. The people's participation is minimum, and there are glaring disparities between the elite class and the masses. The polity is by no means free from any turmoils.[39] This is borne out by the aborted coup against the President, Mamoon Abdul Gayoom in November 1988 that rocked the archipelago. It was the timely assistance rendered by India that saved President Gayoom and Maldives from destabilization.

Religion and State in South Asia

In the traditional societies one of the crucial factors that affects the stability and strength of a regime of any political hue, is the influence of religion on the political system. Experience in many parts of the world both in the past and also at present bears testimony to the fact that the religion (fundamentalism) has been the main destabilizing factor. Religion, acting as an antithetic to equality, social justice and secularism has always weakened democracy. Although the written history of religion had vied with the temporal power and always sought to curb it and thereby influence the destiny of the State.

Any polity that succumbs to the influence of religion readily or without much opposition can be called a traditional one and conversely any political system that successfully remains impervious to the pressures of religion can be called a modern one. Most of the States of South Asia, with the exception of India perhaps fall into the category of the traditional polities. However, the traditional character of many such States of the region has been undergoing changes and the degree of the influence of the religion varies from State to State in the region.

Due to the vision, foresight in the early stages and because of the necessity of the objective conditions prevailing at that time Indian Constitution makers and the top leadership have opted for a secular political system for India.[40] For all legal and constitutional purposes India maintained secular system with all the vigour and enthusiasm and in doing so she was actively assisted by the judiciary and the political parties. The Fundamental Rights under Article 19 (i) and 25 to 28 guarantee complete religious freedom to the people of India without any interference from the State. The Constitution also explicitly prohibits according special status or treatment to any particular religion by the State. Thus, while Hinduism is the religion of the majority of the population, other religions like Islam, Sikhism, Jainism, Buddhism and Christianity etc. exist alongside it with equal rights and status.

However, religion, especially for minorities, has become a focal point or the launching pad for venting out their dissatisfaction against the State and to promote their demands or claims. As far as the Muslims and Sikhs were concerned, this has been the normal practice. Of late, it is used as a rallying point to highlight diffferences with the establishment and to promote the extreme ideas of regionalism and separatism. The fundamentalist factions of Islam and Sikhs have revealed their political ambitions by stoking the fires of separation in Jammu and Kashmir and Punjab respectively.

Today, secularism in India is pitted against the forces of religious fundamentalism in the name of minority interests and nationalism. It is one of the problems of national integration now. The religion is used in politics also, inasmuch as the religious groups are considered as vote banks for the political parties. In the scramble for power the political parties are indulging in opportunistic tactics of supporting one religion against the other.[41] One of the burning issues threatening the communal harmony and national integration of the country is the Ramjanambhoomi-Babri Masjid issue. It was one of the main planks of electioneering in the 1991. The Bharatiya Janata Party (BJP) has fought the election on the slogan *Ram Roti aur Insaf* to underscore the importance of building Ram Temple at Ayodhya. It has actually promised to build Ram Temple in its election manifesto. Even, as on today, the Government of Uttar Pradesh is still trying to woo the Muslims offering concessions to clear its way for the construction of the Ram Temple.[42]

Much has been said about the caste system in India which is an offshoot of the Hindu social system and its influence on politics. Casteism and religious fundamentalism of both majority and minority communities are playing crucial role in the complex power politics of India and they are always a threat to the secular and democratic system of India. The very fact that India survived the divisive forces of religion and casteism indicates the resilience of her political system.

Religion occupies a very important place in Pakistan. It is one and the only factor that has an all pervading influence on the Pakistani State and society. In fact, the evolution of Pakistani State and its nationalism have their roots in the religious identity of its people. The politics in Pakistan are invariably mixed up with religious norms and sentiments.

Right from the beginning, in spite of the secular attitude of Mr. Jinnah, Pakistan has been proclaimed as the Islamic State.[43] Other religious groups like the Hindus and Christians also exist but they are negligible and their numbers are decreasing day by day. For instance, in Sind, there were about 23% Hindus at the time of partition but their share in population has shrunk to 5% now.[44] Obviously, religious tolerance is considered anachronistic in Pakistan and secularism is treated as un-Islamic. Hence, it is believed that opposing secularism is the duty of all Muslims.[45]

The influence of Islam on Pakistani political system has been profound and definite. All the rulers, including those wedded to either to democracy or to dictatorship have accepted the influence of religion and surrendered to it frequently. In fact, whenever there is a crisis of legitimacy of the political power, religion was invoked conveniently to gain the support of the people. Even in foreign policy the Islam has left its mark permanently, inasmuch as opposition to and claim against India are also expressed as Islamic imperatives.[46]

Bangladesh is also a multi-racial and multi-religious polity with a majority of the population (to be precise 87% of them) being Muslims, 12% Hindus and the remaining Christians, Buddhists etc. Initially, during the regime of Shaikh Mujib-ur-Rahman, Bangladesh was declared to be a secular State and the role of religion in the affairs of the State was minimal. With the assassination of Mujib and changing of power into the hands of military, religion had risen to a place of prominence.[47] Both under Zia-ur- Rahman and Ershad religion was used to boost up the sentiments of Bangladeshi nationalism. This was mainly aimed at weaning away Bangladesh from the influence of India. As a matter of fact, during the period between 1975 and late 1980s Islam was used to make Bangladesh adopt anti-Indian postures.

The importance given to Islam is evident by the changes made in the Constitution during Ershad's regime. Bangladesh was declared as an Islamic State and steps were taken to inject Islam into the legal, social and political system of the country.[48]

Nepal is the only State in the world which proclaimed itself as a Hindu State. The Nepalis are proud to call themselves Hindu and they are subconsciously affected by a Pan-Indian feeling as it is India which is the bulwark of Hinduism spiritually and socially. This could be inferred from the words of King Mahendra when he said that the people of India and Nepal together feel happy and proud at the fact that Nepal was a Hindu State.[49]

However, the ruling elite and the State of Nepal do not like to emphasize this link between India and Nepal. Majority of the population being Hindus there is no communal problem in Nepal worth the name. This is also due to the underplaying of religion in political affairs of the State.

Like the other States of South Asia, with the exception of India, which give pride of place to the majority religion, Sri Lanka also gives a prominent place to Buddhism. The other religions in the State, viz., Hinduism, Islam and Christianity do not enjoy equal status with Buddhism. The Sinhalese are the ardent followers of Buddhism and feel that Sri Lanka was their (i.e., Buddhists') country and they exhibited a feeling of antipathy towards the Hindus and Christians.

Bhutan is also a predominantly Buddhist State with a sizeable minority belonging to Hinduism. In both Bhutan and Sri Lanka, Buddhism exercises considerable influence on the State and its decision making process. In Bhutan a good number of members of Tehogdu are nominated from the Lamas. But the other religious groups, mainly the Hindus, the Tamils in Sri Lanka and the Nepalis in Bhutan have a considerable strength to pose a threat to the stability and integrity of the State. However, the kind of influence that is exercised in Pakistan by Islam is not seen either in Nepal or Sri Lanka or Bhutan.

Maldives is an Islamic State with 100% of its population following Islam. The influence of religion on politics in this tiny

State appears to be of least importance. Moreover, the traditions of Islam which are found in the west Asian countries are not visible in Maldives. The Islam of Maldives is quite different and fundamentalism is conspicuously absent there.[50]

By and large it can be said that religion is a source of tensions, disharmony and divisions in the society in the entire region of South Asia without exception. The States of South Asia, being more or less traditional, the people are generally influenced by religion in all walks of life. Hence, it has a telling impact on the political system of this region except where secularism is more steadfastly propagated and adhered to. Even in India, which is a secular State, the religion is not totally devoid of power to disturb the political equilibrium in the State.

Domestic Conflicts in SAARC Countries

All the countries of the South Asian region are haunted by a specture of internal turmoil, instability and separatism. The incapacity to deal with these challenges effectively or inability to find viable solutions to them, makes these States find scapegoats in "external threats". These threats come in handy in diverting the people's attention and save face and maintain political credibility at least temporarily. Generally, this is in fact crisis of the State power in most of the countries of South Asia at present. This naturally has its repercussions on the intra-regional relations in South Asia. It is this crisis and the attendant problems that are threatening not only the internal stability of the existing political regimes but also are hampering the evolution and growth of regional cooperation in South Asia. In this context, it is necessary to throw some light on the domestic conflicts of member countries of the SAARC.

India, the largest and the most powerful of the SAARC members and enjoying an unenviable position, is facing quite a number of problems of gigantic magnitude. It has become a regular phenomenon for India to have some problem or other debilitating the polity, society and the economy. This is particularly so since the early 1980s. The Punjab problem, the Assam problem, the extremist movements etc. have been eating into the vitals of her body politic. Now, the problem of Ramjanambhoomi-Babri

Masjid and the Kashmir problem have been added to the already existing crises.

The problem in Punjab, the most prosperous State of India, started in the late seventies as a sporadic movement, demanding special political and religious rights for the Sikhs, gradually gained strength and turned into a separatist movement by 1982. Various Sikh militant organizations which came into existence in the early 1980s raised the slogan of Khalistan, a separate State for the Sikhs and took the movement to dangerous proportions. The crisis was escalated further by 1984 leading to the Operation Blue Star, the controversial storming and flushing out of the extremists from the Golden Temple complex in Amritsar by the Army. It was a hard decision taken by the then Prime Minister, Mrs. Indira Gandhi. It hurt the sentiments of the Sikh community so badly that it claimed the life of the Prime Minister Indira Gandhi on 31 October 1984 and the communal holocaust sparked by this incident is a dark spot on the history of Indian democracy.

Rajiv Gandhi, succeeded Mrs. Gandhi as the Prime Minister, tried to bring peace to the beleaguered State by signing an agreement with the leader of Akali Dal, Sant Harcharan Singh Longowal on 28 July 1985. But, unfortunately, the peace brought through this agreement was shortlived and Punjab returned to a state of lawlessness with violence and murders becoming a daily feature. During the past one decade ten Governors have been changed and since May 1987 till the last week of February 1992, there was an uninterrupted President's rule in the State, necessitating amendments to the Constitution several times to facilitate the continuation of President's rule. Elections were held in Punjab on 19 February 1992 and a duly elected government is installed in the State putting an end to the President's rule, however pending the resolution of the main crisis. The problem is still haunting the State and nothing is certain until a lasting political solution is found.

Another burning problem threatening the security and the integrity of the country is the crisis in Kashmir. Kashmir is a perennial problem between Pakistan and India (more on this in the ensuing chapter). However, Kashmir remained free from any major problems during the past many years. In the past few years however a separatist movement, instigated and supported by Pakistan[51], has been threatening the peace, stability and security of the country. The separatist movement in Kashmir, spearheaded by the so called Jammu and Kashmir Liberation Front (JKLF) is turned into a bloody war between the armed Kashmiri militants trained by the Pakistani army on the other side of the border, and causing great concern not only to the Government of India but also to the international community as it has the potential of developing into a conflagration between India and Pakistan. This problem has to be solved in the larger perspective of the Indo-Pakistan relations.

The movement in Assam by the Bodos and the United Liberation Front of Assam (ULFA) and the extremist movement in Bihar, Madhya Pradesh, Andhra Pradesh and North-Eastern States are the other problems smouldering quite for some time. Apart from these, religious fundamentalism is raising its head causing concern to the State and society.

Any multi-racial, multi-lingual and multi-religious State is prone to internal turmoils and tensions. In India, these problems have surfaced during the past decade This is indicative of the imbalances that have crept into the system, particularly, in matters of economic development and social welfare.

Pakistan too, is a multi-lingual and multi-religious State. She is also facing problems of internal tensions such as regionalism and separatism. However, being an Islamic country and having the most insignificant portions of other religious groups and having been mostly governed by the military and authoritarian regimes, the internal conflicts in Pakistan have been either less challenging or were kept under leash.

The problem of ethnic conflicts and separatism is more pronounced and has been a cause of alarm to the rulers of Pakistan right from the beginning of independence. The discrimination meted out to the linguistic and ethnic groups other than Punjabis has generated contempt for the Punjabi domination in the Central Government.[52] The complete monopoly of the Punjabis in the army and bureaucracy has been the main feature of the Pakistani political system and this very feature was one of the causes of discontentment among the erstwhile East Pakistanis which ultimately turned into a separatist movement.[53]

Sind is the other major cauldron of the ethnic tensions in Pakistan. The distrust and contempt for the Central Government in this State has turned into a separatist movement called the Jiye Sind Movement.[54] Depending on the political situation at the national level this movement is rising and falling like a wave and yet the current is still alive. Repression against this movement has been very severe. The measures meant to curb the fissiparous tendency in Sind in the past have quite often resulted in eruption of violent riots. It is observed that the ethnic riots in Sind in December 1986 were one of the causes for the dismissal of the then Prime Minister, Mohammad Khan Junejo.[55] The problem of separatism in Pakistan is not limited only to Sind but is also prevalent in Baluchistan and other provinces.

The problems of national integration for Pakistan, on account of the ethnic and communal (Sunni and Shia conflicts) are not as acute as in the case of India. Firstly, it is so because Pakistan is a State with a strong and highly centralized political system and political repression is a commonplace. Secondly, Islam is the main binding factor. In spite of the economic and political contradictions, invocation of a common threat to Islam brings a sentimental unity among the people. Thirdly, the level of participation of the people is low and any movement cannot gain sufficient strength before it is suppressed.

Sri Lanka is the other State bogged down by the internal turmoil which reached the level of a civil war. The Tamil separatist movement in Sri Lanka has its roots in the 19th century and pre-independence ethnic politics of the island State. The Tamils were always the neglected lot in social, cultural, economic and political fields. In fact, they were better off during the British rule as the British had introduced universal franchise which gave the voting right to the Estate Tamils[56] also. They were later on disenfranchised by the Ceylonese government on the pretext that they were not citizens of Ceylon (Sri Lanka). Neither were the Ceylon Tamils allowed to participate in the framing of the Constitution in 1972 and 1978.[73] Presently, the problem of Tamil separatism has reached the boiling point. The Sri Lankan government is engaged in a war (internally) with the main and the most powerful militant organization of the Tamils, viz., the LTTE (Liberation Tigers of Tamil Eelam). The LTTE is in control of the predominantly Tamil populated areas in the North and Eastern provinces of Sri Lanka. The Government of Sri Lanka is also determined to liquidate the LTTE at all costs. Thus, its military is waging a relentless war with the militants at the cost of myriads of lives on both sides. What solution will eventually be found to this question will only be decided by the time. But at the present, it is a point of no return for both the LTTE and the Sri Lankan Government.

It may be mentioned here that India which has a sizable Tamil population and a State for the Tamils, viz., Tamil Nadu, sought to help Sri Lanka to find a solution to the problem under the pressure from the domestic public opinion. After a series of negotiations the Indo-Sri Lanka Agreement was signed by the Prime Minister Rajiv Gandhi and the President J.R. Jayawardene in July 1987. According to the Agreement, India undertook to make the LTTE surrender and lay down arms and Sri Lanka on her part guaranteed to set up North-Eastern Provincial Councils with sufficient devolution of powers to the Tamils. But India faced difficulties in making the LTTE surrender arms and ended up fighting the LTTE itself. The Sri Lankan Government too could not keep up its promises. The Indian Peace Keeping Force (IPKF) which was in Sri Lanka on the mission of disarming the Tamils got itself alienated from the Tamils and the Sri Lankan Government as well. Finally, under pressure from the Sri Lankan Government the IPKF had to withdraw from Sri Lanka without achieving any transible results. In the process considerable damage was done to the India-Sri Lanka relations.

Ethnic disturbances leading to separatist movement are also creating tensions in the ruling elites of Bangladesh. The bulk of the population of Bangladesh is Muslim and 90% of the population speak Bengali language. The Chittagong Hill Tracts (CHT) is a peculiar social, cultural and ethnic formation covering nearly 20% of the area and only 3% of the population of Bangladesh. The Chittagong Hill Tracts districts are the areas covered by hills and forests, inhabited by various tribal groups, viz. the Chakmas, the Marmas, the Chaks, the Khayangs, Tripuras etc. They speak different languages; the Chakmas speak a mixed language of Bengali and Pali, the Marmas speak Arkanese, a dialect of Burmese, the Tripuras speak Kachari etc.[58] These tribals are the followers of Buddhism, Hinduism and other religions through ages and consider themselves as nations.[59] Their economy, culture and political system were distinct from the Bengalis as well as other groups. They have hitherto enjoyed separate identity as they were not disturbed even during the British rule. In fact, the British have protected the political, social and cultural rights of these tribal groups under special Acts made in 1920 and 1935. These areas, encompassing the present districts of Rangamati, Khagra, Chari and Banderban were declared as 'excluded area' and 'totally excluded area' respectively under the above mentioned Acts. Realising the sensitivity of the tribals, the tribal chiefs were made the heads of local administration at the circle, mouza and the para levels.[60]

The 1950s witnessed attacks on the political and cultural identity of Chittagong Hill Tracts (CHT). Gradually, the autonomy of the CHT has been eroded and its integration into the mainstream accelerated. The Kaptai dam which was built in early 1960s inundated a large area of CHT displacing thousands of tribals and rendering nearly fifty-four thousand acres of cultivable land submerged. The rehabilitation of the affected families and the compensation paid to them was meagre in comparison to the loss incurred by them and consequently the tribals felt dissatisfied and cheated. By late 1970s the Bengali migration into the CHT changed the socio-economic character of the area. The internal Bengali colonialism has brought under its control the economy and trade of the area and government too was favouring the trend.[61]

The tribals of the Chittagong Hill Tracts are organized under the Parbattya Chattagram Jan Sangharsh Samithi since 1972. They are waging a relentless battle against the government in Dhaka to regain political and cultural rights. They had to undergo repression on several occasions.[62] To escape the repression some of the tribals have taken refuge in the neighbouring States of India and Burma. But the struggle is still going on. Ever since

Bangladesh has been blaming India for the trouble in CHT. Recently, Bangladesh also witnessed an internal turmoil as the opposition against the Ershad regime turned more vocal and violent. Ultimately, Ershad was forced to resign and elections to the national parliament were held in March 1991. Thus, democracy is restored in Bangladesh.

The people of Nepal also agitated for the restoration of democracy. Against a backdrop of deteriorating economic conditions and growing resentment against the autocratic rule the movement gained momentum gradually and ultimately led to restoration of party system in Nepal. Thus after more than 30 years in May 1991 G. P. Koirala of Nepali Congress became the first elected Prime Minister of Nepal.

The tiny kingdom in the Himalayas, Bhutan, is also not immune from internal troubles. Though, it had the reputation of being an abode of peace, turbulence started brewing up in this kingdom in the recent years. The trouble however started decades ago with the gradual inflow of Nepalis into the southern parts of Bhutan. In fact, the problem lies in the diverse treatment given to the people of Bhutanese and Nepalese origin in regard to the political and civil rights. The problem is made more complex by the enactment of Nationalities Act by the present King, Jigme Singye Wangchuk. The agitationists demand for a change in the political system particularly an introduction of constitutional monarchy and for changes in the composition and powers of the Assembly. Besides, there is a demand for carving out a separate Nepali State in Bhutan.[63]

Internal political squabbles and palace intrigues are said to be threats to destabilizing the monarchy in Bhutan. During the past few years several attempts to stage coup have also been foiled.[64]

Maldives, as was mentioned elsewhere, was also rocked by an attempted coup to overthrow President Gayoom from power in November 1988 which was foiled by the military assistance rendered by India. Since then, there is no apparent threat to the Government in Male. But given the fragile nature of its polity, it cannot be definitely said that Maldives is totally free from troubles.

The impact of the domestic conflicts in the SAARC countries, irrespective of their magnitude, is relative to their size, strength and nature of the political system. While the major States do not face any real danger of destabilization, the smaller ones are more vulnerable to sweeping changes in the political system. Regional cooperation, thus, is useful *inter alia* to ensure the stability of the regimes as far as the small States are concerned.

Foreign Policies of the South Asian (SAARC) Countries

Interestingly, while the foreign policies of the SAARC States are dissimilar and mutually antagonistic the set of factors that determine them are similar, however, with minor exceptions. The most important factors that helped the evolution of the foreign policies of these States are: (i) the colonial legacy, (ii) geographical conditions, (iii) religion, and culture, and (iv) personality factors.

The inter-relationships which form a crucial part of the foreign policies of the South Asian States, is also a colonial legacy. The two-nation theory, the main driving force for the partition of India and the formation of Pakistan is the curse of the history to the people of the Indian sub-continent. This legacy is still haunting the people of India and Pakistan perpetually pitting them against each other and thereby hindering their economic and social progress considerably.

The British had managed the Indian sub-continent as an integral part of the British Empire and had formulated the external policies keeping in view their strategic and security perceptions. India, being the main and the larger successor of the erstwhile British Empire inherited the same security and strategic perceptions. The foreign policy of India in the post-independence period *vis-a-vis* her neighbours has more or less followed the same pattern as that of the British before independence. India's border arrangements (disputes) with China and relations with Nepal, Bhutan and Sri Lanka are the striking elements of such legacy.

Most of the former colonies and protectorates of the British have continued to maintain closer relations with the UK and other western powers. This has been an influential factor in their extern relations. Since early 1950s till today with the exception of In all the members of the South Asian region have maintained explicitly pro-western postures in their international relations. If India wanted to keep out of the crossfire of the two power blocs in the global politics, it was also due to her traumatic experience under the colonial rule. In fact, in the early fifties the Soviet Union (particularly Stalin's regime) branded Indian leadership as the lackies of the western imperialism. Thus, undeniably, all the members of the SAARC with minor variations were immensely influenced by their historical background which invariably included the colonial subjugation in conducting their foreign policies.

Generally, it is accepted that the location of State in relation to her neighbours and her geographical features are the most important determinants of her foreign policy. This generalization is equally applicable to all the States of SAARC without exception. On the other hand, each one of them is also conscious of this factor, especially in dealing with the neighbours.

It is obvious from the statements made by various government functionaries of the SAARC countries either explicitly or implicitly that geographical factors in some cases out-weighed the other influences in shaping their external postures. Pakistan, Nepal, Bangladesh and Sri Lanka have specifically made India as the central concern of their foreign policies. Pakistan's obsession with India is so deep that the Pakistanis complain the political system and socio-cultural system is affected by the presence of the hated neighbour of India. It is no exaggeration to say that Pakistan's foreign policy is solely influenced by this obsession.[65] The landlocked status and its sandwiched position between China and India makes Nepal important disproportionate to its size and strength.[66] Taking advantage of her geographic location Nepal tried to play one big power against the other and thus asserted an independent status in international relations. Bangladesh and Sri Lanka are also conscious of their geographical location which inspired the fear of their bigger and powerful neighbour. Their foreign policies are mainly directed to keep their countries out of the influence of India by building up relationship with countries outside the region.

The Indian sub-continent which was an integrated unit in spite of being a multi-religious, multi-racial, multi-cultural formation, is at present divided into several States of independent status. The complex ethnic, religious and cultural affinity of the people of the sub-continent is cutting across geographical and political barriers. This is one of the complex problems of these States which are often afraid of the centripetal forces underlying these factors. The politically mutually hostile postures are born out of the fear of latent symptoms of 'Pan-Indianism'. This appears to be plausible explanation for the fanatic denial of the existence of social, cultural, racial and religious commonalities by India's neighbours.

Religion, too, has become an integral part of the ideology and value system of most of the countries of this region. South Asia can be divided into three major religious groups. Pakistan, Bangladesh and Maldives are the Islamic States, they are members of the OIC (Organization of Islamic Conference) and their foreign policies are generally directed by the sentiments of Islamic Unity, solidarity and ideology. They use the religion as an interpretor of national interests, the inspiration of patriotism and national solidarity and also to forge a common platform to tackle national and international problems. Secondly, Nepal is a Hindu State, in fact the only self-proclaimed Hindu State in the world, while India is a multi-religious entity following a secular policy. However, India is predominantly Hindu. Bhutan and Sri Lanka fall into the third group which are by demographic composition and admission Buddhist States.

The influence of religion on domestic and foreign policies is more telling in respect of the Islamic States of South Asia. In Pakistan for instance the Islamic identity has definite anti-Indian connotation.[67] In Bangladesh, the change of slogan after the collapse of Mujib's regime from 'Joy Bangla' to 'Bangladesh Zindabad' also implied a change in the external postures. Followed by more numerous people, the existence of more States adhering to it and more steadfast nature, may perhaps be the possible explanation for Islam being more demanding and influential religion in the world.

The influence of personality factor over the foreign policies of the South Asian States (or the members of SAARC) cannot be exaggerated. Being very backward in terms of literacy and levels of consciousness among their people these States are generally dominated by a few individuals in all the spheres of State activity including the foreign affairs.

In case of India, it is a generally accepted fact that Nehru is the main architect of her foreign policy in 1950s and 1960s. His influence of India's foreign policy continued through the 70s and 80s also. Moreover, the policy of non-alignment of which India is considered to be a leader is the brainchild of Nehru himself. After Nehru, it was Indira Gandhi who dominated the Indian foreign policy. Rajiv Gandhi too exercised considerable influence on India's foreign policy during the 1980s.

In case of Pakistan also the influence of some of its leading personalities has been quite significant. Ayub Khan, Zulfikar Ali Bhutto and Zia-ul-Haq have exerted considerable sway over Pakistan's external relations. Benazir Bhutto and now Nawaj Sharif could not do so because of their weak position both in their relations with the army and parliament.

The influence of personality on the foreign policy of Nepal has been great as during the rule of King Mahendra and until recently under King Birendra the political power including the management of foreign relations was practically concentrated in the hands of the monarch. Particularly during 1960s and early 1970s King Mahendra was the main author of Nepal's foreign policy. The same is the case with Bhutan which is still an absolute monarchy.

The influence of leading political personalities has been in the case of Bangladesh, Maldives and Sri Lanka also. Like in all other countries of South Asia in these States also foreign policy formulation has been the exclusive prerogative of their top leaders.

The Economies of the South Asian States

Another uniform feature of South Asia is that all the States of the region without any exception are less developed countries (LDCs) of the world. All the attendant problems of backward economies are present in them and are causing hindrances in the path of their development. The basic economic indicators of the South Asian countries are given in Table -1.

TABLE 1

Basic Economic Indicators of South Asian Countries

Countries	*Population in mid—1989 (in millions)*	*GDP in billion S*	*Per Capita GDP in S*	*Area in sq. km. 1000 sq. km.*	*Country's share in region's GDP %*
Bangladesh	110.7	15.46	160	144	6.00
Bhutan	1.4	0.21	150	47	0.08
India	832.2	203.79	290	3288	79.09
Maldives	210 (thousands)	0.06	310	0.3	0.02
Nepal	18.4	2.20	150	141	0.85
Pakistan	109.9	30.08	350	804	11.67
Sri Lanka	16.8	5.88	400	66	2.28

Source: World Development Report 1988, 1990.

One of the basic features of the South Asian region is the compelling presence of India with a gigantic size in terms of population, area and economy. India shares three fourths of the economy of the entire South Asia. This is both a source of strength and also creating certain discomforts for India as it overawes her smaller neighbours, though India's per capita income and foreign trade as percentage of GNP is lower than most of the SAARC member countries.

The economic backwardness of the region is so universal that except Maldives and Sri Lanka the rest of the SAARC countries, i.e., India, Pakistan, Bangladesh, Nepal and Bhutan consisting of 98% fo the total population of the region figure in the low Human Development Index group of 44 countries prepared by the UNDP.[69]

The overall position of South Asia in the world economy is rather dismal and disproportionate to its size and population. South Asia which consists of 20% the world population and 2.7 percent of world's land surface had a share of mere 0.81 percent of exports and 1.31 percent of imports in the total export and import trade of the world in 1987.[70] Four of the seven member countries of SAARC viz., Bangladesh, Maldives, Bhutan and Nepal, are listed in the category of 'least developed countries'.

The reasons for the economic backwardness of the South Asian countries are historical, structural and to some extent political too. Historically, most of the SAARC countries were under the colonial rule and were subjected to economic exploitation by their colonial masters. They were also kept out of the developments of the Industrial Revolution that had swept Europe and North America. Indeed, the real quest for economic development has begun only after these countries have attained independence.

The structural problems of these countries include the size of their population, their levels of literacy, standards of living, social awareness etc. It is a fact that the bulk of the population of this region is still illiterate and socially and culturally traditional and backward. Another important common feature of these countries is that they are plagued most of the time by internal ethnic and communal conflicts. The demographic composition of the SAARC countries is given in Table - 2. The diverse composition of the population in terms of religious groups cutting across the boundaries of the countries of the region has been a source of problems not only within the respective countries but also a source of discord in the inter-state relations of the region. This had its own impact on the economic development of the region.

In terms of the structure of production of the South Asian countries, agriculture accounts for a major share of their GDP. The structure of production of the South Asian countries is given in Table-3. In case of India, Pakistan and Sri Lanka the share of agriculture in GDP is less than one-third and in the case of others it ranged between 35 percent in case of Maldives to 62 percent in case of Nepal. The manufacturing sector in the countries of the region has been growing but is still very small in its contribution to the GDP.[71]

TABLE 2

Demographic Composition of South Asian Countries

(Mid-1980) Percentage

Country	Hindu	Muslim	Buddhist	Christian	Others
Bangladesh	12.7	85.9	0.6	0.5	0.3
Bhutan	24.6	5.0	69.6	0.1	0.7
India	78.8	11.6	0.8	3.9	4.9
Maldives	-	-	-	-	-
Nepal	89.6	3.0	6.1	0.0	1.3
Pakistan	1.3	96.8	0.0	1.8	0.1
Sri Lanka	16.0	7.2	66.9	8.3	1.6

Figures for Maldives are omitted because her entire population is Muslim .

Source : T.K. Oommen, 'State and Religion in Multi-Religious Nation-States : The Case of South Asia'. *South Asia Journal*, Vol. 4, No. 1, July-Sept. 1990, p.18.

TABLE 3

Structure of Production of South Asian Countries Percentage of GDP

Country	Agriculture	Industry
Bangladesh	47	14
Bhutan	50	18
India	32	29
Maldives	35	13
Nepal	62	12
Pakistan	24	28
Sri Lanka	26	27

Source : World Development Reports 1987, 1988.

Industrialization in South Asia has been based mainly on specialization in the processing of indigenous raw materials. The major industries in the region are : textiles, cement, sugar, fertilizers, cigarettes, paper and newsprint etc. However, considerable disparities exist among the various countries of the region. India and Pakistan are comparatively advanced in terms of industrial growth in the region whereas the other countries are more or less confined to the processing of food, tobacco, cotton and jute products.

One of the main reasons for the industrial backwardness of the SAARC countries is their technological dependence on the Western countries.[72] In fact in this area the stage of development of various countries of South Asia is quite diverse. This, on the other hand, provides for an opportunity for cooperation among the countries of the region while at the same time not totally discarding the latest technology developed in the West for their benefits.

The amount of foreign trade is also an indication of the economic power of a country. As mentioned earlier, the South Asian countries' share in the global foreign trade is quite negligible. However, in the broader context of economic development this follows in tandem with various other factors.

One of the crucial indicators of the state of economy of South Asian countries is their ever-growing burden of external debt. Consequently, the debt servicing ratio (repayments of debt as a percentage of GDP) has also been growing constantly. This has further increased the deficits in the balance of payments of these countries. Table-4 shows the balance of payments position and the external debt of the countries of the South Asian region. The problem of external debt of the developing countries in general, and the South Asian countries in particular, is compelling them to integrate their economies with those of the developed world. This is giving scope for fears of eroding the sovereignty of the developing countries.

Apart from the above mentioned core economic problems, the internal discords among the countries of the SAARC resulting in ever-increasing military allocations and intermittent arms race have been taking the toll of the economies of the countries. This is more so in case of India and Pakistan. It is a universal truth that prosperity and development could be achieved only in times of peace and harmony. It is obvious as to why the South Asian region lags behind in matters of prosperity development and cooperation.

TABLE 4

International Payments Position of SAARC Countries

	Trade in million S	*Debit in million S*	*Debt as % of GNP*
Bangladesh	-2119	10712	53.3
Bhutan		79	
India	-3692	62509	24.0
Nepal	-424	1359	43.5
Pakistan	-2477	18509	46.9
Sri Lanka	-1654	5101	73.5

Source : World Development Report 1990.

However, it may not be out of place to mention here that in spite of the poor state of the South Asia, the divergent sizes of their economic stages of development, patterns of production including geographical location and their attendant problems provide nevertheless a good opportunity for mutual cooperation. Moreover in the context of strained North-South economic relations, the countries of SAARC by evolving strategies for collective economic self-reliance and development could provide a model for South-South Cooperation.

A number of studies by individuals as well as various organizations have been made exploring the trade complementaries of the South-Asian States and the potentialities in expanding economic cooperation in the region.[74] All of them were optimistic about the future of the South Asia.

The foregoing account of various social, ethnic, religious, economic and political characteristics of the South Asian States present a mixed picture of diversity and unity. There is divergence in their political postures, religious attitudes, political systems and strategic perceptions. But at the same time, there is a distinct unity in their combined social fabric, transcendent ethnic and religious structures, historical roots and above all in their geographical cohesion and common economic problems and objectives.

Thus South Asia in spite of its diversity represents a community in the quest of common goals and common destiny. In the pursuit of solution to their common problems of poverty and economic backwardness the South Asian States can achieve better results if only they sink their differences and march ahead unitedly. The present conditions of South Asia are therefore strongly in favour of evolving regional cooperation in a meaningful manner.

References

1. P.C. Mathur (Ed.) *Govt. and Politics in South Asia*, Vol. I, Jaipur, 1985, p.14.
2. Salahuddin Ahmed, 'The Identity of the Subcontinent", *India International Centre Quarterly*, Summer 1987, p. 79.
3. P.C. Mathur, *op. cit.*, p. 14.
4. Rudolph, S. & Rudolph, L. *In Pursuit of Lakshmi*, (Orient Longman, 1987, Bombay), p. 67, also Craig Baxter and others, *Government and Politics in South Asia* (Vanguard Books, Lahore, 1988), p. 51.
5. Ayub Khan, Mohd., Pakistan Perspective, in Betty Burch and Allan B.Cole, *Asian Political Systems*, p.396 and Pandav Nayak, *Pakistan: Dilemmas of a Developing State* (Aalekh, Jaipur 1985), p.2.
6. Denis Wright, *Bangladesh : Origins and Indian Ocean Relations* (Sterling, New Delhi, 1988), p.30.
7. *Ibid.*, p. 36.
8. *Ibid.*, pp. 55-61.
9. A.T. Sibasurunathan, 'Not a polity', in Asghar Ali Engineer (Ed.) *Ethnic Conflict in South Asia* (Ajanta, Delhi, 1987), p. 189.
10. P.C. Mathur, *op. cit.*, p. 16.
11. Paramanand, *Political Development in South Asia* (Sterling, Delhi, 1988), pp. 38-39.
12. *Ibid.*, p. 147.
13. *Ibid.*, p. 148.
14. Baxter and others, *op.cit.*, p. 365.
15. *Ibid.*, p. 367.
16. *Ibid.*, p. 367.

17. The interview with President M.A. Gayoom of Maldives in *The Hindu,* dated August 23, 1991.

18. M.J. Akbar, *India: The Seige within* (Penguin, Bombay, 1985), p. 37.

19. Sibasurunathan in A..A. Engineer, *op. cit.,* p. 189.

20. P. Ramaswamy, *New Delhi and Sri lanka* (Allied Pub. 1987), p. 21.

21. *Ibid.,* p. 22.

22. Denis Wright, *op. cit.,* p. 59.

23. Baxter and others, *op. cit.,* p. 250.

24. Wright, *op. cit.,* p.99.

25. Denis Wright, *op. cit.,* p. 104.

26. Craig Baxter and others, *op. cit.,* p. 51 and Rudolph (s) and Rudolph, *op. cit.,* p. 67.

27. Baxter and others, *op. cit.,* p. 52.

28. *Ibid.,* p. 317.

29. *Ibid.,* p. 203.

30. M.J. Akbar, *op. cit.,* p. 47.

31. Uma Singh, Erosion of Ruling Alliance in Pakistan, *Link,* January 12, 1992, p. 20.

32. Bhabani Sengupta, Pakistan: Towards an Understanding, *Economic & Political Weekly,* Vol. No. 26, December 7, 1991, p. 2798.

33. Craig Baxter and Syedur Rahman, Bangladesh Votes-1991, *Asian Survey,* 31 (8) August 1991, p. 692.

34. Paramanand, *op. cit.,* p. 148.

35. See Narayan Khadka, 'Nepal's Stagnant Economy: The Panchayat Legacy', *Asian Survey,* Vol. 31. No. 8, August 1991.

36. V.D. Mishra, *Bhutan,*

37. Jay W. Scrybe, 'Demand for Carving of Bhutan Unjustified', *Link,* January 12, 1992, p. 23.

38. Baxter and others, *op. cit.,* p. 366.

39. *Ibid.,* p. 366.

40. *Ibid.,* p. 45.

41. C.P. Bhambri, Indian Political System, in Urmila Phadnis, S.D. Muni and Kalim Bahadur (Eds.), *Domestic Conflicts in South Asia*, Vol. I, South Asia Publishers, New Delhi, 1986, p. 102.

42. *The Hindu*, February 13, 1992.

43. Paramanand, *op. cit.*, p. 168.

44. *Ibid.*, p. 172.

45. Kalim Bahadur, Problem of Secularism in Pakistan, in Pandav Nayak (Ed.) p. 35.

46. Religion and State in Pakistan, M.V. Lekhi, in P.C. Mathur (Ed.) *op.cit.*, p. 58.

47. Baxter and others, *op. cit.*, p. 232.

48. Zillur Rahman, 'Islam and Bengali Nationalsim', *Asian Survey*, 25 (8), August 1985, pp. 834-851.

49. A.K. Saksena, Religion and State in South Asia, in P.C. Mathur, p. 39.

50. M.A. Gayoom, President of the Republic of Maldives in an interview to *the Hindu*, dated, August 23, 1991.

51. Sufficient evidence is coming to light to support this view. For instance, see *Frontline*, January 31, 1992.

52. K.P. Mishra, M. Rasgotra and V.D. Chopra, *Southern Asia Pacific Perspectives and Strategies* (Continental, New Delhi, 1988), p. 173.

53. Denis Wright, *op. cit.*, p. 61.

54. Kamran Khan, A Survey of Ethnic Situation in Pakistan, in A.A. Engineer, *op. cit.*, p. 152.

55. Arif Hasan, *Ibid.*

56. There are two types of Tamils in Sri Lanka 1. Sri Lankan Tamils, 2. Estate Tamils.

57. See A.T. Sibasurunathan in A.A. Engineer (Ed.) No. 9, p. 190 and also Marshall R. Singer, New Realities in Sri Lankan Politics, *Asian Survey*, 30 (4), April 1990, p. 411.

58. Syed Azizul Ahsan and Bhumitra Chakma, Problems of National Integration in Bangladesh, *Asian Survey*, 29 (10) October 1989, p. 961.

59. *Ibid.*, p. 960.

60. *Ibid.*, p. 962.

61. *Ibid.*, p. 965.

62. *Ibid.*, p. 968.

63. Jay W. Scrybe, *op. cit.*, 36, p. 23.

64. Baxter and others, *op. cit.*, p. 6.

65. See K.P. Mishra, Regional Peace and Security Coalescene and Clash in Indo-Pak Relations', *India Quarterly*, Vol. 40, No. 3 & 4, July-Dec. 1984, p. 264.

66. Rama Kant, 'Culture versus Geo-politics in Inter-state relations' in P.C. Mathur (Ed.) Govt. and Politics in *South Asia*, Vol. II, January 1986, p. 17.

67. M.V. Lakhi, Religion and State in Pakistan in P.C. Mathur, *op. cit.*, p. 58.

68. N.A. Sarma, 'South Asia and the World Economy: the Emerging Perspectives', *South Asia Journal*, Vol. 4, No. 2, Oct. - Dec., 1990, p. 130.

69. *Ibid.*, p. 131.

70. A.P. Bhuyan, 'Intra Regional Trade Expansion in South Asia : Trends, Obstacles and Prospects', *South Asia Journal*, Vol. 4, No. 1, July-Sept. 1990, p. 39.

71. A.R. Bhuyan, *op. cit.*, p. 37.

72. I. N. Mukherji in Bimal Prasad (Ed.), *op. cit.*, p. 104.

73. The ongoing controversy over the World Bank—IMF Loans in India is a pointer in this direction.

74. To Mention a few : (1) Ponna Wignaraja and Akmal Hussain (Eds.) *The Challenge in South Asia* (Sage Publication New Delhi, 1989). This is a study undertaken by the United Nations University's Asian Perspectives Project (South Asia), (2) Conference on Future of Asia Pacific Economies, Challenges for South Asia : A Report, by Vandana Verma, *South Asia Journal*, Vol. 4, No. 4, April-June, 1991, pp. 435-439, (3) In Mukherji, Economic Constraints and Potentialities', in Bimal Prasad (Ed.) *op. cit.*, pp. 100-136, (4) Rajiv Kumar, 'Coordination of Economic Policies in South Asia : Prospects, Problems and Modalities', *South Asia Journal*, Vol. 1, No. 3, July-Sept. 1988, pp. 99-316, and (5) Pramod Kumar Mishra, 'South-South Cooperation and SAARC', *Monthly Public Opinion Surveys*, July-Aug. 1989, pp. 9-15.

CHAPTER IV

INDOPHOBIA AND THE SAARC

One of the striking and peculiar features of South Asian States is the disparity in their size and their political, economic and military strengths and capabilities. There are tiny and sparsely populated States like Maldives and Bhutan and very larger ones like Bangladesh, Pakistan and India. But of all the South Asian States, India is by far the largest and the strongest one in terms of its area, political stability, economic viability and military capabilities. Thus, India is termed as the core State while the other States are called the periphery of the South Asian regional system.

The size and strength of India is not only the source of embarrassment for India but also a cause of centrifugal tendencies in South Asia. The unenviable position of India emanates from the fact that India is the only State of this region which shares territorial or maritime boundaries with almost all the States of the region, the only exception being the Maldives, the Indian Ocean archipelago located about 1000 miles south-east of India. As India dwarfs all her neighbours by her sheer size, the smaller neighbours of India have developed a sort of inferiority complex, fear and suspicion against India. This unfortunate trend, though without any justification formed basis of the inter-State relations in South Asia. In fact the divide has been such that it was India on the one side and the other South Asian States on the other. The relationship is marked by suspicion, unfriendly postures and at times conflict. The actions and attitudes of all South Asian States except India were conditioned by India's actions and attitudes. The South Asian relations are, thus, fitted into an action and reaction scenario. One may find a clear lack of coordination and cooperation among these States in any meaningful sense. For, whatever proposals are made, there used to be lack of enthusiasm in the opposite camp.

Thus, clearly South Asia is dominated by the actions and reactions by and against India. There is no denying the fact that India is more than twice the other SAARC countries put together in size and nearly four times larger demographically than all the other South Asian countries (SAARC members) put together. Modern States enjoy political, economic and defence capabilities based on their size and resources. This strength may appear to others as mere power and strength. India indeed enjoys such status and power, but not to the disadvantage of any other State in her neighbourhood or in any other part of the globe. India's foreign policy objectives and postures as explained in the previous chapter clearly indicate this fact.

It cannot be denied that India to some extent inherited the security perceptions of the previous British rulers. But the foreign policy of India, inspired and cherished by the ideals and traditions of Indian political and cultural heritage and shaped by mature vision of her first Prime Minister, Jawaharlal Nehru, aimed at evolving friendly relations with her neighbours based on peace, mutual trust and cooperation. In this direction, she tried to lead the newly independent States of Asia and Africa, with a fair measure of success.[1] In spite of this, unfortunately, the attention drawn by India in various international forums and the important place it occupies in the United Nations, coupled with some of her actions in response to the regional crises in the past have been construed by her neighbours and some of the western observers as India's quest for hegemony or domination or Big Brother status in South Asia.

The reasons for the suspicion and fear of India and her actions in the smaller States of South Asia including Pakistan are historical, geographical, political and psychological. These factors dominated the bilateral relations of India with her South Asian neighbours. Only after putting India's relations with all her neighbours (four of which share land borders with India and the other, viz., Sri Lanka, though separated by the Indian Ocean from India by only a few miles, is also a close neighbour of India), we can try to analyse whether or why is the South Asian region affected by Indophobia and how far does it affect the success or failure of SAARC. Hence, let us try to throw some light on the current state of bilateral relations between India and each of her neighbours, in historical perspective.

Bilateral Relations Between India and Her Neighbours : India-Pakistan Relations

It is true that India's relations with all her neighbours is a part of her colonial legacy in general and Pakistan in particular. The resolution of the Congress-Muslim League conflict in the freedom struggle by the British government ultimately manifesting in the Partition Plan left bitter feelings in the consequently emerged new States of India and Pakistan.

The adverse relationship between India-Pakistan has its beginning, in fact, in the 1930 resolution of the Muslim League demanding for a separate Muslim State. This has added a new dimension to the concept of 'Two-Nation Theory' by the then Muslim League Leader Mohammad Ali Jinnah. Jinnah's theory is rooted in his argument that the Hindus and Muslims could never evolve a common nationality.[2]

It is, therefore, evident that the emergence of India and Pakistan as two independent and separate States, is based on certain fundamental differences of ideology and perceptions and beliefs of two sections of elites. While Indian nationalism is based on the idea of unity among different sections of society belonging to divergent ethnic, cultural and religious groups, the basic idea of incompatibility between two dominant religions and the resultant two-Nation Theory is the *raison d' etre* of Pakistan.[3] Though, initially, Jinnah's two-nation approach was political rather than theological, but gradually religious outlook dominated the political perceptions of Pakistani elite. By this logic, the India-Pakistan relations were considered as adverse relationship of two antagonistic religions.[4]

Religious adversity as a factor in India-Pakistan relations has been continuing ever since the partition took place. The communal disturbances in either State are generally attributed to the interference or instigation of the other. While the Indians point out the discrimination meted out to the Hindus in Pakistan, the Pakistanis accuse the Hindu domination for the communal riots in India. One of the basic differences between the India and Pakistan political systems is that while the former is a secular one, the latter is a proclaimed Islamic State. Naturally, the Muslims in India, despite their special status and rights under the Constitution, have sufficient freedom and chance to vent out their discontent and demand for more rights and concessions. This is not the case with the Hindus or any other religious groups other than Muslims in Pakistan. Moreover, professing herself to be an Islamic State, Pakistan takes every opportunity to look at the problems of minorities in India through magnified glasses. No wonder, Pakistan raised an alarm at the imminent dismantling of the Babri Masjid in India at the last meeting of the OIC at Istanbul. It is, thus, no exaggeration to say that Islamic overtones dominate the Pakistan's relations with India. Pakistan using religion as a factor in shaping her external relations is not only in opposing India, but also in mobilizing support for herself against India, especially among the Islamic States of Asia and Africa.[5]

Kashmir is a perennial and the most explosive factor of conflict relationship between India and Pakistan. It is currently a burning problem between the traditional rivals threatening new ruptures all the time. Historically, the Kashmir question is also a fallout of the Partition politics in the immediate aftermath of independence. Kashmir, which was a princely State, with a predominantly Muslim population and a Hindu ruler, was left out by the British rulers while helping the Indian Government in obtaining from the Indian Princes the instruments of accession. The ruler of Kashmir was also undecided about the future of his State. This has provided an opportunity to the Pakistani Government which came into existence on the basis of two-nation theory to covet its usurpation. On 22 October 1947 the Pakistani infiltrators entered Kashmir and the Kashmir Maharaja was caught unawares by the Pakistani invasion. The troops of the Maharaja were so meagre and ill-equipped that there was no hope for survival and the Maharaja was forced to seek assistance from India. In a series of quick developments that followed the Maharaja on 27 October 1947 finally decided to accede Kashmir to the Indian Government.[6] Following this, Pakistan mounted a full-scale invasion and even occupied large tracts of the Kashmir valley. The Indian troops entered Kashmir and repelled the Pakistani attack.

The Kashmir question was taken to the United Nations. The Security Council discussed the issue and asked both the parties to cease hostilities and maintain peace in Kashmir. Subsequently, the UNCIP (United Nations Commission on India and Pakistan) was set up to supervise peace operations in Kashmir. India maintained that accession of Kashmir into India was complete and final.[7] After the cessation of the hostilities also Pakistan kept on demanding for Kashmir. She is still managing to keep the issue alive by raising it in various international forums, especially, the United Nations, the OIC etc.

The differences over the Kashmir question revolve round India's assertion that Kashmir was its integral part and Pakistan's claims on Kashmir. The Kashmir harping has helped Pakistan in the early periods to cool off the tribal revolts in Baluchistan and NWFP and in the later periods to accord legitimacy to the government which was otherwise getting estranged with the people.[8]

Since 1947 Kashmir has remained the centre-piece of India-Pakistan relations. Three wars were fought on this issue. After the 1965 war, both the States entered into an agreement under the mediation of the Soviet Union at Tashkent. But, the Tashkent agreement crumbled amidst the war din in 1971 over the Bangladesh liberation. Pakistan received a good drubbing at the hands of India, during the 1965 and 1971 wars. Though, Pakistan psychologically remained irreconciled to the fate of Kashmir, she had entered into an agreement with India at Shimla in July 1972. The Shimla accord was signed by the then Indian Prime Minsiter Indira Gandhi and the then President of Pakistan Zulfikar Ali

Bhutto. In spite of the continuation of the cold war over the Kashmir issue, both India and Pakistan refrained from entering into another armed conflict. But still, Pakistan accuses India of denying the Kashmiris of their right to self-determination and violating human rights in Kashmir, and India is not even reconciled even to the reality of the existence of Pakistan etc. A perennial propaganda is carried on in Pakistan to create a war-hysteria and hate-India psychology among the people of Pakistan. Pakistan is getting international support against India after its dismemberment and evolution of Bangladesh in 1971 with the support of India.

Currently, the Kashmir issue has assumed urgency and importance becasue Islamic fundamentalist groups loyal to Pakistan (favouring accession to Pakistan) as well as those advocating independent statehood to Kashmir have gained ground in Kashmir. There are a number of militant organizations now operating in the valley and most of them are receiving moral, monetary and material support and military training from Pakistani Government. It would be appropriate to say that Pakistan is waging a proxy war in Kashmir by regularly and systematically infiltrating trained militants into the Kashmir valley. During 1990 and 1991 nearly 6000 infiltrators were apprehended by the Indian army and large quantities of modern arms and ammunitions were confiscated from them.[9] Recently on 5 February 1992 the entire Pakistan observed Bandh in support of the cause of Kashmir. On 11 February 1992 the Jammu & Kashmir Liberation Front (JKLF) tried to cross the Line of Control (LOC) enforced by the Shimla Accord in Kashmir to demand the unification of Kashmir. Pressurized by the international opinion Pakistan had to prevent the Pakistan based JKLF Chief's bid to cross the LOC thereby alienating itself from the JKLF. In spite of this, Pakistan is still persisting on her efforts to keep the Kashmir issue alive and burning. Though, both India and Pakistan are still honouring the Shimla Agreement, Pakistan is of late arguing that Shimla Agreement no longer applies to the Kashmir problem. It is now thinking in terms of supporting the cause of Kashmiri self-determination even if it results in a separate State of Kashmir so that at a later stage it could integrate Kashmir into itself.[10] The Government of Pakistan and its intelligentsia vociferously argue that until and unless the Kashmir issue is resolved to the satisfaction of Pakistan there would not be any peaceful relationship between India and Pakistan nor would there be any meaningful regional cooperation in the region of South Asia.[11]

Irrespective of the form of government, nature of the party or group in power, although the past over four decades, Pakistan has been maintaining the same tempo of Kashmir issue both in the sub-continent and in the international forums. Zulfikar Ali Bhutto and later on his daughter and one-time Prime Minister Benazir Bhutto have gone on record saying that Pakistan would fight for a thousand years to liberate Kashmir.

The Bangladesh liberation in 1971 also had adverse effects on India-Pakistan relations. The events that have led to the struggle for the liberation of East Pakistan (Bangladesh) from the oppressive rule of the West Pakistan and its subsequent liberation and the evolution of Bangladesh as an independent State is a well-known fact of the history of the Indian sub-continent and its importance in the perpetuation of hostile postures of Pakistan towards India.

The happenings in the sub-continent immediately preceding the December 1971 war between India and Pakistan provided a tough and challenging time for India. The repression launched by Pakistan on Bangladeshis turned into genocide resulting in a massive exodus of the affected people into India. The number of refugees, which touched ten million at its peak not only posed political and security risks to India but it was a severe strain on her economy.[12] India pulled out a diplomatic success by signing the Treaty of Friendship, Peace and Cooperation with the Soviet Union (generally referred to as Indo-Soviet Treaty) in August 1971 at a time when the hostilities between India and Pakistan were inexorably bringing to the brink of war. Finally, when the war broke out in December 1971, in spite of political and economic exigencies, India faced the challenge with meticulous care and emerged with a reasonable success. Pakistan left with no alternative surrendered to the Indian troops in Dhaka on 17 December 1971 under the humiliating circumstances of the East Pakistan breaking away formally from Pakistan and emerging as an independent and sovereign State.

Pakistan still remembers the humiliating defeat she suffered in 1971 and is always looking for a chance to pay India in her own coin. However, the Shimla Agreement signed by India and Pakistan in the aftermath of the 1971 war prevented both the countries from entering into another armed conflict. Under this agreement both the parties agreed "to settle their differences by peaceful means through bilateral negotiations or by any other peaceful means mutually agreed between them." It was also agreed that "The basic issues and causes of conflict which have bedevilled the relations of the two countries for the last 25 years shall be resolved by peaceful means".[13] Obviously, so far India and Pakistan have been bound by the Shimla Agreement on the commitment of peaceful co-existence. But the peace has always been precarious. It was rather a no war, no peace syndrome.[14]

Against the backdrop of the natural and traditional hostile postures, India and Pakistan are constantly accusing each other of interference in one another's internal affairs. In fact the ethnic relations in South Asia cutting across all boundaries, the suspicion of interference by outside powers has been a cause of worry in the mutual relations of the countries of the South Asian region. In the context of India-Pakistan relations it is more striking. Especially being a weaker one, Pakistan always looks for an opportunity to stoke the fires of internal conflicts in India. The long border she shares with India comes handy in fulfilling this objective. The same geographical advantage is available for India too and she is also accused of interference in aggravating tensions in Pakistan.

Pakistan had to face many internal conflicts, insurgencies and even secessionist movements in past four decades. Whenever there was a crisis of national integration, Pakistan readily accused India of interference. India was accused to have extended support to the Sindh secessionists in 1987 before the dismissal of the then Prime Minister Mohammad Khan Junejo.[15] In the case of Baluchistan also Pakistan found India as responsible for the tribal insurrections.

The movement for the restoration of democracy organized by the Pakistan People's party and its allies under the leadership of Benazir Bhutto posing a serious threat to the power base of the then military ruler Gen. Zia-ul-Haq received moral support from the Indian public and the Government. This was used by the Pakistani Government not only to accuse India but also to legitimize its power base on the basis of traditional anti-India sentiments of the Pakistani people.[16]

Pakistan's interest in encouraging internal conflicts in India is widely known both within the Indian sub-continent and in the international circles. Mention may be made here particularly of Pakistan's role in the ongoing crisis in Punjab. Pakistan's intentions on Kashmir are too well-known to warrant any emphasis.

The contribution of Punjab crisis in deteriorating India-Pakistan relations has been quite considerable because of the active support rendered by Pakistani Government. The Pakistani involvement in Punjab was revealed by an investigative report published in *India Today* in May 1986.[17] The Indian Government protested to the Pakistani Government on this score and decided to erect barbed wire fence on the Indo-Pakistan border to prevent infiltration of Pak-trained terrorists from across the border. While Pakistan kept denying any interference in the Punjab problem, she continued to abet the terrorist Khalistan movement. Thus, throughout the 1980s Indo-Pakistan relations were marred by the tensions caused by the Punjab crisis.[18]

The involvement of Pakistan in the Kashmir crisis in India, of late, assumed alarming proportions. Pakistan has given moral and political encouragement and military training to various militant organizations operating in the Kashmir valley. It is firm in its intention to see Kashmir wrested away from India at any cost. The active involvement of Pakistan in the Kashmir insurgency is an accepted fact even among the Western countries (particularly US and UK) which have been Pakistan's traditional supporters.[19] Recently, Pakistan mounted a propaganda war against India on the Kashmir question.[20] It insists that the Kashmir issue still remains unresolved and until it is resolved there could not be any peace in the sub-continent.[21] India, on the other hand, asserts that Kashmir was an integral part of India and there was no question of any multilateral approach to the issue. India insists that if there was any contention on the issue between the two countries it should be resolved through bilateral negotiations under the Shimla agreement. But the recent developments in Kashmir especially the attempted crossing of the Line of Control by the people of the occupied Kashmir led by the self-styled President of the JKLF on February 11-12 and his persistent threats to cross the LOC on March 30 again, have opened a new dilemma in Pakistan. While Pakistan's commitment and desires to destabilize India (Kashmir particularly) remain in tact. The demand for a separate State of Kashmir by the JKLF has irked the Pakistani Government.[22] The situation in Kashmir and thereby in the Indo-Pak relations is gloomy and the clouds of war are hovering over the sub-continent as Pakistan is chafing to maintain the tempo of the crisis. Given the military parity and the high-tech and destructive nature of the present day war the two countries may not go to war, but Pakistan is playing its cards cautiously with the only and ultimate aim of dismembering India.

The bilateral relations between India and Pakistan were time and again sought to be balanced by resorting to bring the presence of outside powers in the sub-continent. The sole aim of Pakistan's foreign policy during the past four decades has been only to counter India.

This led to a veritable arms race between India and Pakistan. The post-1971 period has raised hopes of bringing a lasting peace in Indo-Pak relations. This trend was evident as the two countries maintained a reasonable strict adherence to the principles of the Shimla Agreement consequently restraining from resorting to war. This trend unfortunately was halted by the sudden eruption of the Afghanistan crisis and the relative change in the American security perceptions and attitudes towards South Asia in general and Pakistan in particular. Alarmed by the Soviet Union's marching of troops into Afghanistan, the US thought it imperative to arm Pakistan and deter the Soviets to expand further into the South to reach the warm waters of the Arabian Sea. Thus, Pakistan, was regarded as the frontline State in the US security strategy in South Asia and was rewarded generously with large quantities of military and economic aid.[23] This has naturally caused concern for Indian policy makers. While the US military build up in Pakistan was ostensibly aimed at containing the Soviet invasion, it was actually giving Pakistan an opportunity to tilt the military Balance of power in the South Asia in its own favour.[24] As a part of the military aid the US provided Pakistan with a variety of sophisticated arms, including the F-16 deep penetrating strike aircrafts enhancing the capacity of Pakistan air force to reach deeper in to the hinterland of India, including Delhi and other important cities.

The disproportionate acquisition of modern and sophisticated arms, to its size and requirements, by Pakistan has raised suspicion about the intentions of Pakistan in the minds of the Indian decision makers. In fact, while the arming of Pakistan was done by the US, with the aim of forming a bulwark against the Soviets, the actual deployment of troops and the modern (newly acquired) arms took place on the Indo-Pak border.[25] No wonder then, that, this has triggered a vicious arms race between India and Pakistan. As already mentioned Pakistan has been chafing to avenge the humility suffered at the hands of India in the past wars. The Afghanistan crisis and the US perceptions on Pakistan as the frontline State have come in as providential boons for Pakistan. India saw in the arms build up of Pakistan and its changing attitudes a desire to engage India in a limited war and get away with handsome gains.[26] Thus, to restore its military parity with Pakistan, India too had started arms build up. The defence expenditures of both India and Pakistan have increased by leaps and bounds. India's defence outlay reached 3.3% of its GNP and 16% of its total annual budget whereas Pakistan's defence spending reached 6.5% of the GNP and touched 33% of its budget outlay.[27]

The arms race, between India and Pakistan, aggravated the already existing adversary relationship between the two States. Suspicions among each other have increased tensions on the borders and the war hysteria dominated the psychology of the public opinion in the sub-continent. The new cold-war between the USA and the Soviet Union developed in the context of the Afghan crisis has generated a bitter cold war between the traditional rivals, now falling to its ebb and now rising high and thus enforcing an uneasy tension marked by no-war and no-peace syndrome.

The quest for the military build up by India and Pakistan and the desire to maintain the military balance of power with a quest for decisive advantage among both India and Pakistan have not only undermined the security of both these States and that of the South Asian region but also caused a severe set-back to the developmental programmes launched by the respective governments. India and Pakistan while retaining and at times aggravating their hostile postures, have tried to acquire some sort of a legitimacy to their governments which were facing severe crises.

The futility of the arms supplies by the US to Pakistan on the pretext of countering the Soviet onslaught has been proved by the eventual withdrawal of the Soviet troops from Afghanistan and by the subsequent dissolution and disintegration of the Soviet Union. While extending the military aid to Pakistan the US in fact ignored her much vaunted commitments to the virtues of democracy and freedom. America did not mind taking sides with the much maligned and archaic dictatorship of Gen. Zia-ul-Haq. At the same time, it did not heed to the appeals made by the Government of India which is acclaimed by the Americans themselves as the largest democracy in the world. Thus, in the 1980s the USA had contributed quite handsomely to boosting up the aggressive postures of Pakistan and thereby to the further deterioration of Indo-Pak relations (We will deal in detail the role of the major powers in developing hostilities between India on the one hand and her neighbours on the other in a Chapter -V.).

The arms race kicked up by the Afghan crisis and new cold-war relationship between the then super-powers has kept alive the hostile relationship between India and Pakistan. The quest for nuclear weapon capability and its progress has institutionalized the traditional rivalry in a framework of a classical balance of power scenario between India and Pakistan.

The rationale for India in acquiring nuclear capability is that India needed it to strengthen her security *vis-a-vis* China which already possessed nuclear weapons and which was pronouncedly anti-Indian having already fought a successful war against India. The Pokhran Nuclear Explosion by India in mid-1974 triggered the nuclear emotions in Pakistan as Pakistan has the same kind of relationship with India as India had with China.[28] Though yet, Pakistan launched itself on the path of the nuclear quest.

India, on more than one occasion, announced categorically that she did not possess nuclear weapons and her nuclear programme was only meant for peaceful purposes. But it is clear that India did not want to close its options regarding the making of nuclear weapons. This is due to the fact that nuclear weapons are possessed by at least five States in the world including China whose relations with India are not-too-cordial.

Pakistan has persisted on its ardent desire for acquiring nuclear arms capability despite repeated warnings by Washington not to proceed in that direction. Pakistan's desire to acquire nuclear weapons has originally manifested during Bhutto's regime. It is a part of deep rooted rivalry with India. She rather considers it necessary for her survival. Pakistan's political, geographical and economic resources do not permit her to achieve a strict parity with India as far as the conventional military strength and weapon systems are concerned. A parity of military strength or some sort of balance of power is considered an imperative by Pakistan to change the *status quo* in Kashmir and the power politics of the Indian sub-continent. Acquisition of nuclear capability is considered a decisive step for Pakistan in this direction.[29] With this sole objective, Pakistan launched its nuclear programme in the mid-1970s and the Pokhran explosion by India has accelerated a feeling of urgency.

With the Pakistani unclear programme making headlines India too witnessed spontaneous surge of public opinion whether India should or should not make a nuclear bomb. However, India has been advocating from the very beginning that her nuclear programme is meant only for peaceful purposes.

The USA, for its own reasons, felt alarmed at the ongoing quest for nuclear weapons in the Indian sub-continent and as such tried to bring pressure both on India and Pakistan to put a stop to the nuclear quest. Thus Carter administration had ordered for stoppage of supplies of enriched Uranium to India for the Tarapur Atomic Energy Plant which was part of an agreement signed by both India and US at an earlier date and also stopped military aid to Pakistan since 1979.[30] While USA maintained a suspicious attitude towards India all these years and tried time and to coax her into toeing its line by making her sign the Nuclear Non-Proliferation Treaty (NPT), Pakistan got a windfall in the Afghan crisis. In the changed perceptions of the USA, Pakistan got a new lease of opportunity to quench its insatiable desire for military build up and that too without any commitment to nuclear non-proliferation, as the US waived Symington Amendment[31] for period of six years to meet the Afghan crisis.[32] Thus, while the Afghan crisis increased the tensions in the East-West relations, at the same time it has added fuel to the smouldering fire of eternal rivalry between India and Pakistan.

The only respite this race has witnessed was in the initial stages of the Benazir Bhutto's tenure as Pakistan's Prime Minister. The cordiality that existed in the Indo-Pak relations during this period is marked by the agreement reached by both the countries not to attack each other's nuclear installations during Rajiv Gandhi visit of the fourth SAARC Summit in December, 1988.[33] Though, this has brought about a cosmetic improvement for a short period, the suspicions continued to raise the tempers on each side. Recently, Pakistan declared that it had to take to nuclear options because of Kashmir. It has also been acknowledged by Pakistan that it has acquired nuclear weapon capability or even possessed nuclear weapons.[34] With the international opinion taking it for granted that both India and Pakistan possess nuclear capability, there are no signs of relenting hostilities and mutual distrust.

On the question of signing the NPT, both India and Pakistan have been prevaricating for different reasons. India argues that the NPT was a discriminatory arrangement and pleads that nuclear disarmament should begin first with the States that already possess the nuclear weapons. Pakistan, on the other hand, puts the condition that it would sign the NPT if India signed it. The US seemingly giving up the idea of persuading India to sign the NPT, now proposed to hold a conferencce of five countries, viz., USA Russia, China, the major nuclear powers and India and Pakistan. Pakistan has not been receiving aid from the USA since 1990 in nuclear matters, with an intention to please its donor, the USA agreed in principle to attend the proposed summit. But India expressed reservations and sought for certain clarifications.[35]

The Indo-Pak relations, have reached a stage of mutual deterrence due to the nuclear diplomacy. Both the States have been since long developing nuclear weapon delivery systems. Pakistan's F-16 jets are capable of carrying nuclear weapons deeper into the Indian territory. Besides it has been developing its intermediate range missile, Hatf.[36] India too made considerable progress in developing its own indigenous missile systems Agni and Prithvi.

Apart from the above mentioned factors that influence the Indo-Pak relations, there are still many unresolved bilateral problems. The problem which came to the surface recently and resulted in skirmishes on the border, is Siachen glacier issue. Since mid-1980s one finds continuous border clashes between India and Pakistan on this issue. One has to focus attention on the problems and prospects of SAARC in the light of such relations between the major partners of South Asian regional cooperation.

India Sri Lanka Relations

Now let us focus our attention on Indo-Sri Lanka relations. Common cultural heritage and ethnic affinity breeding mutual suspicions rather than strengthening bonds of friendship is exemplified by India-Sri Lanka relationships right from the pre-independence period. Plantation Tamils, the migrant workers from the nearby Tamil province of India, were the bone of contention between the two neighbours during the 1930s. Nehru visited the island State in 1939 on behalf of the Congress Party to plead for the case of the deported Tamil workers but he found the Ceylonese Government and the Sinhalese leaders of the time suspicious and unresponsive to the Indian requests.[37] However, Nehru took it in his stride and advised the Indians to bear with it without any ill-will. That in fact, was the beginning of the love-hate relationship between the two States.

The post-independent era carried forward this love-hate relationship besides the divergence in their ideological and strategic approaches. With the pro-west United National Party of D.S.

Senanayake coming to power and the Congress Party under the leadership of Nehru having a progressive outlook, India and Sri Lanka have found themselves at two different ends of the political spectrum. However, there was apparent calm and cordiality in their relations. But the high profile attitude of India to international problems and issues and her larger size made Sri Lanka harbour feelings of suspicion and fear about India's domination.[38]

Between 1954 and 1964 India and Sri Lanka had several issues of disagreement, most important among them were the question of Estate Tamils (migrant labour) and the trade relations between India and Sri Lanka. The issue of Kachchativu was also one of bones of contention between the two countries.

There were about 975,000 Indian Tamils in Sri Lanka without either Indian or Sri Lankan citizenship. The Shastri and Sirimao Agreement of 1964 tried to resolve this issue amicably. Under this pact India and Sri Lanka were to grant citizenship to the hitherto stateless people at a ratio of 7:4. Again in another agreement between Indira Gandhi and Sirimao Bandarnayake in January 1974 the fate of the other people not covered by the earlier agreement was decided. However, the Sri Lankan Government did not fulfil its commitments, under the agreements.[39]

On the trade issue Sri Lanka was sore with India about its cut in the purchase of coconut from Sri Lanka and not purchasing rubber from the island nation.[40] Sri Lanka, on the other hand, was well disposed towards China despite its dislike for communism because of the Rubber-Rice Agreements reached between the two countries in 1954 and renewed in 1964. The public opinion in Sri Lanka was also generally not very much in favour of India.

The indifference and suspicion towards India and the utilitarian relationship with China was the decisive factor in shaping the attitude of Sri Lanka regarding the Sino-Indian border dispute. At the least, it was neutral and implicitly it was more pro-China.[41] However, during the Indo-Pak wars in 1965 and 1971 Sri Lanka sided with Pakistan. In fact in 1971 Sri Lanka's policy was overtly anti-Indian. First, it was the Indo-Soviet Treaty which was the cause of suspicion and distrust. Further, the crisis in East Pakistan and India's support to the people of East Pakistan made it more serious. Already Sri Lanka was sympathetic towards Pakistan and besides that China, her closest friend at that time, vehemently opposed Indian actions thus influencing Sri Lanka's policy *vis-a-vis* the Indo-Pak conflict of 1971. Alongwith USA and China-Sri Lanka also vociferously argued to contain India.[42] True to this policy, Pakistan was provided refuelling facility and permission of over-flight to its war planes during the war. Later this was acknowledged with gratitude by Gen. Zia.[43]

Subsequently, however, there were some efforts to improve relations with India. But always the suspicion of the Big Brother overshadowing its own identity and security was nevertheless lurking. India on its part tried to assuage the fears of Sri Lanka by settling outstanding disputes like the repatriation of Tamils and the Kachchativu problem etc. But the 1974 nuclear explosion at Pokhran kept the misgivings of Sri Lanka alive.

In an effort to wean away from the influence of India and the centripetal ethnic and cultural forces of the sub-continent, Sri Lanka sought to forge extra-regional links. As a part of this strategy membership of the ASEAN was sought for and allowing oil storage and naval facilities to the US were contemplated. The ASEAN, however, turned down the request of Sri Lanka for membership in that regional organization.[44]

Sri Lanka toyed with the idea of giving naval facilities to the USA in Trincomalee since the early 1980s. This was mainly intended to undercut the growing influence of India in the South Asian region. In fact US ships enjoyed routine access at Trincomalee during the early 1980s. Against the wishes of India, again, Sri Lanka signed an agreement with the US to allow the expansion and upgrading of the Voice of America relay station at Chilav.[45] Sri Lanka voted in favour of the UN resolutions seeking to declare South Asia as a Nuclear Free Zone.

The feelings of mutual distrust and suspicions and the latent hostilities, between India and Sri Lanka have ultimately surfaced into open hostilities with the eruption of the struggle of the Tamils for separate Eelam since the early 1980s. The Tamils are concentrated in the northern and eastern provinces of Sri Lanka. They have been systematically alienated with a sustained policy of discrimination since the dawn of independence. The quest of the Tamils for just and equitale treatment in the united Sri Lanka initially under the leadership of the Tamil United Liberation Front (TULF) on peaceful lines gradually assumed militant postures and slipped into the hands of militant organizations. Notable among them were the Eelam People Revolutionary Liberation Front (EPRLF), People Liberation Organization of Tamils (PLOT) and Liberation Tigers of Tamil Eelam (LTTE). By 1982-83 the struggle turned violent and the leadership went into the hands of the militants and by 1985 the LTTE emerged as the clear pioneer of the struggle.

Because of the strong ethnic affinity, the struggle of the Sri Lanka Tamils naturally evoked sentimental feelings and sympathy among the people of Tamil Nadu in India. As the struggle progressed and turned more violent some of the militants started taking shelter in Tamil Nadu, and many innocent people also started taking shelter in India. The Government of India under the pressure from public opinion had to do something for the cause of the Tamils, at the same time not hurting the sentiments of Sri Lankan government. India took a mediatory stance to the problem and at the same time offered help to the Tamil refugees. Sri Lankan government was sore at the ambivalent attitude of the India though it could not directly accuse India of interference in its internal affairs. At the same time Sri Lanka tried to seek support from outside powers like the USA, Israel and even Pakistan. India had to adopt a cautious approach to the problem because she did not want any outside involvement in the Indian sub-continent.[46]

By 1985 the situation in Sri Lanka went out of control and India's efforts at mediation particularly at the Thimpu tripartite talks between Sri Lankan government, the Tamils and India did not bring any tangible results. Instead, the leadership or the struggle unmistakably passed into the hands of the LTTE popularly known as Tigers. The internal war between the Tigers and the Sri Lankan forces assumed alarming proportions. The repression on Tamils caused a heavy exodus of the affected Tamil people of the northern province of the island into the State of Tamil Nadu in India. The pressure started telling on India but she could not conceive any drastic action for the fear of accusation of interference. Between 1985 and June 1987 nearly 150,000 refugees have come to India, and many more thousands have followed in later periods till the end of 1989. By June 1987 the Sri Lankan forces blockaded the northern peninsular town of Jaffna and did not even allow food supplies to enter the peninsula. The people of Jaffna were threatened with starvation deaths forced on them by the Sri Lankan forces. The public opinion in India in general and in Tamil Nadu in particular reached a crescendo and forced the Government of India to do something about it. The Government of India was very much aware of the implications of any action at this stage and was left with no option than to extend some help with people of Jaffna whose lives were endangered by the Sri Lanka. Under these circumstances, India airlifted food supplies to Jaffna on June 5 1987 after unsuccessful persuation of the Sri Lankan authorities to permit Indian fishing vessels to deliver supplies to the beleaguered people of Jaffna. The June 5 operation coded "Operation Pawan" resulted in the already intemperate abuses pouring on India turn into a vitriolic attack on India by all sections of the Sri Lankan Government, press, political parties and public. It was the lowest ebb of Indo-Sri Lankan relations, short of war actual.[47] Every opportunity was grabbed by Sri Lanka to attack the Indian action as a violation of her territorial integrity, sovereignty and independence. Even it was decided to boycott the SAARC Council of Ministers meeting scheduled to be held at New Delhi in June 1987.[48]

However, due to vigorous and sutained efforts rapprochement between the two estranged neighbours could be achieved by July 1987. The swift succession of diplomatic activity finally culminated in the Indo-Sri Lankan Accord signed by Prime Minister Rajiv Gandhi and President J.R. Jaywardene at Colombo on July 27, 1987.

The Indo-Sri Lankan accord hailed as an harbinger of peace for the island nation and the beginning of a new era of friendship, mutual good will and cooperation between Sri Lanka and India, proved with the passage of time to be a self-imposed trap by India. It was a marked departure from the hitherto Indian policy of mediation and support from outside to an active involvement in the quagmire of the ethnic conflagration in Sri Lanka. Under para 6 of the Annexure to the Agreement, India committed to send a peace keeping contingent to Sri Lanka to guarantee and enforce the cessation of hostilities.[49] Accordingly, India sent the Peace Keeping Force to Sri Lanka to oversee the surrendering of arms by the LTTE and guarantee cessation of hostilities so that Sri Lanka could fulfil the obligations undertaken by her in the July 27, 1987 Agreement. The Indian Peace Keeping Force (IPKF) faced the intriguing task of disarming the LTTE in its own land. The deployment of the IPKF was resented by the Tamil militants as it was done without the participation of theTamils in the conclusion of the Agreement. Thus the LTTE viewed the Indo-Sri Lankan Accord as a device to dilute its struggle and as a device to snatch away the fruits of the hard-fought struggle over the past five years. The IPKF, thus, faced a hostile situation in an alien land. In the process of making the Tamil militants, especially the LTTE surrender its arms the IPKF ended up fighting the LTTE itself in the jungles of the Vavuniya and other areas of the northern province of Sri Lanka.

Sri Lanka on its part, in pursuance of the Indo-Sri Lankan Agreement, conducted elections in the northern and eastern provinces and devolved some powers to the Provincial Councils. The EPRLF, a rival organization of the LTTE came to power in the shortlived honeymoon of the Sri Lankan government and Tamil rapprochement.

The folly of the Indo-Sri Lankan Agreement coupled with the support to the EPRLF in sharing power in the North-East Province further estranged the LTTE from the IPKF and the Indian Government. In the ostensible war with the LTTE in the northern and eastern provinces the IPKF lost control of the situation and in the process was accused of many commissions and omissions. The IPKF which was doing a thankless job became the target of abuse by both the Sinhalese dominated Sri Lankan Government and the Tamil militants and the Tamil people. The LTTE which enjoyed the support of over 80 - 90% of the population of the northern province accused the IPKF of trying to annihilate the Tamils on the pretext of peace keeping.[50] The Sri Lankan Government, especially the more hawkish sections led by the then

Prime Minister Premadasa opposed the Accord from the very beginning and made India and IPKF their target of a vicious verbal abuses and attacks.[51] The IPKF was called the "occupying force" trampling the sovereignty and independence of Sri Lanka.[52] Premadasa who succeeded Jayawardene as President of Sri Lanka entered into negotiations with the LTTE and the two hitherto antagonistic forces with one voice demanded the immediate withdrawal of the IPKF and advised India not to meddle in the internal affairs of Sri Lanka. The *volte face* of the Sri Lankan Government irked the Indian Government and inflicted a severe setback to the India-Sri Lanka relations. The change of government in New Delhi in late 1989 resulting in the withdrawal of the IPKF by March 1990 somewhat helped ease the tensions between the two governments. But still the question of Tamils' struggle for their political and economic rights remains unresolved.

The Sri Lankan fiasco posed many questions about foreign policies and mutual attitudes of both India and Sri Lanka. While it was a clever policy on the part of Jayawardene to bait India into entering the muddle which was exclusively his own, on the part of India and Rajiv Gandhi it was a great folly prompted by lack of understanding and desire for false prestige. The assassination of Rajiv Gandhi on 21 May 1991 by the LTTE was the tragic end result of the overt military involvement of India in Sri Lanka.

The crackdown on the LTTE and the other Tamil militants taking shelter in Tamil Nadu by the Tamil Nadu government has assuaged the suspicions of the Sri Lankan Government in the recent period. But the tensions in the bilateral relations between the two countries are still simmering. The impact of the prevalent mood of mutual distrust and dislike particularly in the case of Sri Lanka, reflected in the aborted SAARC Summit at Colombo in November 1991.[53]

Indo-Bangladesh Relations

Bangladesh is one of the closest neighbours of India, which not only shares a land border of about 400 miles but also inherited a common cultural, ethnic and historical background alongwith India. Besides, India played a very crucial role for several reasons,[54] in the emergence of Bangladesh as an independent State. For the interference in the Bangladesh affair in 1971, India had to face a spate of rebukes from her South Asian neighbours as well as the USA and her Western allies. In fact with the US deployment of its Seventh Fleet in the Bay of Bengal and the counter move by the Soviets to deter the Americans, 1971 witnessed the cold war tensions threatening the Indian sub-continent. Naturally, one expected from Bangladesh fair amount of enthusiasm in maintaining friendly and cordial relations with India for a long time to come. However, the India-Bangladesh relations which indeed began on the rhetoric of India's magnanimity and the sentimentalities between the people of the two countries, have taken a zig-zag path over the past two decades. Having lost the labours of love, India is now in an unenviable position of finding her eastern neighbour joining the euphoria created in the name of Indian hegemonism.

The relations between the two largest neighbours of South Asia (in terms of population) have begun with all sincerity and friendly intentions. This phase lasted between 1971-75, i.e., during the period of Shaikh Mujibur Rahman's rule in Bangladesh. Bangladesh under Mujib took to a democratic path with a secular approach. This was the main point of convergence for both the countries. The personal relations between Indira Gandhi and Shaikh Mujibur Rahman dominated the official policy of India-Bangladesh relations.[55] India was quite generous in giving aid to Bangladesh during this period. However, it cannot be said that Indo-Bangla relations during the Mujib regime were totally devoid of any irritants, they were now and then raising their heads. One such problem was the Islamic identity or Muslim nationalism which dominated the pre-1971 India-Pakistan relations. It was in essence an anti-Indian current gaining momentum below the surface. Moulana Bhashani, a prominent leader known for his uncompromising anti-Indian postures has in fact declared a *jihad* on June 3, 1973 on Indian 'exploiters' and urged the army, police and paramilitary forces to oppose the Indian influence in Bangladesh.[56] Besides, India was subjected to a vilification campaign because of the problem of smuggling across the border.[57] In spite of this Bangladesh maintained friendly ties with India till the end of the Mujib regime which came to an end abruptly in August 1975 when he was assassinated.

Gen. Zia-ur-Rahman, the military ruler of Bangladesh, who took over the reigns of power shortly after the August 1975 coup changed the character of the Constitution from a secular one to an Islamic oriented one. Article 12 of the Constitution now proclaimed that Bangladesh would be guided by the "Principles of absolute trust and faith in the Almighty Allah, nationalism, democracy and socialism." The Awami League slogan of "joy Bangla" was discarded at it was a secular expression and in its place the new slogan "Bangladesh Zindabad" was brougth in.[58] These and other related measures, meant to Islamize the Bangladesh polity and society, were invariably followed by the anti-Indian propaganda. Thus friendly relations were replaced by feelings of antagonism and hostile postures. It was this period when the Farakka barrage issue was the main source of tension and discord between the two neighbours. However, the conciliatory attitude of the Janata regime during 1977 made it possible to arrive at an amicable solution to the Farakka problem. But certainly India was not as pliant and accommodative towards the already metamorphasized neighbour as she was in the earlier periods. The changed political ambience of the Bangladeshi domestic scene had its impact on the hardened attitude of India.[59]

The Ershad regime, which followed the regime of Zia-ur-Rahman through another coup followed the Islamization more vigorously and in the same vein the anti-Indian tirade. It was a necessity for the military rulers of Bangladesh without exception to rouse the anti-Indian sentiments in order to claim some semblance of legitimacy and public approval.[60] This went hand in hand with the growth of fundamentalism. This is coupled with an attack on hitherto cordial cultural intercourse between the two Bengals on either side of the border. This trend was stretched further in banning Indian films, music, books and newspapers in Bangladesh. Bangladesh's cultivation of friendly relations with Pakistan during the Ershad period was meant to counter-balance the influence of India in the South Asian region.[61]

Thus in the earlier period democracy and secularism were the main factors in forging good neighbourly relations between India and Bangladesh. As long as the cultural and ethnic unity of the people cutting across the borders is sought to be divided on religious lines, the discords and mutual suspicions in Indo-Bangla relations will remain. All other factors, like peace, human rights, non-alignment etc. do only serve as cosmetic covers incapable of hiding the real colours of discordant attitudes and postures.[62]

India and Bangladesh have, apart from the basic causes of mutual antagonism mentioned above, had quite a few bilateral problems. Most important among them are: (a) the sharing of Ganga waters, (b) the dispute over the New Moore (South Talpatti) islands, (c) controlling of floods, (d) Chakma refugee problem, and (e) the Tin Bigha corridor.

Bangladesh argues that river Ganges was an international river and hence its waters should be shared by India, Nepal and Bangladesh. She has raised the issue at the OIC conference, the NAM Summit and the United Nations also. Bangladesh also proposed in 1978 that Nepal and Bangladesh should together negotiate with India regarding the sharing of the Ganges waters.

The issue of sharing of Ganga waters has been a nagging problem in the Indo-Bangla relations since last two decades. In the past a few temporary agreements were arrived at. But the problem used to come to the fore after the expiry of the short term arrangements. And permanent solution were not in sight. The Indo-Bangla Joint Commision has been meeting during the past several years but the intransigent attitudes have defied any solution to the problem.

The New Moore island issue first emerged in 1980. The New Moore island (Purbhasha or South Talpatty island were the names given by Bangladesh) is a new configuration sighted in the estuary of river Hariabangha of the Sunderbans. In May 1981 Bangladesh tried to challenge the ownership of the island by India by deploying three gunboats which approached the island menacingly as the Indian survey personnel were carrying experiments in the area. To counter the Bangladesh gun-boats India had to deploy INS Andaman.[63] Subsequently too, Bangladesh tried to physically intervene in the Indian possession of the island but such attempts were thwarted. Bangladesh still disputes the ownership right of the New Moore island and on that count the question of maritime boundary is also unresolved between the two countries.[64]

The Chakma refugees problem is another important cause of worry in the Indo-Bangla relations. The Chakma refugees numbering more than 1,50,000 crossed the border into the neighbouring Indian States to escape the repression of the Bangladesh authorities. India has been experiencing difficulties in dealing with the influx of the refugees as they pose economic as well as law and order problem to the concerned Indian States. As the Chakmas under the banner of hardline Shanti Bahini have intensified their struggle against the Bangladesh government (and the non-local Bengalis) the problem of refugees is getting further aggravated. Bangladesh has yet to create conditions conducive for the return of Chakma refugees who have taken shelter in India. On the other hand, a strange theory of 'Lebensraum' (a copy of Hitler's theory for the expansion of the Germany into other areas) is sought to be circulated to defend the influx of the Bangladeshi refugees into India. The main thrust of the theory goes like this: "There is no reason why regional and international cooperation could not be worked out to plan and to execute population movements and settlements to avoid critical demographic pressures in pockets of high concentration".[65] Its protagonists also accuse India of instigating the Chakmas and Shanti Bahini[66] which is well in tune with the official line of Bangladesh. While Bangladesh is sitting pretty on this problem it is ironical that she is worried about the similar problem of influx of the people of Myanmar into Bangladesh. Khaleda Zia, Prime Minister of Bangladesh was on a tour to the USA to apprise the Americans of the problem and to seek their assistance to meet the situation.[67]

The Tin Bigha problem has since been solved with the handing over of the corridor in June 1992 to the Bangladesh government on a perpetual lease.

As mentioned above the crux of the problem in the bilateral relations of India and Bangladesh is the incongruity of the social philosophy of the ruling elites of Bangladesh and India. The incongruity or divergence is the main outcome of the conflict between the modern and traditional elements of the social system and also due to the legitimacy crisis faced by the autocratic political structure particularly in Bangladesh.

India-Nepal Relations

The cultural and social homogeneity of India and the Himalayan Kingdom of Nepal is so striking that Nepal has always been obsessed with the fear of domination by India. The Rana rulers of Nepal, apprehensive about the fate of Nepal after the success of the Indian freedom struggle tried to maintain good relations both with the British rulers of India and the nationalist elements.[68] Thus, India right from the beginning, is the main determinant of Nepal's foreign policy.

India and Nepal entered into a special bilateral relationship through the Indo-Nepal Treaty signed in 1950. The Treaty recognized Nepal's independence but in matters of security and import of arms and ammunition especially through the territory of India she is supposed to act in consultation with the Government of India. The special relations according to this Treaty is marked by the undertaking of both the parties to grant each others nationals, national treatment and the rights of ownership, residence, participation in trade and commerce and employment etc.

The special relationship between India and Nepal lasted throughout the 1950s. However, the elements of suspicion, the fear of the giant neighbour and differences in the political systems and divergent interests were slowly getting articulated in the minds of the ruling elite of Nepal. The sentiments of gratitude for helping the Nepalese in restoring the authority of the King gradually disappeared. King Mahendra, the absolute monarch of Nepal, always had the lurking suspicions about the democratic political system of India and her rulers. Naturally, Mahendra decided to repose his trust in the Chinese rather than the Indians whose democratic principles endangered his position. The full support he needed for his authority was not forthcoming from India. Thus India is identified as his main threat whereas China was considered less dangerous.[69] King Mahendra, in such circumstances, entered into negotiations with the Chinese and in 1961 signed an agreement with China.

The policy of balancing between China and India by King Mahendra and later on his son King Birendra irked the Indian Government. India has high security stakes in Nepal as Nepal is considered the gateway of India for the Chinese. The result was a solid support for Nepal from China.[70] This had given Nepal a taste of independent identity. She has got more leverage in her dealings with India. The policy of playing India and China one against the other also brought rich dividends to the Nepalese rulers in consolidating power within the Kingdom.[71]

Indo-Nepalese relations ran into rough weather in 1970s as the assertive monarchy started denouncing India's policy as 'Big Brother attitude'. Using the China card, King Birendra blew hot and cold against India. Except acknowledging the role of India in the revolution of 1950 in Nepal, Birendra finds no positive aspect in India's relations with Nepal. He accused India of cheating Nepal in the construction of Kosi and Gandak projects.[72] The then Prime Minsiter of Nepal, Tulsi Giri commented euphemistically that Nepal was not land locked but India-locked.[73]

The crux of Indo-Nepalese relations is the Nepal's quest for identity and its clash with Indian strategic interests. Nepal is desirous of expanding its area of operation as far as possible with the sole aim of reducing her dependence on India which she thinks is crucial to its survival and development.[74] However, in spite of the less importance attached to India, Nepal is aware that China is not a substitute to India as far as the economic ties are concerned.

Paradoxically, while Nepal insists that India recognize Nepal as a zone of peace, she acquired large quantities of arms and ammunitions from China to the dislike of India.[75] Obviously, Nepal's proposal of declaring itself as Zone of Peace is only meant to attract international attention whereas the acquisition of military hardware is aimed at asserting its power both internally and externally.[76]

The friction in the bilateral relations of the States in the recent past was due to the differences over the Trade and Transit Agreements which expired on March 23, 1989. India refused to renew the agreement as she insisted on a single treaty while Nepal wanted to have two different treaties. Subsequently, India increased vigilance at the crossing points between the two States and refused to provide railway wagons for the movement of goods between Nepal and Bangladesh.[77]

Nepal was also jittery about the alleged involvement of the Indians in the struggle for the restoration of democracy and party system in Nepal. The democratic system providing opportunity to criticize repression and authoritarian system anywhere in the world through free press in India is the main cause of suspicions about the imminent interference in the internal affairs of Nepal. Thus, the systemic divergence surfaced as the main source of friction in the Indo-Nepalese relations in the late 1980s. The resolution of the problems related to the systemic changes in 1990 in Nepal have, understandably, contributed to the easing of tensions in the bilateral relations of India and Nepal.

The visits of two Prime Ministers of Nepal, in the aftermath of the restoration of democracy in Nepal have eventually resolved most of the bilateral problems between the two neighbours especially the ticklish issues of Trade and Transit treaties.

However, alleged Big Brother attitude of India, its size, 'India-locked' nature of Nepal's geography and the issues relating to the tapping and distribution of water resources may cause worries in the future relations of India and Nepal.

India'a Relations with Bhutan and Maldives

Bhutan and Maldives are the two States of the South Asian region which do not have any apparent cause of complaint in their bilateral relations with India.

Bhutan, the tiny Himalayan Kingdom, entered into a bilateral Treaty of Friendship with the Government of India on August 8, 1949. Under this Treaty India undertook to exercise no interference in the internal administration of Bhutan whereas Bhutan agreed to be guided by the advice of the Government of India in regard to its external relations.[78]

The treaty also provides for free trade and commerce between the territories of the two States and India agreed to grant all facilities to carry the produce of Bhutan by all means throughout the territory of India.[79] India also agreed to permit Bhutan to import arms, ammunition, machinery or any warlike material that may be required or desired for the strength and welfare of Bhutan with the assistance and approval of the Government of India.[80]

The bilateral relations between India and Bhutan were mutually satisfactory and good neighbourly. Neither had any room for complaint against the other. In fact, India's security concerns were well in line with the thinking of Bhutan. For instance, Bhutan put a total ban on trade with Tibet quite in tune with the China policy of India, even though it caused hardship to its people who had traditional links with Tibet.[81]

Besides, the cooperation in external relations, India extended considerable economic assistance to Bhutan. Initially, India was the only external donor to Bhutan. Even now the dependence of Bhutanese economy on the external aid is as high as 95%. Bhutan with the guidance and help of India launched economic planning for its economic development. Her first five year plan started in 1961. The mainstay of Bhutan's economy currently, the Chukha hydroelectric project was built with 100% financial assistance from India, out of which 60% was grant. Besides, India purchases a sizable portion of its produce which brings considerable revenue to Bhutan.[82]

In spite of the fact that Bhutan is guided by India for her external relations, Bhutan started looking outward. It has entered the United Nations in 1971 and established diplomatic relations with other countries gradually and made its external aid dependence broadbased. Surprisingly in 1981 Bhutan entered into direct negotiation with China with the approval of New Delhi. Bhutan now enjoys an equal status with India and other States of South Asia in the SAARC and the United Nations.

As of now, Bhutan does not have any complaint against India nor does it pose any security threat to India. However, the current turbulence in Bhutan over the question of Nepali population in Southern Bhutan and the imminent settlement of border questions between China and Bhutan may change the security perceptions and attitudes of Bhutan.

Maldives, the Indian ocean archipelago, the only State which does not share either land or maritime boundaries with India has perfectly cordial and friendly relations with India. Though Maldives is a predominantly Muslim State it does not fall into the category of the other Islamic States which are invariably affected by the fundamentalist thinking.

Maldives and India do not share either historical, or cultural or ethnic commonalities and hence there is no chance for Maldives of any fears of cultural or Pan-Indian domination over her. Hence, the element of suspicion and the lurking fear of the Big-Brother-next-door is completely absent in the case of Maldives. Thus a totally clean slate gave an opportunity to formulate their mutual policies objectively. Thus until November 1988 though there were no extremely cordial or warm relations between the two States, both India and Maldives were tied in good neighbourly relationship.

However, the aborted coup by the Sri Lankan mercenaries in November 1988 brought about a warmer current in the India-Maldives bilateral relations. Now, Maldives, being grateful to India for the timely help rendered by her in repelling the attempt to overthrow the existing government, regards the friendship with India as valuable.[83] Maldives is receiving assistance from India on various programmes. The Indira Gandhi Memorial Hospital is nearing completion in Male with India's assistance.

South Asia - A Phenomenon of Indo-Phobia

To any casual observer, the position of India—its size and geographical location—clearly appears to be of a definite significance in the region of South Asia. Commensurate with its size and strength, India is expected to play an important role in the global politics in general and in South Asian politics in particular. To quote Nehru:

> "Now, India is very curiously placed in Asia and her history has been governed a great deal by the geographical factors plus other factors. Whichever problem in Asia you may take up, somehow or other India comes into the picture. Whether you think in terms of China or the Middle East or South East

Asia, India immediately comes into the picture. It is so situated that because of past history, traditions, etc. in regard to any major problem of a country or a group of countries of Asia, India has to be considered. Whether it is a problem of defence or trade or industry or economic policy, India cannot be ignored. She cannot be ignored because, as I said, her geographical position is a compelling reason. She cannot be ignored also because of her actual or potential power and resources".[84]

Evidently, right from the beginning, the policy makers of India were convinced that India was destined to play a key role in the international and Asian political system. But it cannot be construed as an ambition to exercise power and to dominate the regional politics. Nehru did not envisage such a scenario for the coming decades in the post-independence era. It was more contemplated in active and positive response to any international situation depending on its exigency and merits. It was in line with this thinking and in response to the ongoing rivalry between the two power blocs that the concept of non-alignment came into being.

Nehru, being a visionary and a statesman of high calibre, conceived of a rightful role for India in the world affairs. The active role that India played in the international politics in the 1950s was solely due to the political idealism and consciousness of the contextual imperatives on his part. However, neither Nehru nor India had any vision of acquiring the status of a 'power' and dominating the region. For, India was obsessed with her economic problems in the 1950s and her military strength was negligible. Neither was India accused of regional domination by her neighbours during the 1950s or 1960s.

The reasons for the pre-occupation of 'indophobia' in the smaller States of South Asia have their origins in the political, demographic, ethnic, economic, geographical and psychological factors that influenced their evolution and existence during the past few decades.

Size and strength made India the most striking culprit in the eyes of her smaller neighbours in South Asia. Firstly, India distinctly out weighs all her neighbours individually and collectively in terms of size, population and economic strength. The very realization of the existence of a giant neighbour next door inspires awe in the minds of the ruling elites of the smaller neighbours of India, especially when their domestic existence is precarious due to various inherent weaknesses. Secondly, curiously enough, India shares borders with all the countries of South Asia (except Maldives) but no two among them share borders with each other. Naturally, the trade and commerce and demographic movements are more often than not directed towards India. This is a cause of the fear of domination by India without however, appreciating the potential of cooperation based on the comparative industrial and technological progress achieved by India.

Added to this the economic strength of India, her industrial advancement, scientific and technological development created in the minds of her smaller neighbours suspicions of the (imperialistic) domination by India. Already, most of the neighbours of India particularly Nepal, Bangladesh, Bhutan and Sri Lanka have been facing balance of payments deficit *vis-a-vis* India during the past few decades. Nepal and Bangladesh have been particularly worried about their dependence on India both for trade and commerce and economic assistance. Of late these two States have been deliberately trying to diversify their links with countries outside South Asia or other than India.

One of the most important causes of suspicion and vocal denunciation of the hegemonistic designs of India by the smaller States of South Asia is the domestic conflicts that have been plaguing the political, social and economic systems of these countries. Most of the South Asian States except perhaps Sri Lanka have had fragile political systems and the political stability of the regimes has always been open to doubts. In most of the cases, the domestic conflicts, other than ethnic, were due to lack of accountability of political authority, the consequential legitimacy crisis followed by frequent changes in the power bases.

Besides, except Maldives no State whether smaller or big in South Asia could boast of monolithic ethnic composition of people. The heterogenic ethnicity varies only in degree in its acuteness. The conflicts arising out of these internal diversities have quite frequently posed problems of national integration in these countries. The smaller States of South Asia, including Pakistan and Bangladesh always found the ubiquitous foreign hand—invariably India in all cases—responsible for their troubles. History stands witness to the fact that whenever there were turbolences in these States, there were repressions on the minorities and the disgruntled people and this naturally led to the demographic flows into India. In order to underplay their own weaknesses and inability to deal with the domestic problems, these countries always accuse India of causing destabilisation and hegemonism.

The cultural and ethnic linkages between the people of the entire region of South Asia poses a peculiar problem particularly to India. This is one reason for magnifying the fears of the smaller States of the region. India, the heartland of the Indian sub-continent, which is now divided into several States is historically the mother of different ethnic and religious groups. It is borne out by the reality that the different ethnic and religious groups of the neighbours of India, again, with the exception of only the Maldives, have connections with India. In most cases the cultural linkages are alive and active. This has created a fear of cultural imperialism by India in these countries. The fear of some sort of Pan-Indianism transcending the national loyalties, coupled with the fear of the Big-Brother-next-door or Indian hegemony, have been causing anxiety in the ruling elites of the smaller States of South Asian region. In fact, Pan-Islamic feelings posing the problem of extra-territorial loyalties manifest sometimes in India also. Buy, India does not have the advantage of blaming anybody of hegemonism.

However, the bilateral approach generally followed by India in her dealings with the South Asian neighbours has been the subject of severe criticism.[85] While the advantages of bilateralism in removing misunderstandings and thrashing out mutual problems easily cannot be overemphasized, it is construed by the critics of India as a device to take on the smaller neighbours one at a time and manoeuvre them with the natural advantage of political, economic and strategic superiority. In fact, India did not at any time try to take undue-advantage of its position in her relations with the South Asian neighbours. Moreover, India's relations with her neighbours have not consistently been in any senseless cordial. During the time of Janata Party's rule at the centre[86] and in the subsequent periods during Mrs. Gandhi's second tenure and since past over two years till now India have made persistent efforts to improve relations with the neighbouring countries of Asia in general and South Asia in particular. However, the changing international political ambience makes it imperative for India to reorient her foreign policy, particularly regarding her relations with her neighbours. But bilateralism is not as sinful as it is projected to be by the western observers because it is the West which followed the policy of bilateral in matters of giving aid to the Third World countries, in contrast to the demand of the developing countries for multilateral aid.[87] However, as long as the bilateralism relations are conducted on the basis of mutual goodwill, trust and understanding there will not be any chance to brand it as a tool of domination.

India's Monroe Doctrine?

The frequent recourse to the invocation of the extra-regional relations by the smaller countries as a counterpoise to the perceived Indian domination has been continuing. This has been the general feature in South Asian relations since 1950s. Pakistan's relations with USA, Nepal and Sri Lanka's relations with China and the Western powers and Bangladesh's with the West, China and Pakistan have been the main instances of the extra-regional power infiltration in the bilateral problems of India and her South Asian neighbours. India was always averse to the intrusion of any outside power in the affairs of the Indian sub-continent or Indian Ocean area.[88] It is generally believed by the Western scholars that India, explicitly or implicitly, systematically pursued the policy of denial in South Asia, *a la* the United States in the Western Hemisphere.[89] This undeclared policy is called as India's Monroe Doctrine.

The so called India's policy of denying extra-regional approach to the smaller countries of South Asia, together with her security perceptions regarding South Asia and Indian Ocean region is utilized to rake up the bogey of India's quest for domination and the much publicized fears of Indian hegemony.

While India's concern for security is based on the reality in the context of the existing international political environment the talk of India's hegemonic intentions and the talk of India as the major power[90] or centre of power of South Asia, is either a simulated psychological perception of the critics of India or only a rhetoric which is invariably used to undercut the importance of India or psychologically demoralize India in her bilateral relations with the smaller States of South Asia. This is a trap which India generally likes to avoid, while conducting her foreign policy *vis-a-vis* the South Asia and the outside world.[91]

Some of the events involving India which were indicative of India's military strength, political ambition, commitment to the humanitarian issues and desire to be in the limelight, have confounded the fears of her smaller neighbours. Though India several times assured that the security of the smaller States of South Asia is complementary to the security of India, they were suspicious because of the past record in which they saw an (alleged) assertion of power by India. The events in reference are the India-Pakistan war of 1971 and the active part taken by India in liberating Bangladesh, the integration of Sikkim in 1975, the deployment of Indian Peace Keeping Forces to Sri Lanka and the airlifting of food to Jaffna in May 1987 and of course the intervention in Maldives in November 1988 to thwart the coup attempt against the incumbent government in Male.

While India is accused of intimidating her smaller neighbours assuming hegemonic intentions and formulating her own security doctrines, the reality of the power politics in South Asia points to the other way round. Realistically speaking, Indo-Pak relations occupy the centre stage of the South Asian relations. The entire gamut of the foreign policies and bilateral relations of the South Asian relations hinge on the perceptions of power equations between India and Pakistan.

In fact, with Pakistan having challenged India right from the beginning, initially with the support of USA and China[92] and now with the newly acquired nuclear weapons, the South Asian regional politics are taking a bipolar dimension. Pakistan's ability to challenge India has actually been a morale booster to the smaller countries of the region. They are now more assertive than ever and are adopting more independent course of policies playing the two regional powers one against the other.[93] Thus, the concept of Indian hegemony is nothing more than a piece of fiction. In fact the smaller neighbours of India are playing more intelligent power games, in that they derive benefits from the magnanimity of their larger neighbour but refuse to accept the mutual obligations.

The smaller States of the region, quite often, have taken advantage of the differences of perceptions and bilateral problems between India and the major powers of the world, especially the USA and China. Irrespective of the political diversity these powers tried to support the smaller States of the South Asian region in their claims against India.

These inherent factors are contributing to aggravate the effects of inequality in size and strength and to overplay the political, economic and strategic differences in the bilateral relations of India on the one hand and the other States of South Asia on the other. SAARC has inherited these weaknesses from the history of the past over three decades prior to its evolution. How far and how effectively India will be able to dispell the misunderstandings and suspicions of her small neighbours and to what extent she could sacrifice for the well being and development of the people of the South Asian region and how far fairplay, goodwill, accommodation and understanding overtake the passions of fear and suspicion in the smaller States of South Asia, are the moot questions the answers to which will spell the nature of the prospects for the infant South Asian organization, the SAARC. The role of Pakistan will also be very crucial in shaping the future of the SAARC. Continuous harping on the anti-Indian policies and raking up religious and historical differences and dogged persistence to see the bigger neighbour dismembered or eternally infested with troubles are not only going to hamper the future of SAARC but also severely affect the socio-economic progress of the people of the entire Indian sub-continent.

It is interesting to note that the smaller States within the region have played a very significant role in the evolution of the SAARC. In fact, the initiative for the launching of South Asian Regional Cooperation came from Bangladesh. At that time, the major States of the region India and Pakistan were not very enthusiastic about the idea.

Against the backdrop of the prevalent hostile sentiments against India in most of the countries of the region the mooting of the idea of a formal organization of the regional cooperation appears to be a surprising development. However, this idea can be explained as the result of a search for an alternative to bilateralism insisted by India in dealing with her neighbours in resolving of the bilateral issues. Bangladesh, which at that time was unhappy about the problems of trade and commerce and the sharing of Ganga's waters issue, found it worthwhile to engage India somehow in multilateral negotiations. In this connection one may cite Bangladesh's proposal for the inclusion of Nepal in the negotiations on the sharing of Ganga waters which was rejected by India. The proposal for regional cooperation in South Asia amidst increasing discords in the bilateral relations between India and Bangladesh and other smaller States like Nepal and Sri Lanka has a definite political connotation.

Such are the circumstances under which the SAARC has emerged. By and large, under the changed political and strategic environment of South Asia the perceptions or intentions of any particular country dominating the region or its members is unrealistic and out of question. Hence, the much publicized Indo-Phobia remains only as imaginary problem.

References

1. The Asian Relations Conference in New Delhi in 1949, The Conference on Indonesia and the Bandung Conference and mooting the policy of Non-Alignment are some of instances worth mentioning.

2. Partha S. Ghosh, *Cooperation and Conflict in South Asia* (Manohar, Delhi, 1988), pp. 10-20.

3. K.P. Misra, 'Regional Peace and Security : Coalescence and Clash in Indo-Pak Relations', *India Quarterly*, Vol. 40, No. 3, July-Dec. 1984, p. 263.

4. Partha S. Ghosh, *op. cit.*, p. 26.

5. *The Hindu*, August 8, 1991.

6. See Sisir Gupta, *Kashmir : A Study in India-Pakistan Relations* (Asia Pub. House, 1966, Bombay), pp. 111-27.

7. Amitava Mukherjee, *India's Policy Towards Pakistan* (Associated Book Centre, New Delhi, 1983), p.25.

8. Sisir Gupta, *op.cit.*, pp. 117-19.

9. *Frontline*, January 31, 1992, p. 61.

10. Kesava Menon, 'The Third Option' *Frontline*, pp. 37-39.

11. Abdul Sattar (Pakistan's Ambassador to India), "Imperatives for a Better Future", *Mainstream*, 3 August 1991, p. 35.

    S.M. Mujtaba Razvi, "Conflict and Cooperation in South Asia", *Round Table*, 1986 (299), p.278.

12. Amitava Mukherjee, *op. cit.*, p. 44.

13. The Text of Shimla Agreement is reproduced in Amitava Mukherjee, pp. 115-16.

14. See Niranjan Khilnani, 'India's Political and Economic Policies towards her Neighbours', *Round Table* 1987 (301), p. 55 and P.K. Srivastava and Rajni Kothari, SAARC, *Seminar* (324), August 1986, p. 22.

15. An interview with the then Prime Minister of Pakistan, Mohd. Khan Junejo in *India Today*, 15 June, 1988, p. 104.

16. P.R. Chari, 'Security Aspects of Indian Foreign Policy', in *The Security of South Asia*, Ed. by Stephen Philip Cohen (Vistaar Publications, Delhi, 1988), p. 58 and see Partha S. Ghosh, *op. cit.*, p 42.

17. *India Today*, 15 June 1986.

18. Partha S. Ghosh, *op.cit.*, pp. 45-46.

19. 'Britain asks Pak not to encourage terrorism (in Kashmir), *The Hindu*, February 8, 1992, and Pran Chopra, 'New U.S. focus on South Asia', *The Hindu*, October 5, 1991.

20. *The Hindu*, September 28, 1991.

21. *The Hindu*, February 24, 1992.

22. Kesava Menon, 'The Third Option', *Frontline*, March 13, 1992, pp. 37-39.

23. J.P. Anand, 'India's Indian Ocean Neighbours', *Monthly Public Opinion Survey*, May 1989, p. 9.

24. Selig Harrison, 'US Policy in South Asia', in Stephen P. Cohen (Ed.), *op. cit.*, p. 37.

25. K. Subramanyam,'Prospects for Stability and Security in South Asia', in Stephen P. Cohen, *op.cit.*, pp. 209-10.

26. Selig Harrison, *op.cit.*, p. 137.

27. S.M. Muztaba Razvi, *op. cit.*, p. 270.

28. P.R. Chari, *op.cit.*, p. 53.

29. Barry Buzan, Gowher Rizvi *et al. South Asian Insecurity and Great Powers*, p. 122.

30. R.R. Subramaniam, "US Policy and South Asia", in Stephen P. Cohen, *op.cit.*, p. 143.

31. The Symington Amendment to the Foreign Assistance Act restrains the US administration from giving economic aid to any country which has unsafeguarded nuclear programmes. It was in force during Carter regime and its present successor is the Presler law.

32. Narottam Gaan, "Superpower Involvement in Indo-Pak Relations", *India Quarterly*, 46(4), Oct-Dec. 1990, p. 14.

33. *Indian Express*, January 1, 1989.

34. *The Hindu*, March 17, 1992.

35. *The Hindu*, March 15, 1992.

36. S.U. Kodikara, 'The International Environment and Indo-Pak Power Struggle in 1990s: A view from Sri Lanka, *South Asia*, 4 (2), Oct.-Dec. 1990, p. 159.

37. V. Suryanarayan, 'India's Sri Lanka Policy: A Need for Reappraisal', *South Asia Journal*, 4 (4), Apr.-June 1991, p. 418.

38. Vijay Kumar, *India and Sri Lanka-China Relations* (1948-84) (Allied Publishers, New Delhi, 1986), p. 25.

39. Partha S. Ghosh, *op. cit.*, p. 158.

40. Vijay Kumar, *op. cit.*, p. 62.

41. Vijay Kumar, *op. cit.*, pp. 59-60.

42. *Ibid.*, pp. 129-30.

43. Partha S. Ghosh, *op. cit.*, p. 174, also J.P. Anand, op. *cit.*, *p.* 12.

44. Partha S. Ghosh, *op. cit.*, p. 175.

45. J.P. Anand, *op. cit.*, p. 11.

46. V. Suryanarayan, "A Policy for Peace: On India-Sri Lanka Relations" *Frontline*, Sept. 28-Oct. 11, 1991, p. 44.

47. J.P. Anand, *op.cit.*, p.12.

48. Narayan Khadka, "SAARC : A Nepalese Perspective", *Round Table*, 1989 (309), p. 69.

49. Indo-Sri Lankan Agreement, dated July 27, 1987, in M. Mahmood, *Regional Integration in South Asia* (S. Chand Aligarh, 1987), pp. 93-98.

50. Marshall, R. Singer, "New Realities in Sri Lankan Politics", *Asian Survey*, 30(4) April 1990, pp. 417-422.

51. V. Suryanarayan, *op. cit.*, p. 46.

52. Shelton U. Kodikara, "The Continuing Crisis in Sri Lanka: The JVP, The Indian Troops & *Tamil* Politics", *Asian Survey*, 29 (7), July 1989, p. 721.

53. See Thomas Abraham, "Indo-Sri Lankan ties at the Nadir, "*The Hindu*, Nov. 23, 1991.

54. Partha S. Ghosh, *op. cit.*, p. 63 and Jayadeva Uyangoda, in Shelton U. Kodikara (Ed.), *South Asian Strategic Issues : Sri Lankan Perspectives* (Sage, New Delhi 1990), pp. 72-3.

55. Denis Wright, *Bangladesh : Origins and Indian Ocean Relations*, 1197-1175, p. 157.

56. *Ibid.*, p. 142.

57. *Ibid.*, p. 141.

58. Partha S. Ghosh, *op. cit.*, p. 69.

59. Barry Buzan, Gowher Rizvi *et al.*, *op. cit.*, p. 173.

60. *Ibid.*, p. 133.

61. *Ibid.*, p. 133.

62. The Indo-Bangladesh Friendship Treaty Signed by Mujibur Rahman and Indira Gandhi in March 1972 is still in force but it is observed in its blatant disregard.

63. J.P. Anand, *op. cit.*, p. 13.

64. *Ibid.*, p. 13.

65. *The Hindu*, October 29, 1991.

66. *Ibid.*

67. *The Hindu*, 19 March 1992.

68. Leo E. Rose, 'Nepal's External Relations' *Pacific Affairs*, 47 (2), Summer 1974, p. 193.

69. Leo E. Rose, 'The Himalayan Border States: "Buffers" in Transition', *Asian Survey*, 3(2), Feb. 1963, p. 117.

70. D.P. Kumar, *Nepal : Year of Decision* (Vikas, Delhi, 1980), p. 172.

71. *Ibid.*, p. 179.

72. *Ibid.*, pp. 207-8.

73. *Ibid.*, p. 209.

74. Dhruba Kumar, 'Managing Nepal's India Policy', *Asian Survey*, 30(7), July 1990, p. 699.

75. *Ibid.*, p. 708.

76. Bhabani Sengupta, 'Heat in the Himalayas', *Monthly Public Opinion Surveys*, April 1989, p. 10.

77. John W. Garver, "China-India Rivalry in Nepal : The Clash over Arms Sales", *Asian Survey*, Vol. 31, No. 10, October 1991, p. 960.

78. Article 2 of the Treaty of Friendship between Bhutan and India, dated 8 August 1949.

79. *Ibid.*, Article 5.

80. *Ibid.*, Article 6.

81. Partha S. Ghosh, *op. cit.*, p. 141.

82. Sukhdev Shah, 'Bhutans' Economy', *Asian Survey*, 29 (8), August 1989, p. 820.

83. Interview with President M.A. Gayoom of Maldives published in *The Hindu*, August 23, 1991.

84. From the speech delivered at the Indian Council of World Affairs, New Delhi, 22 March 1949, published in *India Quarterly* Vol. 44, No. 1 & 2, Jan.-June 1986.

85. Leo E. Rose, 'India's Regional Policy : Non-Military Dimensions', in Stephen P. Cohen (Ed.), *The Security of South Asia*, p. 4.

86. See S.D. Muni, 'India's "Beneficial Bilateralism" in South Asia', *India Quarterly*, Vol. 35, No. 4, Oct.-Dec. 1979, pp. 417-433.

87 There is a vast amount of literature on the adverse characteristics and effects of Foreign Aid.

88. For instance see S.D. Muni, 'India's security stakes in Nepal' in P.C. Mathur, Ed. *Govt. & Politics in South Asia*, Vol. II, Jaipur 1986, pp. 238-50 and Dilip Dobb, On Indo-Sri Lanka Accord in *India Today*, 31 August 1987.

89. Devin T. Hagetry, 'India's Regional Security Doctrine', *Asian Survey*, 31(4), April 1991, pp. 351-63 and also see Surjit Mansingh, *'India's Search for Power : Indira Gandhi's Foreign Policy*, 1966-82, New Delhi, 1984.

90. M.V. Bratersky and S.I. Lunyov, 'India at the end of the Century: Transformation into an Asian Regional Power', *Asian Survey*, 30 (10), October 1990, p. 941.

91. C. Raja Mohan, 'India's Strategic Environment in the 1990s' *Monthly Public Opinion Surveys*, April 1990, p. 15.

92. Rasul B. Rais, *'Pakistan in the Regional and Global Power Structure'*, *Asian Survey*, 31 (4), April, 1991, p. 378.

93. Barry Buzan, Gowher Rizvi *et al.*, *op. cit.*, p. 129.

CHAPTER V

MAJOR POWERS—SOUTH ASIA—REGIONAL COOPERATION

The ramifications of the post-world war politics have made the whole world into a single and unified international system. The major powers of the post-war international system, who were better known as super-powers sought to ordain the global politics according to their wishes and interests. Irrespective of the ideological commitments and leanings of the individual actors (states) the major powers or super powers, viz., the USA and the Soviet Union plus China tried to extend their influence virtually overall the countries of the world. These alignments of power politics have even cut across the non-aligned nations.

South Asia which occupied a very important place in the international system of the contemporary times was not an exception to this modern version of the politics of balance of power. South Asia, a well defined and coherent region, however, has in the post-colonial era developed a peculiar system of power politics for itself. The political sub-system of this region cannot strictly be called a subordinate of the global system. However, it has become a fertile ground for the power games of the major powers.

In their bid to out-smart their rivals in the global system the major powers sought to influence the politics of the South Asian region. The effect of this influence has, alongwith other factors, critically affected the prospects of cooperation among the important actors of this region.

The diversity of political systems, interests, mutually contradictory claims, suspicions and fears among the South Asian States indeed provided an easy opportunity to the major powers to make inroads into the politics of this region. This in turn has aggravated the differences among the States of the region. Particularly, as was explained in the previous chapters, the chasm that existed between the core State viz., India and the other States of the region was widened as a result of this.

The most important reason for the significance attached to this region by the major powers is its strategic location and proximity to the two most powerful socialist giants who themselves are two major powers. The other important reasons include the ideological factors and the territorial claims. But the convergence of interests between the outside powers and the local States appears to be vague.

As has been mentioned above, the most important powers that have developed keen interest and consistently tried to influence the power equations of this region are the United States of America, the People's Republic of China and the Soviet Union.

This chapter analytically narrates the instances of the interference or exertion of influence by each of these major powers in this region and the effect it had on the relations between the core and the periphery of this region. Our main interest, in doing this, of course, is to relate these sets of influences on the growth and prospects of regional cooperation in South Asia in a historical perspective.

The United States and South Asia

Emerged as a superpower in the post-war period, the United States took upon itself the responsibility of leading the 'free world' in countering the threat of communism and to provide security to the world by adopting appropriate policies. This perception became the basis of the cold-war politics and prompted the strategy of containment of communism. This strategy encompassed all parts of the world, especially those surrounding and in the vicinity of the rival superpower, USSR, the bulwark of communist system. America and its allies expected all the countries, which did not follow the path of socialism (Marxism-Leninism) to toe its line and join hands in a bid to contain communism. In other words, the US looked for a strong and viable power to combat communism in South Asia and the first and foremost attraction was India. The views and perceptions of the newly emerging Indian State were of course, quite different.

The policy makers of the United States were disheartened to hear the talk of non-alignment, i.e., joining neither of the power blocs and adopting an independent policy based on the merits of the issues, mainly articulated by the architect of India's foreign policy, Jawaharlal Nehru. Nehru's idea of non-alignment was not only meant to give India an independent approach but also to keep the Indian sub-continent away from the interference of the superpowers. However, India came under bitter attack from the United States and its allies for this. The policy of non-alignment, announced by Nehru even before India actually got independence, made India subject to the US suspicions and even contempt. On the contrary, Pakistan was less outspoken about its proposed foreign policy and its basic tenets. Moreover, Pakistan and the Muslim League before the partition were consistently supported and sympathized by the United Kingdom, the staunch and closest ally of the US. Soon after the partition, the United States got an opportunity to punish the forlorn and to reward the obedient one. The first major diplomatic clash between the US and India took place in 1947 at the United Nations. The first diplomatic problem between the US and India in the United Nations was on the issue of Kashmir.

India was shocked at the US attitude on the Kashmir issue in the United Nations.[1] The US attitude strengthened the case of Pakistan. Thus the US helped to formalize the rift between India and Pakistan and extended the much needed initial support to Pakistan's desire to grab Kashmir from India and also to perpetually challenge the position of India in the South Asian region. However, that was not the real beginning of the involvement of USA in the

India-Pakistan relations. The crucial step came at a later date.

The early 1950s saw the shifting of cold-war theatre to Asia with the outbreak of the Korean crisis. It was the first major international problem erupted in the vicinity of South Asia. India, true to its non-aligned philosophy took a neutral stand and even presided over the UN peace keeping force in Korea. The US which was going through the most hawkish times of the cold-war diplomacy under John Foster Dulles as the Secretary of State was seriously unhappy at the attitude of India. During the period of the Korean crisis not only the India-US relations received a setback[2] but India's policy of non-alignment was bitterly criticized by Dulles.[3]

During the early 1950s, thanks to the new awakening among the newly emerged Afro-Asian nations, the India-Pakistan relations were gradually getting brighten up through the efforts made by Jawaharlal Nehru, and his counterpart in Pakistan, Liaqat Ali Khan and his successors. However, the US had a surprise up its sleeve for India and Pakistan. The India-Pakistan efforts at rapprochement and the resolution of the Kashmir dispute received a severe jolt with the US offer in 1953 of 25 million dollars of military aid to Pakistan[4] and thus unleashing the dormant aggressive tendencies of Pakistan. The peace efforts were left in shambles.

The US might have conceived the move to arm Pakistan as a part of its large (global) security concerns. But its effects were undoubtedly felt on the India-Pakistan relations which were on the softening course. Pakistan accepted the offer made by the US too willingly. The interests of Pakistan and the US at the regional level and the global level respectively converged and the relationship took firm ground. The US Pakistan relations were to become an important determinant of the India-Pakistan relationship in general and the military balance in particular. The India-Pakistan adversorial relations since then were set on the path of no-return.

While India wanted to keep the superpowers out of the sub-continent, Pakistan deliberately wanted to involve the US in the affairs of the Indian sub-continent. In pursuance of this policy,

Pakistan signed the Mutual Defence Assistance Agreement with the United States of America on 19 May 1954. Pakistan also joined the US sponsored collective security arrangements viz., the SEATO and the CENTO. The US involvement in South Asia in the 1950s, particularly with the formal alliance with Pakistan was more an encirclement of India than anything else.[5]

The US-Pakistan relations flourished through the 1950s, though there was a slight slump before the taking over of power by Gen. Ayub Khan. Again in 1959 US signed an Executive Agreement with Pakistan thus entrenching itself in the South Asian regional politics and reinforcing the strength and confidence of Pakistan.

The interest of the US in South Asia remained in tact all through, but the Pakistan's turning towards China in the late 1950s and early 1960s made the US a little cautious in its approach. The Sino-Indian border conflict resulting in war between the two countries in 1962 provided a chance to both India and the US to come together. The Chinese agression on India in 1962 made the US spontaneously come to the aid of India. This was the only time when the US has willingly tried to help India to build its defence. The reason is quite obvious, the desire to prevent the expansion of the power of Communist China down southwards. The US continued to help Pakistan with military and economic aid with the same intention. This proved to be strategic to the US in gaining a decisive leverage in South Asian politics. In fact by that time, already Pakistan came to be regarded as an important ally of the United States.[6] The reasons for the US military aid to Pakistan apart, the arms supply had a direct impact on the intra-regional relations in South Asia. Pakistan, was looking for an opportunity to realise the dream of occupying Kashmir and entered into an adventurous war with India in 1965. The US and its ally, the UK solidly supported Pakistan. But the war ended in an ignominious defeat for Pakistan.

In contrast to the US stoking the fires of conflagration between India and Pakistan, the Soviet Union offered to mediate between the two States in 1965 and in the presence of the then Soviet Premier Alexie Kosygin India and Pakistan signed an agreement at Tashkent.

The Johnson administration in the 1960s extended uninterrupted military and economic assistance to Pakistan. This also put severe impediments on the economic aid to India. The aid under the PL 480 funds was deliberately delayed to such an extent that India had to lead an existence of ship-to-mouth.

The Nixon administration also continued the same policy. It was during this period that Pakistan was regarded as the "most allied of the allies" to US. India was on the other hand regarded as a threat to the US power at the global level.

In 1971 the US involved itself in the affairs of the Indian sub-continent in support of the military regime of Pakistan during the war of Bangladesh liberation. By doing so the US tried to intimidate India by despatching its Seventh Fleet to the Bay of Bengal. This has provoked the Soviet Union to move its Indian Ocean fleet closer to India to counter the US threat. Thus, the cold war was brought to the door-steps of South Asia in 1971 courtesy United States of America.

The events of 1971 were the culmination of the continued military, economic and political support extended by the US to Pakistan particularly in its bid to upset the military superiority of India. The US argued that the assistance to Pakistan was modest.[7] It also accused India of deliberate attempts at dismemberment of Pakistan. Thus the relations between India and the United States reached the lowest ebb in 1971. In fact, the Indo-US relations were never as low as in 1971-72. But in the subsequent years the US tried to smoothen her relations with India. In the wake of the Shimla agreement the US adopted a policy of indifference towards India. This has given way to the policy of 'benign neglect'. The American administration perceived that the Indians were too proud or arrogant to want their country to be a satellite of the Soviet Union,[8] and hence no direct threat to the US or its security system.

The intrusive policies of the US in South Asia, were ostensibly intended to protect the security interests of the West in the context of the global power balance. They inevitably ignited the tensions between India and Pakistan, the two most powerful States of South Asia. Most of the military assistance extended to Pakistan was misused, not without the knowledge of its donor causing constant strains in the Indo-Pak relations resulting in an unabated arms race making heavy demands on the already fragile and backward economies and intermittantly erupting into armed conflicts. The peace, security and stability of the South Asian region was always affected thus by the military aid provided by the US to its 'ally Pakistan. This invariably led to the conclusion that as long as the US regards Pakistan as an ally and attaches importance to it in the wertan security persepctive peace and cooperation in South Asia will be subjected to severe uncertainties.

The superpower rivalry, between the US and USSR (now defunct and disintegrated) too has caused severe impediments to the peace, security and economic well being of South Asia. The Soviet Union intervened in Afghanistan in late 1979. The Afghanistan crisis brought about a new predicament to the world, which came to be known as the second cold war. Viewing it as a blatant expansion of the Soviet communism and as a serious threat to its security interests worldwide in general and in South Asia in particular, the US resorted to massive dumping of arms in Pakistan as a deterrant to the Soviet Union. This in fact proved to be a windfall to the militarily hungry Pakistan, she was happy to be graded by the US as a frontline State in the Afghan crisis and enthusiastically espoused the cause of American supported war of Mujahideens against the puppet regime of Afghanistan. Consequently Pakistan continued to receive massive military and economic aid from the US. The US Government waived the 1978 Symington Amendment to facilitate the military package to Pakistan. A wide range of sophisticated weapons, tanks, aircrafts including the most powerful F-16s were given under this package with the intention of countering the Soviet military threat to Pakistan.

While America justified the arming of Pakistan from the point of its global security interests, Pakistan always perceived India as her major threat. Hence, for Pakistan the US military aid was a welcome development in a bid to achieve a military parity with India and if possible to over-take it. In other words, the Afghanistan crisis created a new threat to the stability, peace and security of South Asia. The arch-rivals India and Pakistan were thrown into an unprecedented arms race, with the induction of the most modern an sophisticated warfare into Pakistan by the US. If the US is Pakistan's main source of the fresh supply of arms, for India it was the Soviet Union, France, UK and Sweden. The mad race for the weapons build-up inevitably increased the burden on both the economies and also added to the growing external debt. Yet the race was to go on.

India protested to US on the dangers of disproportionate supply of arms to Pakistan. The Indians tried to impress upon the US administration the need to apply restraint on the arms supplies. In spite of the Indian protests the US continued, rather increased, the supply of sophisticated weapons to the Pakistani military regime.

During his visit to the United States, the Prime Minister of India, Rajiv Gandhi impressed upon the US administration to realise the implications of arms build up in Pakistan. President Reagan in his raply stated rater perfunctorily. "On the subject of US security assistance to Pakistan, I assured Mr. Gandhi that our objective is stability and reduced tension in South Asia and that our assistance is not directed at India."[9]

In spite of such assurances, the US arms build up had the effect of encouraging yet another show down with India. The Siachen limited war and the 1987 Zarb-e-Momin[10] are evident of the Pakistani intentions. It may be mentioned here that on several occasions the military assistance offered by the superpowers has resulted in diversion of arms to fulfil the limited ambitions of the recipient countries. Pakistan's is one of the most striking instances of this. Pakistan indulged in misadventures in 1960, and again in 1971.[11]

The Soviet Union withdrew its troops from Afghanistan in late 1980s. Subsequently it ceased to be a superpower and even became a non-entity literally followed by its disintegration. This has changed the basic character of the Afghan crisis from the US strategic point of view. Thus, prompted by these developments the US stopped military aid to Pakistan in 1989 under the Presle amendment. The new development put a stop to the arms race between India and Pakistan atleast temporarily. Yet, the imbalances generated by the Afghan crisis have not totally disappeared and the tensions between the two major States of South Asia are not totally relented. In the meanwhile there are reports that the US is planning to arm Pakistan again.[12]

The Pokhran experimental nuclear explosion of 1974 by India has raised alarm in the US administration. Being a superpower the USA never liked the prospect of any new State acquiring nuclear weapons. Being a non-aligned country and a close friend of the Soviet Union, India's joining the nuclear club was definitely not a welcome sign for the monopolist of the global power, the US. India, however, made it clear in no uncertain terms that her nuclear programme was meant only for peaceful purposes. Unconvinced with this the US continued to believe that India had acquired nuclear weapons.

Spurred by the advance made by India, Pakistan too embarked on the path of nuclear race during the Bhutto regime and picked up momentum and with the passage of time reached an advanced stage during the rule of Gen. Zia-ul-Haq.[13]

The Carter administration unilaterally stopped the supply of enriched uranium to the Tarapur power plant in 1978, thus violating the bilateral agreement committed with India. At the same time the aid to Pakistan was also stopped under the Symington Amendment. But in 1980 US aid to Pakistan was revived waiving the Symington Amendment on a large scale, while India was denied the uranium supply. The US has since been more vigorously insisting that India should sign the Nuclear Non-Proliferation Treaty (NPT).

India's stand on the NPT has been clear and consistent. Even during the formative stages of the NPT India expressed her disagreement with the draft prepared by the superpowers.[14] India argued that the NPT is discriminatory and the problem of nuclear weapons should be treated in the global context. While asserting that India was committed to non-spread of nuclear weapons and to the peaceful uses of the nuclear energy she has been consistently refusing to sign the NPT.

Pakistan recently declared that she has acquired the nuclear capability. Though officially there were contradictory statements about the nuclear programme and its progress in Pakistan, a leading nuclear scientist of that country Dr. A.Q. Khan declared that Pakistan has acquired the nuclear power whether anyone believed it or not.[15]

The recent visit to South Asia, especially India and Pakistan by the US Senator Larry Pressler, the author of the law forbidding the US administration to offer aid to any country possessing nuclear capability too has confirmed that Pakistan was in possession of nuclear bomb and advised her to dismantle it.[16] At the same time he gave a clean chit to India saying that she did not possess the bomb.

The US attitudes towards India and Pakistan have been varied and discriminatory. While it has been insisting that India should sign the NPT and agree to the international safeguards and inspection of the nuclear installations since the mid-1970s, its attitude towards the Pakistani nuclear programme was that of benign neglect.[17] In fact, during the 1980s when the US was vigorously trying to arm Pakistan to its teeth, Pakistan was on the thresh-hold of the nuclear capability. The US was quite aware of the development but pretended ignorance and continued the arms supply.[18] Even now the US seems to be ready to accommodate Pakistan provided the latter signs the NPT without looking for the Indians to sign it.[19]

Having reconciled to India's reluctance to sign the NPT the US has put forth a proposal for holding a Camp David type of summit of five nations viz., the US, Russia, China, India and Pakistan to resolve the nuclear issue of the South Asia. India is averse to the idea, though no firm negative answer has been given.[20] The US is still keenly pursuing the matter, with the fond hope that some regional arrangement (for South Asia) could be worked out.

US Interests in South Asia

It has always been a matter of keen interest for Americans to secure bases in South Asia for their naval and air force. Towards this end they have always tried to take advantage of the hostilities between the two South Asian States, India and Pakistan. As mentioned earlier while India asteadfastly opposed the idea of military bases to superpowers in the South Asian and Indian Ocean region, Pakistan has been opposing India's idea. Taking advantage of the differences between India and other States of the region, the US enjoyed facilities in different parts of the region at different times. The US had airfields near Peshawar during the late 1950s. Karachi port was used for the visits of its worships in the 1970s. Trincomalee port of Sri Lanka was also used as a port of call by the US naval ships in the latter part of 1970s.[21] The US has and still is maintaining a fullfledged military base in Diego Garcia in the India Ocean.

As a corollary of the policy of the opposition to the erstwhile Soviet bloc, the US consistently followed the policy of containing the growing power of India. The US-Pak relations have played a significant role in isolating India in the South Asian politics. Interestingly, the interests of the US and China have converged in this aspect[22] even prior to their rapprochement. Closer Indo-Soviet relations have given the much needed motivation to these major powers and most of the smaller States of South Asia to play up the factor of Indophobia.

In the changed scenario of the international relations particularly after the disintegration of the Soviet Union their appears to be a change in US attitudes in respect of South Asia. If this change in attitude means equi-distance between itself and India and Pakistan, then it will go a long way in bringing about the necessary peace in Indo-Pak relations and in paving way for a more meaningful cooperation under the aegis of SAARC.

But the situation is still in a state of flux. The change in international relations however has not so far affected positively the existing India-Pakistan relations.[23] The policy proposals prepared by the Pentagon officials under the supervision of the Secretary of State himself, popularly known as the Pentagon document has raised doubts about the future attitudes of the US towards India, Pakistan and South Asia. As regards the South Asia, the document says: "The US should try to bring all nuclear facilities in both India and Pakistan under the international safeguards and to discourage Indian hegemonic aspirations over the other States in South Asia and on the Indian Ocean."

It also calls for "restoring full military ties with Pakistan to promote stable security conditions in South West Asia and Central Asia."[24]

Though officially the Pentagon document has been declared as not authentic, the contents of the document if implemented or given effect to will portend a grim future for South Asia. Thus the intrusive and divisive policy of the US may continue and the Indo-Pak conflicts would be perpetuated. Thus it is anybody's guess that the SAARC will hardly go beyond the cultural cooperation.

Given the current mood of the United States, its state of economy, growing competition and protectionism in the developed world, its interest in South Asia does not appear to be limited to the security and strategic concerns. Its most important interest is to gain access to the vast markets of this region. As the most important State and the most industrially advanced country of the region, India has the potential of posing a threat to the US penetration of the South Asian markets. This may provide a rationale and motivation for its continued involvement in this region and also in keeping the Indo-Pak rivalry and the phenomenon of Indophobia alive. Whichever way the pendulum swings South Asian cooperation depends on the policy orientations of the only superpower of the day, the US.

China and South Asia

China too alongwith the US and the Soviet Union, is actively interested and involved in South Asia. Her interest in South Asia is not merely due to strategic and ideological reasons, but due also to the common borders she shares with at least four countries of this region. Most of the northern neighbours of India, viz., Nepal, Bhutan and Pakistan. The integration of Tibet into China in 1950 has considerably enhanced the territorial and strategic interests of China in the region of South Asia.

China's involvement in South Asia during the early 1950s was minimal, except the friendly ties with India. Behind the cordiality of Indo-Chinese relations, there was a latent suspicion about the growing power and prestige of India in the international relations. In fact, by mid-1950s India was regarded as the leader of the Asian, particularly the South Asian region. China, being the largest and the most powerful State of Asia, with close geographical links with both South and East Asia, had the ambition of being an unrivalled leader of Asia.[25] The zeal to extend the influence of communism in the early 1950s also prompted China to harbour the desires of extending her influence over other regions of the world.

Obviously, the main rival to China in South Asia was undoubtedly India especially in terms of exercising political influence over this region. Gradually her policy had undergone perceptible changes from that of outspoken friendship based on the five principles of peaceful coexistence (Pancha-sheel) to that of claiming to have disputes over the settlement of border and finally to that of an aggressor. This is preceded by the Bandung Conference and the subsequent attempts by Nehru and other Asian leaders to organize the Afro -Asian group of States committed to the policy of non-alignment and maintaining peace in the world. Once identification of the rival i.e., India, is over, China systematically tried to tarnish the image of India both within the region and at the global level. As a part of this policy a special emphasis was laid on building up relation with India's neighbours and thus, isolate India in her own region.

With the war in 1962, China appears to have achieved the twin objectives proving the weakness of India in the eyes of her neighbours and weaning them away from her and also proving herself (China) as the major power of the region. Sino-Indian conflict has brought out the nature and extent of support or lack of it for India in her neighbourhood. Rather it was proved how lonely India was left in South Asia.[26]

China's strategy of building up friendly relations with the countries of South Asia particularly with Pakistan, Nepal, Sri Lanka, and during the last one decade or so, with Bangladesh and Bhutan worked quite smoothly because of the bilateral problems and disputes these States had with India in spite of Indophobia.

That is, Chinese diplomacy made an adept use of the internal discords in South Asia to isolate India and weaken its political prestige.This has contributed to a great extent in keeping South Asia a divided house bereft of chances for an effective regional cooperation in political, social and economic fields.

Let us try to recount briefly how China forged strong links with some of the South Asian States and thereby created a hostile environment for India.

Pakistan with its open conflict with India since its birth readily provided China an opportunity to find a naturally. Though, China ignored the overtures made by Ayub Khan government since 1959 she showed keen interest to enter into a strong relationship with Pakistan only after the escalation of the Sino-Indian border dispute during 1960-61. In fact, it was during 1961- and 1963, shortly before and after the Sino-Indian border conflict, that China signed border agreements with Nepal and Pakistan respectively. Sino-Pak relations in the aftermath of the Sino-Indian war improved steadily and by 1965 China was regarded as a strong and reliable ally of Pakistan. True to this, China supported Pakistan in the 1965 Indo-Pak war to its hill. This was notwithstanding the close links of Pakistan with the US at that time.[27] It is quite evident that the anti-Indian factor was the main element in motivating the two countries to build up close links.

One of the main factors that influenced the Chinese hostility towards India was the growing relationship between India and the Soviet Union and the increasing chasm between the Chinese and Soviets at that time. Thus, the Sino-Pak alliance was intended to counter-balance the growing influence of the Soviet Union in South Asia apart from weakening India.

China's special relationship with Pakistan continued through the 1960s to 1980s with same tenacity and commitment China actively supported Pakistan in the 1971 war and strongly condemned India for the role it played in liberation of Bangladesh. China could have opened another front on its borders with India or attacked India during the 1971 war but for the Soviet warning against such move.[28]

Subsequently the Sino-Pak special relationship flourished with the active involvement of Pakistan in bringing about a detente in the relations between China and the United States.[29] The outbreak of the Afghan crisis also helped the cause of closer ties between the two countries. All along, China had been helping Pakistan in building its military might to match the main rival in the region, India. China is also reported to have helped Pakistan in its nuclear programme.[30] Even at the present moment, the Sino-Pak relations are considered to be quite influential in shaping the Sino-Indian relations and even the South Asian relations as a whole.

China's opening up of friendly relations with Nepal, a State sandwiched between the two giants of the region, China and India, was also carefully timed and analogous to the development of the Sino-Pak relations. China with its indifference to the political system of Nepal, appealed more to the ruler of the Himalayan Kingdom, King Mahendra, in comparison to India which laid emphasis on democratic systmes and opposed autocratic regimes.[31] Having found convergent points in regard to their opposition to India, Nepal and China vigorously tried to forge close and cordial relationships. There were exchange of visits by the Chinese Premier Chou-en-lai to Kathmandu and King Mahendra to Beijing in 1960 and 1961 respectively. In Septemebr 1961 China and Nepal signed a border treaty.

The Nepal-China relations have caused worry in the Indian political circles. This has further increased the necessity for China to maintain its hold on the Nepalese. Then onwards China supported the repressive monarchy in Nepal despite its commitment to oppose the exploitative regimes and to support the revolutionary movements all over the world. The Sino-Nepalese relations have cooled down to some extent during the 1970s. However, during 1980s there was a new thrust to strengthen the bonds between the two countries again. This zeal was prompted by the simmering suspicions between India and Nepal—as Nepal has been accusing India of interfering in its internal affairs by encouraging the anti-monarchy and anti-Panchayat Movements.

The revived friendship between Nepal and China was thus

marked by the growing anti-Indian feelings in Nepal and also by the purchase of arms by Nepal from China. China supplied large quantities of arms, sophisticated firearms and anti-tank and anti-aircraft guns to Nepal during 1988-90 causing severe strains in Indo-Nepalese relations.

India regards Nepal as extremely important from security and strategic points of view because of her geo-political conditions. The Indo-Nepal Friendship Treaty of 1950 was considered by India as a bond of good relationship between the two countries. However, in the latter part of 1980s Nepal's purchasing of arms from China altered not only this special relationship but also the strategic environment of India. In spite of protests from India, Nepal proceeded with the arms purchases from China with the hope that it can have economic assistance also if the same is denied by India. However, China did not promise any economic assistance matching the loss due to the displeasure of India.[32]

It is not possible and necessary to go into the details of the Sino-Nepal relations and its impact on the Indo-Nepal relations, but suffice it to say that the China factor has been a negative factor in the sensitive relationship of India and Nepal. Counting on the friendly and supportive relationship with China, the Nepalese Kings, Mahendra and Birendra have explicitly tried to extract favours from India,[33] thus vitiating the cordial atmosphere in the relations of the South Asian States in general. It can be said without any doubt that the trend of countering the influence of India started with Pakistan, and spread to Nepal also, and all this with active involvement of China.

The classic trend of balance of power relations, with the colossal of China, throwing its weight with any smaller States of South Asia and automatically turning them anti-Indian continued. Sri Lanka and Bangladesh also have become prey in the latter period. It is not that these States did not have reasons to be afraid of India. But the fact that the biggest power of Asia was on their side made these smaller States more recalcitrant and more outspoken in their hostile postures against India.

The role of China in influencing Bangladesh to turn anti-Indian is not that effective. But Sri Lankan-Chinese relations systematically developed since the early 1950s, despite much publicized pro-western attitudes and anti-communist postures of Sri Lanka, imperceptibly contributed to the growth of adverserial relationship between Sri Lanka and India.

All-through the 1960s and 1970s Sri Lanka and China maintained cordial relations. Their ties include a strong economic orientation mainly rooted in the Rubber Rice agreements reached between the two countries in 1950s and renewed subsequently. From the beginning, China took a patronizing attitude towards Sri Lanka. In spite of Sri Lanka's support to Farmosa (Taiwan) during the early 1950s, China adopted a softer posture towards Sri Lanka and in fact always tried to strengthen friendly relations with it. This, coupled with the fear of India for geographical and ethnic-cultural reasons, brought about a natural tilt in Sri Lankan Foreign Policy towards China.

Sino-Sri Lankan relations are marked by a consistent mutual support and common regional security perceptions. The occasional spells of friendly and cordial relations of both Sri Lanka and China with India, did not come in the way of their mutual political commitments. During the Sino-Indian war of 1962, despite the public opinion being strongly in favour of India, the official Sri Lankan attitude was that of neutrality.[34] During the 1971 India-Pakistan war and on the Indo-Soviet Treaty also there was a striking identity of views between Sri Lanka and China.[35] They in fact supported Pakistan and opposed Indo-Soviet treaty. Even in the Sino-Soviet differences also Sri Lanka was more inclined towards China. During the current ethnic struggle in Sri Lanka the Chinese have been consistent in their stand that it was the internal affair of Sri Lanka and that no outside interference was justified. The Chinese have been opposing the Indian mediation since the early 1980s itself on basis of this attitude.[36]

Thus, China because of her geographical proximity and political aspiration, have throughtout the past four decades, sought to play a key role in the shaping of the cooperation-conflict relations in South Asia. Its role in this region has been strikingly similar to that of USA.[37]

While China played the role of the wrecker of the South

Asian good-neighbourly relations and cooperation, in the past its role in strengthening mutual confidence and thereby paving way for future cooperation in South Asia is also quite important. Its future policies and attitudes will have deciding effects on the emerging trends in the region in general and on SAARC in particular.

There is a welcome change in the attitude of China during the past few years. It has been more receptive to the idea of improving relations with India based on mutual goodwill and accommodation. The recent postures of China cannot be interpreted as its acceptance of India's preeminent role in South Asia. It is, more of an outcome of identity of views on various international crises such as Afghanistan and Kampuchea. The realisation of the fact that India was not a stooge of the Soviet Union seems to have impresed China in recognizing the potential of India.[38]

The Sino-Indian relations were severely paralysed after the 1962 border conflict. However, they were revived in 1976 and have received a favourable consideration in the 1980s. Currently China appears to be keen on improving its relations with India. The recent visit by the Chinese Premier Li Peng to India opened a bright new chapter in Sino-Indian relations as well as in the political and economic cooperation in South Asia. Coming after a gap of 30 years, the visit of the Chinese Prime Minister to India certainly raised hopes of better prospects for South Asia with the evolution of friendly relations between India and China.[39]

However, the basic factors of China's common borders with the smaller States of the South Asian region, China's friendly relations with them and the fear of India's domination over the region continue to give leverage to China in influencing the intra-regional relations of South Asia. The settlement of disputes between India and China and India and Pakistan can certainly alter the situation but the situation being in a state of flux nothing can be predicted certainly except hoping for the better.

Soviet Union* and South Asia

The Soviet involvement in the region of South Asia during

---

* The reference to Soviet Union is only a thing of part with its disintegration in December 1991.

the past four decades has been more of a reaction to the enthusiastic and vigorous anti-Soviet and anti-communist strategies of the Western bloc and America. Unlike America, the USSR was not willingly harboured by the States of this region except India. Particularly, in the initial period of the cold-war era the Soviets were more keenly engaged in consolidating their position and influence in the Eastern Europe. Hence, its interest and involvement in this region was minimal whereas the US was tenaciously trying to extend its containment policy into South Asia also.

The attitude of the Soviet Union during the early 1950s was more of a reaction to the US postures rather than active support or opposition to the local actors involved in the problem. On the Kashmir question the Soviet activities varied between support and indifference in the initial stages, but later on once the US-Pak alliance was finalized in the mid-1950s it was more forthcoming to support India.[40]

However, after the formalization of Pakistan's alliance with the US and the West, the USSR started showing interest in India. This also coincided with the change in the leadership in that country. The Indo-Soviet relations gained new and firm ground under the leadership of Khrushchev. In 1955 the Soviet Union entered into an agreement to build a steel plant in India and in the same year Khrushchev visited India. Even during this period Indo-Soviet relations were not as firmly based as the US-Pak relations at that time were. But that was a sincere beginning for the future bonds of deep commitment and reliable friendship.

As a matter of fact, the Soviet Union was equally eager to maintain friendly relations with Pakistan during the 1950s. The Soviet Union quite early extended invitation to the Pakistani Prime Minister to visit their country. But due to various problems from time to time the visit had to be postponed and finally it did not materialize. A special mention may be made about the Soviet mediation in easing the tensions between India and Pakistan after the 1965 war. It is under the sponsorship and in the presence of the then Soviet Prime Minister Kosygin that the Indian Prime Minister late Lal Bahadur Shastri and the Pakistan President Ayub Khan signed the famous Tashkent Agreement.

Even after the Tashkent Agreement also the Soviet ambivalence continued for some time. They have even offered to supply arms to Pakistan in 1968[41], which could not materialize because the Americans and Chinese could divert the attention of Pakistan from the Soviets. But by that time the Indo-Soviet economic and military relations started gaining roots.

Then came the war of Bangladesh liberation in 1971. Even as the trouble started brewing up, India sensed an imminent alliance between China, Pakistan and the US to thwart any involvement from India. The Indo-Soviet Treaty of Friendship and Cooperation (with the much talked of Article 9 dealing with mutual assistance during the times of war or threat to security) of either party proved to be a diplomatic success of both India and Soviet Union. It was justified on the ground that it was a counterweight against the US and Chinese involvement in the region.[42]

The Indo-Soviet Treaty was a subject of much criticism both within the region of South Asia and at the international level as well. Pakistan denounced it in strongest terms and Nepal too was critical of it. Sri Lanka too did not conceal its displeasure about the implications of the treaty.[43] The Chinese were also critical of the Treaty and the non-aligned status of India in the wake of it. Truly, the Indo-Soviet Treaty was a subject of serious debates both for and against it for quite some time. Even now, in retrospect critics quite often differ on the nature and implications of this Treaty. However, one thing could be said that this treaty was one of the few controversial subjects with raised quite some dust in South Asia. It was a balancing factor in South Asia which ensured peace and stability in the region.

Based on the success of the Indo-Soviet Treaty, Soviet Union later on floated the idea of forming an Asian collective security system.[44] Naturally, they wanted India to play a significant role in it. But India was not quite enthusiastic about the idea. This idea of the Soviet Leader Leonid Brezhnev remained a still-born child.

By far the most blatant and controversial involvement of the Soviet Union in the region of South Asia came in the last few days of 1979 in the shape of military involvement in Afghanistan to protect the communist and pro-Soviet regime of Tarakki. The consequences of this intervention have considerably affected the peace and cordiality of the relations between the South Asian States in general and India and Pakistan in particular. The involvement of the United States to counter the Soviet intervention and the status of frontline state assigned to Pakistan followed by the offer of enormous military build up of Pakistan caused severe tensions in the region. The ostensible overarming of Pakistan triggered an unending arms race between India and Pakistan heavily draining their meagre resources.

The Soviet intervention in Afghanistan received a widespread opprobrium in almost all the States of South Asia. China was the bitter critic of the USSR's involvement in Afghanistan. Pakistan also raised the alarm that it would be the next target of the Soviet attack, which appeared quite in line with the American perceptions. This, however, provided the Pakistanis an opportunity to transform their country into a strong military power capable of posing threat to their much hated neighbour, India. The Indian reaction on this issue was quite guarded and cautious and at the same time not an approval of the Soviet action. In fact, India was surprised at this development in its vicinity involving her own trusted friend, the USSR. An annoyed Mrs. Gandhi is stated to have privately suggested the Soviets to withdraw.[45]

The Afghan crisis raised the tensions in this region for over a decade. It has reached a transitional stage with the withdrawal of the Soviet troops in the late 1980s. But the unalterable consequence of the Soviet action, the military build up of Pakistan remained in tact and continued to be a source of tension in the sub-continent.

The Soviet interest in the Indian Ocean and maintaining its military presence there has been a counter product of the American presence in the area. While the US had its permanent base at Diego Garcia and facilities of port of call at Karachi in Pakistan and Trincomalee in Sri Lanka, the Soviet Union did not have any base. Friendly relations with India were construed as India's offering facilities to the USSR, but India explicitly offered no base or facilities to either of the superpowers keeping her non-aligned status in tact. The Soviet Union had its naval fleet permanently deployed in the India Ocean to counter the US presence. India was always averse to the presence of superpowers and the deployment of nuclear submarine in the region. The US and the USSR, however, continued their military presence in the Indian Ocean despite the requests from the littoral States and the UN resolutions declaring the Indian Ocean as a Zone of Peace.

The USSR showed willingness to reduce or withdraw its military presence from the Indian Ocean provided the US also did the same. In his response to the Indian politicians on this matter Gorbachev, the then President of USSR wrote :

> "The Soviet Union, as you know, is for scaling down the non-littoral States naval activity in the Indian Ocean, for freeing it of foreign naval squadrons. In the quest for ways to solve this problem, we are prepared for cooperating with all countries concerned".[46]

The motive for the Soviet involvement in South Asia or in the Indian Ocean region was mainly in the context of the cold-war politics and the superpower rivalry. The desire to support and to protect the progressive and pro-Soviet regimes was also one of the prime motives. The Soviet presence or influence in the Indian sub-continent was only limited to India. The Indian support was always circumscribed by its own independent foreign policy guided by the principles of non-alignment. The Soviet Union too respected the non-alignment policy of India.

The Soviet desire to keep goodwill, influence and military presence in South Asia and Indian Ocean was not only to counter the American influence but also to face the challenge posed by China. The reason for the Soviet interest in harbouring India was that it was only India which had the capacity and motivation to assist the USSR in balancing China.[47] However, in the recent years India too was showing interest in maintaining good relation with the U.S. This kept the USSR tied to India because it cannot risk severing relations with India despite its desire to disengage the earlier relations particularly in the context of the internal problems coupled with the turbulence in the Eastern Europe.

Now, with the dissolution and disintegration of the Soviet Union, its involvement in South Asia remained only as a thing of past. The successor States of the USSR are too busy in grappling with their own economic and political problems to be able to extend their influence to any part of the world. Even if they like to do so, their capacity to influence the political equations of the region is open to doubts.

South Asia in World Politics

The above narration of the great powers' involvement and its consequences in South Asia clearly confirms the general pattern of international relations set in practice in the post-war period. That is, the international relations at all levels are ordained and controlled by the superpowers generally. The superpowers, had a definite and relentless hold on the intra-regional relations of South Asia. Everything went according to their game plan and both the superpowers had a complicity in this.

China, which could not be considered as a superpower by the standards of the US and the USSR, was nevertheless the only major power of Asia and particularly so in the case of South and Southeast Asia. Ironically these powers, having a monopoly of global hegemony, have created the bogie of 'Indian hegemony' in South Asia, which ultimately helped the smaller States in reinforcing their anti-India feelings.

In other words, South Asia, a region with a fair degree of cohesive and collective identity, was in effect functioned as a subordinate of the international system operating at the global level. The States of South Asia, knowingly or unknowingly served the strategic, security and hegemonic interests of the major powers who were involved in the region. It was done so effectively that most of the countries of the region (except India) did not feel the pinch of such political and economic subjugation. The main powers were always treated by these States with respect and expectation because these States of the region were generally not in close relations with each other. On the contrary the major countries of the region (India and Pakistan) were traditional rivals. Most of the other States of South Asia had some or other bilateral problems with India. This suited the major powers to gain a free opportunity to interfere in the region.

The major powers needed control over all the regional systems including South Asia not merely because they wanted to protect and maintain their influence but they also had crucial economic interests in these regions. America and Britian and sometimes USSR gave more importance to secure access to raw-materials and markets throughout the world. The Americans wanted to control the high seas to ensure a free flow of oil supplies to their industries. The USSR wanted to have access to warm water ports which it did not have.

This apart, one of the common features of the major powers and other imperialist powers in the post-war period is the growth of the military industrial complex (MIC). This had created strong vested interests in gaining a strangle-hold over the developing countries. The US and the USSR at the global level and China within Asia have emerged as leading suppliers of arms and weapons, military aircrafts and warships etc. to the developing countries which are their allies, friends or surrogates in various regions. The mutual conflicts and hostilities among the developing countries were always a veritable source of arms markets for the MIC of the major powers. It was very much in the interests of these outside powers to keep the mutual conflicts among the developing countries alive and in tact. Thus any change in the *status quo* or any attempt to bring about a state of harmony in South Asia was considered detrimental to the interests of the major powers.

This explains how Pakistan was made a surrogate of the US and to a lesser extent India of the USSR. It was also in the interests of the major powers to prevent the emergence of any regional or global power. Hence, the possibility of India acquiring a status of preeminence in South Asia was always an anathema particularly to the US and China, each of which considered this region as its own sphere of influence. The USSR also cherished the same desire to a lesser extent. Thus the interests of both the US and the USSR conversed in insisting on India to sign the NPT. It is understandable that acquisition of the nuclear capability will alter the power equation at the regional level and also at the international level thus upsetting their undisputed supremacy.

The breath-taking changes that have taken place in the last three years leading to the cessation of rivalries between the US and the USSR and the consequential reduction of nuclear arms deployments, the collapse of communism in Eastern Europe and finally the disintegration of the USSR have changed the international relations drastically. However, it did not alter substantially the situation in South Asia.

The New World Order (NWO) contemplated and controlled by the US envisages only a *status quo* for South Asia. That is, South Asia is supposed to remain a subordinate to the US dominated global system. It is also expected to serve the strategic and economic interests of the US and its allies. The New World Order aims at containing the growth of India as a regional power. To ensure this the US attaches more importance to make India and Pakistan sign the NPT and submit themselves to the international safeguards.

The Pentagon document, which came to light recently, which was discounted by the US officials as an obscure position paper and not (yet) a policy[48], sought to spell out the American plans for the global order in the coming few years. This document proposes the use force, if necessary against India to destroy its nuclear capability.[49] It is also proposed to continue military aid to Pakistan to maintain the security and strategic concerns of the US in South Asia. Thus America clearly intends to maintain a *status quo* in this region by isolating India and helping Pakistan to counter-balance it.

In the light of this thinking the US is averse to the idea of enhancing the number of permanent members in the UN Security Council to facilitate *inter alia* India to become a permanent member of the Security Council. The US is not interested in the proposal for the restructuring the UN because it does not want the world body to undercut its (US) importance as the only superpower of the world.

The New World Order of the US also includes the strengthening of the free market system throughout the world. This is only to ensure new markets to the crisis ridden US industries. Even in the changed strategic environment the US does not want to neglect the interests of the military industrial complex.

China, the only major power of Asia also shows keen interest in maintaining *status quo* in the region. In the recent times China is striving to improve relations with India. But its ties with the other States of the region are likely to cause problems to India. Like the US, China is also averse to the idea of India becoming a permanent member of the UN Security Council. Thus, there is still a grim suspense over China's attitudes and its impact on the intra-regional politics in South Asia.

Apart from being a strategic prey, the vulnerability of South Asia is further increased by the poverty and economic backwardness of its component States. All the members of SAARC without exception are underdeveloped mainly with agrarian economies and a fragile industrial base. Most of these States are economically appended to the western countries. Low levels of industrialization, high unemployment rates, low per capita incomes, poor standards of living, illiteracy and disease are major features of these countries. Naturally, social backwardness, low levels of participation, lack of legitimacy in political systems and instability follow in tandem to the deep rooted economic and social problems. The ruling elites of these States which are generally of autocratic nature, irrespective of the outward features of the political systems, fall a natural prey to the temptations of aid and assistance from the extra-regional powers.

The external problem of adverse balance of trade and the ever growing debt problem of these States is also a contributory factor in the impulsive desire of these countries to approach for aid from the developed countries of the West. A glance at the external trade and debt position of the States of South Asia will serve as an indication of the magnitude of the problem.

TABLE 5

(Figures in 1989)

Name of the country	*Trade balance m dollars*	*External debt in m dollars*	*Debt as % of GNP*
India	—3692	62509	24.0
Pakistan	—2477	18509	46.9
Sri Lanka	—4654	5101	73.5

Bangladesh	—2119	10712	53.3
Nepal	—424	1359	43.5
Bhutan	-	79	-
Maldives	-	-	-

Source : World Development Report, 1990.

The commitment to economic development and the internal political problems are said to be important reasons for the dependence of these States on the external aid. But the key to the problem of the external interference and the dependence on the external assistance lay in the mutual rivalries and suspicions among the States of South Asia. Unless this basic problem is resolved an atmosphere conducive to economic development free from external interference cannot be created in this region. Regional cooperation will be possible only in such an atmosphere.

References

1. Sisir Gupta, Kashmir : *A Study in India-Pakistan Relations* (Asia Publishing House, Bombay, 1966), pp. 163-164.

2. S. Nihal Singh, 'Can the US and India be Real Friends?', *Asian Survey*, 23(9), Sept. 1983, p.1013.

3. See Baljit Singh, *Indian Foreign Policy : An Analysis*, (Asia Publishing House, Bombay, 1975), pp. 25-32.

4. Narottam Gaan, 'Superpower Involvement in Indo-Pak Relations', *India Quarterly*, Vol. 46, No. 4, Oct-Dec. 1990.

5. S. Nihal Singh, *op. cit.*, p. 1014.

6. President Kennedy is also said to have commitments to Pakistan based on his security perceptions. See Henry A. Kissinger, *Years of Upheaval* (Vikas, New Delhi, 1982), p. 304.

7. *Ibid.*, p. 677.

8. Nihal Singh, *op. cit.*, p. 1019.

9. Statement by President Reagan on October 20, 1987 during the visit of Mr. Rajiv Gandhi to Washington. *American Foreign Policy Current Documents 1987*, (Department of State, Washington 1988), p. 491.

10. Zarb-e-Momin is the code name given to the military exercizes conducted by Pakistan on Indo-Pak border. Narottam Gaan, "Superpower Involvement in Indo-Pak relations." *India quarterly* Vol. 46, No. 4, Oct-Dec. 1990, p. 17.

11. Howard Wriggins, 'US-Soviet Relations : Across the Arc of Rimland Asia, *Asian Survey*, 23(8), August 1983, p. 909.

12. *The Hindu*, September 21, 1991.

13. K.L. Kamal & Prabha Arun, *Pakistan : Democracy at The Cross Roads* (Yuwraj Publishers, Jaipur, pp. 75-79.

14. B.M. Kaushik, in P.C. Mathur, *Government and Politics in South Asia* (Jaipur 1986), p. 235.

15. *The Hindu*, 23 October 1991.

16. *The Hindu*, 24 January 1992.

17. K.L. Kamal & Prabha Arun, *op. cit*, p. 75.

18. *The Hindu*, 20 March 1992.

19. *The Hindu*, 23 Sept. 1991.

20. *The Hindu*, 15 March 1992.

21. Shantha K. Hennayake, 'The Peace Accord and the Tamils in Sri Lanka', *Asian Survey*, 29(4), April 1989, pp. 405-406.

22. K. R. Singh, *The Indian Ocean* (Manohar, Delhi, 1977), p. 115.

23. Rasul B. Rais, 'Pakistan in the Regional and Global Power Structure', *Asian Survey*, 31(4), April 1991, p. 379.

24. Despatch by R. Chakrapani from Washington in *The Hindu*, March 11, 1992.

25. See Vijay Kumar, *India and Sri Lanka-China Relations (1948-84)* (Uppal Pub. House, New Delhi, 1986), p. 67.

26. While Pakistan supporting India was out of question, India could not enlist the support of her close neighbours with whom she had no serious disputes, viz., Nepal and Sri Lanka. Both Nepal and Sri Lanka remained neutral, while both had sympathies for China off the record. *Ibid., pp.* 59-60, See also Partha S. Ghosh, *op. cit.*, p. 127.

27. Shelton U.Kodimara (Ed), *South Asian Strategic Issues, Sri Lankan Perspectives* (Sage Publ. 1990), p. 61 (Mahinda Wirake, China in South Asia).

28. Mehrunnisa Ali, 'Soviet-Pak Ties since the Afghan Crisis', *Asian Survey*, 23(9), Sept. 1983, p. 1032.

29. Henry Kissinger, *op. cit.*, p. 362.

30. *Frontline*, April 10, 1992, p. 24.

31. P.S. Ghosh, *op. cit.*, p. 107.

32. John W. Garver, 'China-India Rivalry in Nepal : The Clash over Chinese Arms Sales', *Asian Survey*, 31(10), Oct.1991.

33. D. P. Kumar, *Nepal : Year of Decision* (Vikas, Delhi, 1980), p. 179.

34. Vijay Kumar, *op.cit.*, pp. 59-61.

35. *Ibid.*, p. 124.

36. *Ibid.*, p. 164.

37. G. W. Choudhury, 'China's Policy towards South Asia', *Current History*, April 1979, p. 182.

38. Mahindra Wirake, in Kodikara (Ed.), *op.cit.*, p. 64.

39. See *Frontline*, 'A Step Closer' by Manoj Joshi, pp. 4-10 and interview with Chinese Premier Li Peng, pp. 120-122.

40. Sisir Gupta, *op.cit.*, pp. 300 and 320.

41. Nihal Singh, *op.cit*, p. 1017.

42. P. S. Jayaramu, 'Foreign Policy Behaviour of India, Afghanistan and the Himalayan Kingdoms : A Balance of Power Interpretation, *The Indian Journal of Political Science*, Vol. 50, Oct.-Dec. 1989.

43. Vijay Kumar, *op.cit*, p. 124.

44. Stephen P. Cohen, 'Growing Soviet Interest in South Asia' in Ray S. Cline, James A. Miller and Roger E. Kanet (Eds), *Asia in Soviet Global Strategy* (London, 1987), p. 132.

45. *Ibid.*, p. 137.

46. Darshan Singh (Ed.), *Soviet Foreign Policy Documents 1987*, pp. 434-435.

47. Cohen, *op.cit.*, p. 133.

48. *Frontline*, 10 April, 1992, pp. 18-23.

49. *Ibid.*

CHAPTER VI

SAARC AT WORK — RETROSPECT AND PROSPECT

Having considered the evolution of SAARC (including the conceptual framework of regionalism) and various problems of SAARC viz., the political, social, ethnic and cultural diversity of member States of SAARC, their bilateral problems and the external influences on the intra-regional relations and regional cooperation in South Asia, let us now turn to the actual functioning of SAARC and its achievements so far.

In this chapter, we deal with the (a) political dynamics of SAARC summits held till-date, (b) the major decisions taken and breakthroughs achieved during various summits, (c) the Integrated Programme of Action, the main areas covered and the progress made in each area, and (d) the general impact of SAARC on the political, social, cultural and economic relations among the countries of the region outside the purview of SAARC. In a way, this chapter brings out the impact of various factors of discord in South Asia, discussed in the preceding chapters, on the actual functioning of SAARC. Thus, it is a precursor of the conclusions of the present study in content and spirit.

The launching of the SAARC in December 1985 at Dhaka amidst fanfare and diplomatic euphoria was the culmination of the five years of slogging efforts to formalize the regional cooperation in South Asia. The adoption of the Charter of the SAARC at the historic summit of the South Asian countries at Dhaka on 8 December 1985 institutionalized the regional cooperation which began in August 1983 under the acronym SARC. The Dhaka summit was symbolic of the will and desire of the South Asian countries to embark on the path of cooperation and collective development.

The declaration issued at the end of the Dhaka summit spelt out the basis, rationale and necessity for the regional cooperation among the signatories. It considered the SAARC 'to be a tangible manifestation of their (the members) desire to cooperate regionally, to work together towards finding solutions for their common problems in a spirit of friendship, trust and mutual understanding and in the creation of an order based on mutual respect, equity and shared benefits'[1] And the 'fundamental goal was to accelerate the process of economic and social development in their respective countries through the optimum utilization of their human and material resources so as to promote the welfare and prosperity of their people and to improve their quality of life'[2] And it was also reiterated that "they were conscious that peace and security was an essential prerequisite for the realization of this objective."[3]

It was also noted that these countries were bound by many common values rooted in their social, ethnic, cultural and historical traditions and the regional cooperation provided a logical response to the problems faced by them. On the economic front the Dhaka Declaration 'acknowledged that the countries of South, which constituted one-fifth of humanity, were faced with the formidable challenges of poverty, economic backwardness, low levels of production, unemployment and pressure of population compounded by exploitation of the past and other adverse legacies'.[4]

It was also emphasized that 'strengthening of regional cooperation in South Asia required great involvement of their people. They agreed to increase interaction and further promote people-to-people contacts at various levels among their countries.'[5]

The Dhaka summit approved the Integrated Programme of

Action already under-way and welcomed the progress already made in the implementation of the programme of action in the mutually agreed areas (nine at that time). Another new area viz., Women in Development was also added at the Dhaka Summit.[6] Exploration of new areas of cooperation, decision making, coordination and implementation is done by various committees specified in the Charter as mentioned in Chapter II.

The summit of the Heads of States and Governments is attached with greater importance for decision making at the highest level, breaking new grounds for cooperation and for creation of an ambience of goodwill conducive for cooperation. The Dhaka Summit also recognized the importance of the periodic meetings at the summit level as central to the promotion of mutual trust, confidence and cooperation among the member countries.

That was the beginning of the regional cooperation in South Asia under the aegis of SAARC. The declaration issued at the end of the summit was the pious document of laudable objectives, principles and great platitudes. All nice things were said and impressions were sought to be created that the people of the region were going to witness happier days in the future. The Dhaka summit, however, was not totally devoid of discordant notes. But on the face of it, it was claimed to be a great success opening new vistas of peace, security and progress in the region. This euphoria was continued to dominate the real achievements at all the subsequent summits also. The success and failure of the SAARC is more or less reflected in the way the summits were held in the past seven years.

The second summit was held in India in November 1986 at Bangalore. The Bangalore declaration, issued at the end of the summit, reaffirmed the determination of the people and governments of the South Asian countries to work together on the lines laid down in the SAARC Charter with a view to devising common policies and approaches for finding common solutions to their common problems. It was also stressed that progress and prosperity of each of the countries would rebound to the benefit of the others.[7]

Apart from the normal euphoria of goodwill, mutual trust

and enthusiasm for cooperation that overflowed at the Bangalore summit, a few more areas also sought to be brought into the fold of the cooperation under SAARC. A new topic viz., Prevention of Drug Trafficking and Drug Abuse was added to the already agreed upon areas of Integrated Programme of Action.[8] In addition, approval was given in principle to such ideas as (a) launching of a South Asian Broadcasting Programme covering both radio and television (the present SAVE programmes), (b) taking necessary steps to promote tourism in the region, (c) exchange of students, scholars and researchers, (d) establishment of SAARC Documentation Centre to collect and store reliable and up-to-date information on technical, scientific and developmental matters relating to South Asia, and (e) establishment of Organized Volunteers Programme in SAARC.

One of the significant achievements of the Bangalore summit was the signing of the Memorandum of Understanding on the establishment of the SAARC Sacretariat at Kathmandu. Subsequently on 17 February 1987 the SAARC Secretariat with the Secretary-General and Four Directors was inaugurated at Kathmandu.

The Bangalore Declaration reaffirmed all the good things that were zealously included in the Dhaka declaration. The importance of the increasing involvement of the people for ensuring the success of regional cooperation was reiterated. It was also recalled that the countries of South Asia had been linked by age-old cultural, social and historical traditions, and these commonalities constituted solid foundations for regional cooperation for addressing more effectively the economic and social problems.[9]

While expressing satisfaction that considerable progress had been achieved in the implementation of the Integrated Programme of Action (IPA) the Heads of States or Governments agreed about a progressive movement towards more concrete and action-oriented benefits from the SAARC to the people of the region.[10] This was indicative of the desire for making the regional cooperation more meaningful and people-oriented. However as we find in the course of our discussion even after a lapse of six years after the Bangalore summit, this remained only as a pious desire and a hollow promise.

The same euphoria and the spirit of enthusiasm for consolidating the cooperation was carried on at Kathmandu summit, which was held on 2-4 November 1987. The implementation of the 11 already agreed upon areas of the IPA was pursued and the action on the new areas identified at the Bangalore summit was also followed up at Kathmandu. Concretizing the concern expressed and efforts made at the earlier summits, the SAARC Regional Convention of Suppression of Terrorism was signed at Kathmandu.[11] This was expected to tackle the burning problems of internal conflicts in various States of South Asia. Another important achievement at Kathmandu was the signing of Agreement establishing South Asian Food Reserve. This reflected a consensus among the members of SAARC to tackle their urgent common problems collectively.

Surprisingly the spirit of SAARC was maintained and the impression of all-is-well-and-nice sought to be created at both Bangalore and Kathmandu summits, despite the simmering differences between India and Pakistan and between India and its other neighbours viz., Sri Lanka, Nepal and Bangladesh. However, attempts were made to highlight bilateral problems. We shall discuss the political differences that have vitiated the cooperative spirit of SAARC during various summits at a later stage. Suffice it to mention here that in the dichotomy of the desire for achieving a tangible cooperation (whether the desire is simulated or real is open to doubts) and the urge and enthusiasm to score a diplomatic victory over the political adversary (undoubtedly India in the case of all other members of SAARC), a facade of cordiality however was presented while the feelings of mutual suspicion were not totally concealed.

As is well known the bilateral relations between India and Pakistan touched lowest ebb during the period between the Bangalore summit and the Islamabad summit (1988). India's bilateral relations with Sri Lanka, Nepal and Bangladesh were also experiencing severe strains during this period. The sudden disappearance of Pakistan's President Gen. Zia-ul-Haq from the scene, the conducting of elections and the taking over of Miss Benazir Bhutto as the Prime Minister of Pakistan brought a refreshing change in the political climate of the Indian sub-continent and raised hopes of a bright period of genuine cooperation between India and Pakistan in particular and South Asia in general. The signing of Indo-Sri Lankan Accord towards the resolution of the Tamil separatism in Sri Lanka also brought about a spirit of good-will between India and Sri Lanka. Thus, the aura of mutual good-will and trust permeated the political atmosphere of South Asia on the eve of the Fourth Summit of Heads of States or Governments held at Islamabad in late December 1988.

The Islamabad summit held between 29-31 December 1988 intended to transform the fledgling SAARC from a forum of debate to a forum of action. In line with this, the basic needs perspective plan, SAARC 2000, covering food, clothing, shelter, education, primary health care and population planning was proposed to be given a concrete shape at the next summit at Colombo. The Islamabad declaration also enunciated the commitment of the SAARC leaders to all-out war against terrorism in all its forms and it was also proposed to root out the evil of narcotics which posed a grave threat to political and social stability of the region.[12] To begin with, the leaders called for adoption of enabling measures by the member States to implement the Convention on the Suppression of Terrorism.[13]

No particular decision, however, was taken about the core economic areas of cooperation, viz., trade, manufacturers and services. But the Heads of States or Governments expressed satisfaction at the progress in the studies underway regarding the feasibility of cooperation in those areas.[14]

Though, there was no significant breakthrough regarding the cooperation among the member States in any meaningful way it was once again recognized that there was need for focusing attention on more concrete and result-oriented activities within the framework of SAARC.

The significance of Islamabad summit was in the atmosphere of good-will and the feelings of optimism that filled the air especially regarding the bilateral relations between India and

Pakistan. This raised expectations among the other members of the SAARC and rightly so, that it would favourably affect the SAARC. However that has come out to be a shortlived optimism as the period subsequent to the Islamabad summit witnessed a temporary setback in the general functioning of the SAARC and the fifth summit that was scheduled to be held in Colombo in 1989 could not take place at all. The next summit, the fifth one in the SAARC series, was held in November 1990 at Male, the capital of Maldives. For a critical eye it may appear that SAARC came to Male from Islamabad in a somewhat limping fashion.[15]

The Male summit was held in an atmosphere of rapid political changes that have been taking place in various member countries of SAARC. There were significant changes in India, Nepal and Pakistan all of which were represented by their new Prime Ministers. Sri Lanka was represented by its Prime Minister Wijetunga. Unlike in the previous years Nepal was represented by its Prime Minister, symbolizing the changes that have taken place in that country. The Male summit, like the previous ones was also a star-studded extravaganza. Some of the important decisions taken at Male include, the consensus on setting up of a Fund for Regional Projects which could make available credit on easy terms for the identification and development of regional projects.[16] At Male the Heads of States or Governments noted with satisfaction that the national studies on Trade, Manufactures and Services had been completed and they underlined the need for expeditious action for completing the Regional Study within the stipulated timeframe.[17] The need for giving proper attention to the matters of environment and bio-technology was also recognized. Decision was also taken to complete the study on causes and consequences of natural disasters and the protection and preservation of environment.[18]

The penchant for making idealistic statements and catchy slogans and the general euphoria symbolizing the proverbial much-ado-about-nothing was very much evident at Male also. The usual reaffirmation of the convictions that regional cooperation was a necessity for the well-being of the people of South Asia and the reiteration that more action-oriented programmes should be taken up etc. were invariably included in the declaration issued after the summit.[19]

The Journey from Male to Colombo was not really a smooth one. The summit which was to be held in November 1991 could not be held. It was cancelled just before one day because of the inability expressed by the King of Bhutan to attend the summit. The King suggested that his representative would attend the summit on his behalf if accepted. But there was disagreement on this issue and the summit had to be postponed. It was alleged that it was India which caused the fiasco. There was quite a bit of flutter which was somewhat alarming (more on this at a later stage).

The damage done to SAARC with the sudden postponement of the summit in November was quickly redressed by the successful holding of the summit (for only one day) on 21 December 1991 at the same venue, Colombo.

The Colombo summit, the Sixth Meeting of the SAARC Heads of States or Governments, was held on 21 December 1991 in a sombre and business like atmosphere. Contrary to the expectations, the summit passed off without much mutual accusations about the November fiasco. The leaders in a day of hectic deliberations tried to cover all the important issues. A few significant decisions were also taken during the summit. It was agreed to set up a South Asian Commission on Poverty Alleviation and a proposal for examining the plan to set up a regional development fund was also agreed upon. The need to eliminate and stem the evil of terrorism from the region was once again reiterated. A new thrust was given to the environmental issues and the need to promote cooperation among themselves was emphasized.[20]

For the first time in the history of SAARC summitry a new thrust was laid on the economic cooperation, especially on the core area of trade and development. Though no break-through was achieved in identifying the exact areas of economic cooperation, the major achievement of the Colombo summit was the consensus on looking into the proposal made by Sri Lanka (supported by India) for forming the SAARC Preferential Trade Area (SAPTA) by 1997.[21]

The Colombo summit also touched upon many more issues

of mutual concern of non-controversial nature. As usual a wide range of issues were covered by the deliberations and decisions taken at the Sixth SAARC Summit at Colombo. Though the Colombo summit could be regarded as a success like the previous five summits, it was also not devoid of the undercurrents of mutual suspicions and antagonism.

One of significant common feature of all the six summits held so-far was the wide coverage and importance given to the international issues of both general and contextual importance. The declarations issued at the end of all the summits invariably mentioned the collective views of the SAARC members on a wide range of international problems, like the super-power relations, the issues of nuclear arms control and disarmament, Nuclear Test Ban Treaty, the international economic problems, the importance of the North-South Dialogue, the emerging new world order etc. On each occasion the Heads of States or Governments reiterated their commitment to the principles and ideals of Non-Alignment and the United Nations.

The brief survey of the SAARC Summitry presented above, gives an impression that the deliberations held and the decisions taken at the meetings of the Heads of States or Governments held so far (as well as the other levels) were rather drab and devoid of any serious intention to get to the core of cooperation. All the crucial and central issues were avoided deliberately to avoid differences. The main reason shown for this has been the basic principles agreed to and enshrined in the SAARC Charter that (a) all decisions would be taken unanimously, and (b) bilateral and contentious issues should be avoided. Throughout the past seven years no efforts were spared to unscrupulously adhere to the above mentioned principles. This actually symbolized the 'SAARC Spirit' (of cooperation). It was justified on the ground that there were differences in the bilateral relations of the member States.

Obviously, the members of SAARC while professing the virtues of regional cooperation and advocating for more action-oriented programmes etc. were actually playing a 'zero-sum-game' on the SAARC platform. But the persisting differences and the growing urge to score diplomatically and corner the main rival taking advantage of conference diplomacy nevertheless gave rise to the contentious issues and discordant notes, thus exposing the fledgling SAARC to the rumblings of political turmoils.

On many occasions the members of SAARC, did not hesitate to rake up controversial issues or to drag bilateral problems into the SAARC forum. Apart from sounding esoteric and veiled references on some issues blatant accusations were also made at various levels of the SAARC meetings.

The politics of subversion began at the very first meeting of the Heads of Governments or States at Dhaka in December 1985. The publicity material distributed by the Pakistan Embassy in Dhaka prior to the summit spoke of 'not so subtle' anti-India media campaign raising the Kashmir issue, defending Pakistan's nuclear programme and depicting India as a 'hegemonist' which was taking a negative attitude on SAARC proposals.[22] Gen. Zia was reported to have spoken of India's disputes with 'every country in South Asia' at the end of the Dhaka summit.'[23] The speech of the King of Bhutan clearly mentioned that it was not desirable to limit the discussions to the issues of non-political nature. President Zia's talk of 'Collective pledge' was aimed at gaining support from the smaller States of South Asia in his anti-India campaign.[24]

The cancellation of the stamp releasing ceremony at the end of the Dhaka summit was only because of the fact that the stamps issued by some States especially Pakistan, Maldives were objectionable to India.[25]

Thus right from Dhaka the summits were sought to be used to canvass for political support on bilateral problems, especially with India. Even in the meetings of the Council of Ministers the bilateral problems played a disruptive role. Particular reference may be made of Sri Lanka's threat to boycott the New Delhi meeting of the Council of Ministers in June 1987 but later changed its stand.[26]

The political overtones aimed at focusing the bilateral differences continued at Bangalore and Kathmandu summits also. At Bangalore the Prime Minister of Pakistan (President Zia did not attend) accused India of unwarranted military movements along the border. The Indian Prime Minister late Rajiv Gandhi on the other hand denied the Pakistan Prime Minister's allegations and expressed apprehensions about the latter's plan for making the 'Islamic bomb'.[27] The bilateral differences were the main hurdle for the SAARC leaders in their bid to expand the areas of cooperation to include trade, industry, energy, money and finance.[28] The Sri Lankan ethnic problem also overshadowed the Bangalore summit despite the general agreement that bilateral and contentious issues should be kept out of SAARC.[29]

The Kathmandu summit also witnessed the bilateral differences between India and Pakistan coming in the way of taking decisions significant to the intra-regional relations. Pakistan did not like to see India coming out with flying colours on the Indo-Sri Lankan accord and it also blocked India's support to the Afghanistan's request for entry into SAARC. The only reason for the kicking up of the controversies was the political rivalry between India and Pakistan and Pakistan's desire to play-up its leverage with the other members of the SAARC. By and large, Kathmandu also kept up the general trend of the South Asian politics affecting the noble sentiments and the general significance of the SAARC.[30]

The SAARC summits and other meetings have been used as the launching pads for political propaganda on the bilateral differences. It has been a regular feature ever since the first summit held at Dhaka in December 1985. The complete paralysing of the SAARC and the cancellation of the proposed summit took place in 1989 because of the belligerent and intransigent postures adopted by Sri Lanka over the issue of the IPKF. Sri Lanka did not to host the fifth SAARC summit at Colombo until the withdrawal of the IPKF which was stationed in Sri Lanka on its own request under the Indo-Sri Lanka Agreement of 1987. The differences of opinion between India and Sri Lanka on this issue resulted ultimately in the cancellation of the Colombo summit. It was only after the withdrawal of the Indian troops from Sri Lanka that the fifth summit took place at Male in November 1990. The Sri Lankan President sent his Prime Minister to Male whereas normally the President used to attend the SAARC summits.

The latest and the most serious set back received by SAARC, though recovered later, was when the Colombo summit was suddenly postponed just one day before the summit was to be held in November 1991. The roots of the fiasco were in the expression of inability to attend the summit by the King of Bhutan Jigme Singye Wangchuk due to some internal problems. Floundering on the technicality that the summit required the presence of all the Heads of States or Governments, the summit was postponed at the last minute. The reason for the postponement was the reported objections raised by India over the inability of the King of Bhutan to attend the summit.[31]

The postponement of the summit was a disappointment to the people of the region and it was a temporary set back to the fragile Association. The major damage, however, was done by the subsequent events that have taken place at Colombo. In spite of the postponement of the summit, the President of Maldives, the Prime Minister of Pakistan and the Prime Minister of Bangladesh, gathered at Colombo on the day of the postponed summit, ostensibly to express solidarity and sympathy with the host State Sri Lanka. But what transpired there was nothing but India-bashing. The Prime Minister of Pakistan Nawaz Sharif took the opportunity to forge a strong alliance with Sri Lanka apparently to counter the influence of India. He was very generous and effusive in his praise of the Sri Lankan President Premadasa for his dynamic and farsighted leadership. He declared : "Pakistan considers Sri Lanka a true and tested friend sharing a commitment to principles and justice. We shall link arms with you in peace and in adversity."[32] He was only short of presenting India as the villain. The Pakistani Prime Minister took the opportunity to raise the Kashmir issue also.

Sri Lanka took full advantage of the situation to unleash vehement attacks against India. It was alleged that the hidden hand of India worked behind the scenes to prevent the summit from being held.[33] In its battle of wits against India, Sri Lanka went ahead with according the pomp and pageantry reserved for the SAARC summit and virtually hosted a 'mini-SAARC',[34] in the absence of India. It was a clear indication of the emerging anti-India grouping within the SAARC. In fact it already existed right from the beginning but the Colombo incident was a blatant exhibition of its strength.

The past record of the SAARC summitry and other political level meetings bear a clear reflection to the fact that the members of SAARC did not exhibit the required commitment for realising any meaningful cooperation in the region. In fact they lack any regional identity or the SAARC identity or spirit which is the first step in the direction of forging regional cooperation. The only purpose most of the members of SAARC desired and achieved was gaining an international identity and equal status (and some influence at the regional level) *vis-a-vis* the bigger States of the region.

SAARC also came in handy for the smaller neighbours of India, in fact all the neighbours of India including Pakistan, to bait, bash and isolate India within the region. They found it easy to focus their bilateral problems and try to articulate an anti-India grouping under the aegis of SAARC. This is how in spite of the formal restrictions in the Charter against bringing the bilateral and contentious issues before SAARC, every occasion was used to rake up some or other controversy at the political gatherings of the SAARC. Pakistan, Sri Lanka and Nepal have particularly tried to do so on one or more occasions.

Against this scenario it is self-explanatory as to why the SAARC could not touch upon any core areas of cooperation but only tried to play with just peripheral and volatile issues. Given the present state of affairs and the mood of the main actors there is hardly any likelihood of SAARC entering into any core areas of cooperation transcending their mutual suspicions. However, all the members of SAARC without exception show a keen interest in keeping the organization alive. Especially the smaller States of South Asia have a political stake in its existence and perpetuation of SAARC despite its drawbacks. Hence the need for maintaining a facade and off the record pursuit of ones own parochial national interests.

The Areas of Cooperation and Achievements

The political dynamics of SAARC, as explained above,

remained complex and without any clear direction. The programmes of cooperation were, however, very carefully maintained so as to avoid any sensitive issues. The activities of cooperation of the SAARC were brought under the so-called Integrated Programme of Action (IPA). The various mutually agreed areas were included under the IPA and after completion of feasibility studies at various levels were put to implementation. The identification of the areas of cooperation and their formal approval or inclusion in the IPA has been done at the political level. The follow-up action is taken at the levels of Technical Committees, the Standing Committee under the control of the Council of Ministers.

The Integrated Programme of Action as upto the Colombo summit covered 12 mutually agreed areas. And some other proposals for future cooperation were also approved. The areas included in the IPA are : (1) Agriculture, (2) Education, (3) Health and Population Activities, (4) Meteorology, (5) Postal Services, (6) Prevention of Drug Trafficking and Drug Abuse, (7) Rural Development, (8) Science and Technology, (9) Sports, Arts and Culture, (10) Telecommunications, (11) Transport and (12) Women in Development.

In order to gain a clearer understanding of the nature and usefulness of the activities undertaken by the SAARC in the name of regional cooperation we must go into the details of the IPA in the aforementioned areas.

(1) *Agriculture*

Scientific and technical exchange of information and materials of research, conducting of seminars, workshops and training programmes were the main activities taken up so far in the field of agriculture. Scientific and technical knowhow was sought to be exchanged in regard to various crops, particularly for improving the methods of cultivations, improvement of seeds, output and the use of pesticides, insecticides etc. The same activity in regard to the maintenance, development and protection of livestock is also under-way. Various areas having good potential for joint ventures or joint collaborative efforts have been identified. Meeting of counter-part scientists and surveys are included in the future activities.

The SAARC Agriculture Information Centre (SAIC) the first and the only regional institution has been set up at Dhaka. It is engaged in establishing an Agricultural Institutional Network which will serve the needs of SAARC countries by identifying and documenting pertinent literature in the field of agriculture.

(2) *Education*

The activities in the field of education covered the primary education, literacy programmes, continuing education, educational research and science and technical education. The activities were confined to conducting seminars, conferences and group meetings only.

SAVE (SAARC Audio Visual Exchange Programme) is expected to work closely with the Technical Committee on Education so as to produce programmes of common interest to the member countries in this field.[38]

(3) *Health and Population Activities*

In this area also the main activities are confined to seminars, workshops and preparation of status papers. Exchange of status papers on common interest or importance is underway in a general format. Papers were prepared by India on the welfare of handicapped persons, family welfare and traditional systems of medicines etc. Bhutan also prepared a paper on handicapped people.

It was decided to establish a Regional Centre for Tuberculosis in Nepal and another proposal for a similar centre on Malaria is also under active consideration.[39]

A lot interest is generated on the child development and child care. However, much needs to be done in this area to realize a purposeful cooperation.

(4) *Meteorology*

Among the activities undertaken in this area so far are limited to seminars on Inter-comparison of Barometers, Meteorological Instruments, Agricultural Meteorology, Weather Prediction, Crop Weather Relationship, Short-Range Prediction of Monsoon, Rainfall, etc. In essence the cooperation envisaged is only exchange of information and know-how.

The long-term project on the setting up of a Regional Meteorological Research Centre (in India) to conduct joint research on different aspects of monsoon meteorology and atmospheric sciences in the tropics with emphasis on operational forecasting of tropical weather systems is yet to be finalized.[40]

(5) *Postal Services*

The programmes undertaken, as usual, include seminars, training, consultancy, technical assistance, studies on various related matters like International Money-Order System, International Air Letter Mail and International Surface Mail etc. The Technical Committee recommended a long-term programme envisaging a regional postal union, regional data bank, commemorative postage stamps etc.[41] But not much progress has been made in this innocuous area also.

One activity which has been regularly held since 1985 is the Letter-Writing Competition among the School children.

The proposal for the establishment of a Postal Research and Development Centre has been under consideration.

(6) *Prevention of Drug Trafficking and Drug Abuse*

This area has attracted the attenion of the SAARC Heads of States or Governments at the Dhaka summit itself in 1985. The problem of drug trafficking and drug abuse has been a cause of worry not only from the health point of view but also because its links with the countries of the Indian sub-continent. Various programmes including seminars, workshops and meetings of expert and non-government groups were held to study the legal, medicinal, economic and sociological and other implications of the problem. Efforts were made to coordinate the laws relating to punishments and preventive measures in the member countries. A large scale publicity campaign was launched in December 1988 on the day of the Fourth Summit at Islamabad for Combating Drug Trafficking and Drug Abuse. It was also decided to observe 1989 as the SAARC year for Combating Drug Trafficking and Drug Abuse.[42]

The SAARC Convention on Narcotic Drugs and Psychotropic Substances was signed by the Foreign Ministers of the Member States at the Fifth Summit of SAARC at Male in November 1990.[43] It is yet to come into force as many member countries have still to ratify it.

(7) *Rural Development*

Most of the cooperative activities under this head have been of academic interest only. A number of seminars, workshops and meetings were held on a wide range of subjects covering this area. The SAARC Youth Volunteers Programme has also been brought under the purview of Rural Development.

(8) *Science and Technology*

This is one of the areas in which cooperation began way-back in 1982. A number of long-term and short-term activities were planned and carried on. The areas in which cooperation was successful include Energy Problems, R&D in Non-conventional and Renewable Sources of Energy, Food Technology, Transfer and Adoption of Appropriate Technology, Survey of Natural Resources and Remote Sensing, Forestry Development and Erosion Control, Mining, Micro-electronics, Instrumentation, Solar Technology, Genetic Engineering etc. Recently Energy Modelling Techniques have also been brought within the purview of this area.[44] Joint projects in the fields of Development of Low Cost Instant Food, Bio-gas Technology, Informatics, Bio-technology and Micro-electronics were also envisaged.

A number of areas were indentified for exchange of information and for extending cooperation. Specific importance is being given to Bio-technology and Genetic Engineering for exchange of expertise in genetic conservation and maintenance of germplasm banks.

Generally the type of activities conducted in this area were again confined to seminars, workshops, conferences and Meetings of Experts. More such activities are planned for future also.

(9) *Sports, Arts and Culture*

The SAARC activities under this area have aimed at promoting contacts among the people of the region through regular and frequent meetings of scholars, academicians, artists, authors and professionals. Workshops, seminars, coaching camps, clinics for players in various sports and games, painters camps, exhibitions of handicrafts, crafts, Photographs and Monuments of Natural Heritage have also been conducted.

India's proposal for holding periodic cultural festivals in SAARC countries has been welcomed by the Heads of States or Governments. India is supposed to hold the South Asian Cultural Festival in 1992.

(10) *Telecommunications*

This is one area which has helped most of the member countries of the SAARC in improving the quality of services. There has been a marked improvement of telecommunication links within the region.

The areas of cooperation included Satellite Technology, Trainings of Packet Switched Data Network, Study Tours of Maintenance Facilities, Telecommunication Services etc.

As a result of the cooperation in this area, ISD services were available among six member States and ISD telephone and automatic telex services are currently in operation in all the member States. Bureaufax service has already been introduced in all the member countries and common collection charges and media independent tariff have been introduced in most of the member States.[45]

(11) *Transport*

The majority of activities that have taken place in the field of transport have been in the nature of conducting workshops, expert group meetings, short-term training courses etc. The major segments of transport included in this area, are Land Transport, roads and railways, sea-transport (including inland waterways and shipping) and Air Transport.

Various aspects of land, sea and air transport and the related matters of technology, operational methods and management, safety, efficiency, training programmes and energy conservation etc. are discussed at various levels to improve the transport in the region and within the member countries.

(12) *Women in Development*

A lot of significance has been attached to this aspect by the member States of the SAARC. Detailed studies on the status of women and all aspects of problems of women have been conducted and the programmes of Women's Development have been included in "SAARC 2000—A Basic Needs Perspective" of all the member countries.

A number of seminars, workshops, conferences, meetings and discussions were held under the aegis of SAARC both by the Government and non-Government organizations throughout the region of South Asia.

The Fourth SAARC Summit held at Islamabad declared 1990 as the SAARC Year of the Girl Child. Further it was decided to observe the 1991—2000 decade as the " SAARC Decade of the Girl Child" . It was also decided to focus on the concerns of the Girl child in various activities of the IPA, viz, Agriculture, Education, Health and Population Activities, Prevention of Drug Trafficking and Drug Abuse, Rural Development, Sports, Arts and Culture.[46]

Several decisions to give importance to this area have been taken at various meetings of technical committees, ministerial meetings and also at the Male summit of the Heads of States or Governments.

Apart from the above mentioned areas included in the Integrated Programme of Action a number of steps were taken and actions were proposed in several important areas to foster cooperation among the countries of the region. SAARC Food Security Reserve was established with more than 200,000 tonnes of food-grains to meet the contingencies of food scarcity in the member countries of SAARC . It is a step in the right direction, though no member State has had occasion to draw from the SAARC Food Security Reserve so far.[47]

Keeping in view the implications of economic problems, security and territorial integrity the SAARC Heads of States or Governments have attached much significance and urgency to curb the menace of terrorism and drug abuse and drug trafficking. Accordingly regional conventions on the Prevention of Terrorism and SAARC convention on Narcotic Drugs and Psychotropic Substances were signed at the Kathmandu and Male summits respectively. The former was ratified by all the member countries, while the latter still awaits ratifications by some of the member countries.

Decisions were taken to establish SAARC Documentation Centre in India, the Nuclear Centre for Human Resource Development in Pakistan and the Regional Centre for Tuberculosis in Nepal.

It was decided at the Islamabad summit to introduce a SAARC Travel Document to facilitate initially the members of Parliament and chief justices of the member countries to travel in all the SAARC countries without any visa or such document. A formal decision to launch the SAARC Document covering the Supreme Court judges, members of parliaments and heads of national academic institutions, was taken at the Male summit.[48]

SAARC has consistently been trying to draw public attention towards the burning issues of social and economic importance in the entire region by observing various calender years in the name of the respective topics. The year 1989 was observed in the entire SAARC area as the Year for Combating Drug Trafficking and Drug Abuse; 1990 was observed as the Year of Girl Child; 1991 was observed as the SAARC Year of Shelter and 1992 is being observed as the SAARC Year of Environment. It is also decided to observe 1993 as the SAARC Year of Disabled Persons.[49] Besides, as mentioned earlier, the entire decade of 1991-2000 is observed by all the member countries of SAARC as the Decade of Girl Child.

At the Sixth Summit of SAARC Heads of States or Government held at Colombo on 21 December 1991, the crucial economic issues were given more importance. It was decided to examine the proposals for the establishment of the SAARC Preferential Trade Area (SAPTA) and it was also decided to set up a South Asian Commission on Poverty Alleviation. And the SAARC Fund for Regional Projects came into effect with contributions from the member countries as per the decision taken earlier.

The details of the IPA and the measures of implementation and the decisions and actions taken in regard to various other matters may appear to be impressive, but the net benefit derived out of cooperation among the member countries is rather negligible and insignificant. The areas covered and the activities undertaken during the past few years have been either peripheral or limited to interactions at the academic, official or other fringe levels only. Most of the activities mentioned in the IPA and the measures taken were generally appealing to academic interest and remained paper statements without any involvement of the people of the member countries.

While meagre or lack of availability of funds may be one of the reasons for the poor performance in implementing the cooperative measures in the agreed areas. To quote the Secretary-General of SAARC the major and the most important drawback coming in the way of achieving the desired results has been the lack of commitment on the part of the member countries (their governments).[50] The reasons are not far to seek. The existing differences stemming from the deep rooted rivalries hardly allow them to seek any gainful cooperation. Thus, not surprisingly, in spite of a lapse of considerable time after the ratification of the SAARC Convention on the Suppression of Terrorism, no concrete enabling measures have been taken so far to curb the menace.

Similarly, the SAARC Convention on Narcotic Drugs and Psychotropic Substances which was signed at Male could not be ratified even to-date. The decisions on the establishment of the SAARC Documentation Centre, SAARC Regional Centre on Tuberculosis and on the core issues of Trade, Manufacture and Services have not yet come to fruition.

Whatever cooperation SAARC is trying to implement among the member countries is more or less confined to academic discussions, issuing of statements, signing of conventions or declarations and coining of slogans etc. only. Generally SAARC is confining itself to innocuous areas leaving the core areas of cooperation for fear of raking up contentious and bilateral issues. Thus SAARC cannot yet be described as being fully geared to the tasks of promoting the welfare of the people of South Asia and improving their quality of life; accelerating economic growth; social progress and cultural development in the region; and providing all individuals the opportunity to live in dignity and to realise their full potentials-objectives enshrined in the SAARC Charter adopted at Dhaka and reiterated invariably at every summit held subsequently.[51]

One of the striking features of the SAARC has been that while an aura of pomp, ceremony and grandeur had been attached to the various meetings of SAARC, there had been no matching response as far as the financial commitments for the general and developmental activities of SAARC. This is reflected in the financial contributions of the member countries for the SAARC activities (See Table).

Ironically, while crores, of rupees are frittered away by the countries of South Asia on activities like sports, cultural programmes, visits to foreign countries by officials and politicians, arrangements for VIPs publicity, meetings, conferences etc., they have been maintaining an uncalled for frugality and miserliness in allocating funds for the SAARC activities. In the absence of sufficient financial support, naturally it cannot be expected to achieve substantial results even in the limited sphere of the mutually agreed areas not to talk of to carry out exploratory studies for future cooperation. This being so, interestingly, some of the members of SAARC have been keen on seeking financial support from the countries and organizations outside the region for the activities and projects of SAARC.[52]

The crux of the problem is the ever smouldering mutual suspicions and antagonism between India and her neighbours. The general luke-warm interest on SAARC and its activities is symbolic of the political turmoils within South Asia. Most of the key issues of cooperation are bogged down in the din of political differences between the member countries of SAARC, especially between India and the other members.

Another serious draw-back of SAARC lies in its general prohibition on the issues of contentious and bilateral nature. While most of the crucial areas of cooperation are left out because of this prohibition, the existing bilateral problems and controversial issues are being given a protective cover by allowing them to continue in future. Thus, it has not only hampered the progress of SAARC but is likely to come in the way of strengthening cooperation among the member countries.

While the achievements or progress of SAARC have been none-too-satisfactory, what has been its effect on the general political, social, cultural and economic interaction among the member countries and their peoples? Naturally with the formation of SAARC one would expect a general ambience of goodwill pervade over the entire gamut of relations among the SAARC member countries. One would expect favourable changes in matters of trade, exchange of information media and peopel-to-people interaction. But the record of the past seven years presents a near dismal picture on all counts.

On the political front, the launching of SAARC does not seem to have even a salutary effect on the bilateral relations and attitudes of the member countries. Bilateral relations between India-Pakistan, India-Nepal, India-Sri-Lanka and India-Bangladesh during 1985-1991 have witnessed more turbulence than the preceding period. Especially, during 1986-88 India-Pakistan relations have been characterized by an alarming arms race and at times there were fears of eruption of war. Again involvement of Pakistan in the secessionist movements in the

TABLE - 1
Financial Contributions of Member Countries for SAARC Activities

(Amount in Millions)

Country	*1983-84*		*1984-85*		*1985-86*		*1987-88*		*1988-89*	
	Amount in NC	*Amount in IR*	*Amount in NC*	*Amount in IR*	*Amount in NC*	*Amount in IR*	*Amount in NC*	*Amount in IR*	*Amount in NC*	*Amount in IR*
Bangladesh	0.5	0.2	6.25	2.8	7.5	3.36	7.5	3.15	8.0	3.47
Bhutan	0.5	0.5	1.0	1.0	1.5	1.5	2.0	2.0	2.0	2.00
India	5.0	5.0	7.5	7.5	10.0	10.0	15.0	15.0	17.5	17.50
Maldives	0.084	0.12	0.084	0.12	0.084	0.118	0.252	0.36	0.325	0.52
Nepal	1.5	1.0	2.5	1.7	2.5	1.72	7.0	4.16	7.0	4.19
Pakistan	4.0	2.32	5.5	8.2	10.5	8.7	10.13	9.72	15.0	11.76
Sri Lanka		-	2.5	1.1	3.0	1.3	5.0	2.23	7.0	3.18

Notes: NC - National currency and IR - Indian Rupees.
The National currencies of member countries are Bangladesh-Taka, Bhutan-Ng, Maldives-MRF, Nepal-Rupee, Pakistan-Rupee and Sri Lanka-Rupee.

Source: I.N. Mukherjee, "Towards Financial and Monetary Cooperation in South Asia", *South Asia Journal*, Vol. 4, No. 2, Oct.-Dec. 1990, p. 147.

States of Punjab and Jammu & Kashmir have created tensions between the two countries. The problem is further aggravated by the new-dimension acquired by the nuclear politics with the confirmation beyond doubt that Pakistan has the nuclear capability. The atmosphere of hide and seek is still going on and there is no let up in the tensions between India and Pakistan. The recent developments in Kashmir have been brought them to the brink of war. All this in spite of the commitments made by India and Pakistan in the SAARC Charter to the literal principles of peaceful settlement of disputes, non-interference in internal affairs and non-use of threat of use of force against the territorial integrity and political independence of other States.

India-Nepal also had some problems over the treaties of trade and transit. The issue of Nepal purchasing arms from the Chinese also caused strains in the bilateral ties between India and Nepal. The general fear of India's domination and the urge to reduce dependence on India have made Nepal to distance herself from India. The political turbulence in Nepal for the restoration of democracy also raised the suspicions in the ruling elites of Nepal against India. Thus, while Nepal was also an enthusiastic supporter of the cause of SAARC it worked in the direction of creating discord between herself and its major partner in SAARC, India. The situation however seems to have improved with the changes that have taken place in the Nepalese political system in the past two years. But still there is no scope for complacency. There seems to have no significant change in the public opinion of Nepal. A letter published in *Frontline* recently from a citizen of Nepal is an indication of this trend.[53]

The Indo-Sri Lankan relations, instead of taking a favourable turn with the evolution of SAARC, have taken a sharp twist resulting in increased tensions. SAARC instead of facilitation solution the Indo-Sri Lankan bilateral problems had on the contrary been affected adversely by the increased tensions between the two countries over the issue of Tamil movement and the IPKF. It was Sri Lanka's intransigence over the IPKF issue that caused the cancellation of the proposed Colombo summit in 1989. The irritant bilateral problems have spilled over the postponed Colombo summit in November 1991 blowing it up out of proportions.

India-Bangladesh relations were also witnessing irritants over the issue of Ganga waters, Chakma refugees,trade imbalances and the Tin Bigha corridor. The political changes in Bangladesh in the past one year have brought about some respite in the strains. With the settlement of the Tin Bigha issue recently there are signs of improvement in the bilateral relations between the two countries. But still the chasm that has developed over the past one half decades remains unbridged to a large extent.

On the social and cultural front also the impact of SAARC has been not satisfactory by any count. The people-to-people interaction has been kept at the minimum level because of the restricted travel facilities within the region. In fact, it is not easy to travel within South Asia. The flow of information, which is vital in bringing people across the borders together psychologically has been rather discouraging. Mutual availability of publications of the member countries has been deliberately restricted. In fact in some cases exchange of information is prohibited.[54]

The intra-regional cultural relations did not witness any breakthrough. In fact the levels of cultural exchange between the SAARC member countries both at the formal and informal levels are quite insignificant in comparison to the cultural exchange these countries have with the countries outside the region.

Even in the field of sports which is quite non-controversial, the experience of the interaction among the members of SAARC, has not been encouraging.

One of the encouraging features since the evolution of SAARC has been the gradual progress made by the member countries towards a broad convergence of their external postures. On almost all the matters of international concern, like the changes in the global order, the North-South economic relations, containing the proliferation of nuclear weapons, support of anti-racial movements, NAM etc., the members of SAARC have been expressing in identical terms and these opinions were invariably included in all the declarations issued at the end of all the past six summits. However, SAARC has not yet emerged into a formidable group of solidarity to deal collectively with the problems of both intra-regional and extra-regional nature.[55] The divergent approaches adopted by the SAARC member countries towards the Kampuchean and Afghanistan problems at the extra-regional level and the Sri Lankan Tamil Problem at the intra-regional level is a clear evidence of this drawback. It is again the inherent differences among the members of SAARC coming in the way achieving any significant improvement in these areas.

The core economic issues of trade and commerce have been continuously avoided by SAARC implicitly putting them in the category of contentious issues. Thus, naturally, the evolution of SAARC did not raise expectations of any dramatic improvement in the trade relations of the member countries. However there was hope that atleast the existing trade in manufactured goods among the countries of the South Asian region would increase.[56] However the reality has been to the contrary. It is disheartening to note that the intra-regional trade has consistently declined during the past one decade, i.e., since the evolution of SARC.

It is striking to note that all the SAARC countries have shown as steady decline in their exports and imports within the region.

The following table shows how this has occurred during 1976 and 1987.

TABLE 7

Dwindling Intra-SAARC Trade (Exports) % in World Trade

Year	*Bangla-desh*	*India*	*Maldives*	*Nepal*	*Pakistan*	*Sri Lanka*
1976	4.63	3.05	41.66	69.47	6.91	8.14
1985	7.65	2.23	17.08	33.45	6.01	4.14
1987	4.11	2.05	18.14	32.11	3.92	3.81
		Imports % of World Trade				
1976	8.02	1.06	17.46	66.00	2.86	9.99
1985	3.45	0.71	9.12	33.12	1.58	6.64
1987	4.28	0.47	7.44	23.90	1.61	6.50

Source: Compiled from World Development Report (Various issues)

Interestingly the past few years have witnessed changing directions even within the intra-SAARC trade. Significant changes have occurred in the case of Nepal, Bangladesh, Pakistan and Sri Lanka. Particularly, Nepal has tried to diversify its external trade links reducing its dependence on India. It has entered into trade relations with Bangladesh and has been steadily maintaining the same. Bangladesh too reduced its dependence on India and forged trade links with Pakistan and Nepal. Pakistan emerged as its major partner sharing 62.97 and 31.9 percent of its exports and imports (in 1987) respectively. Sri Lanka also has been maintaining strong trade relations with Pakistan during the past two decades. Thus, the emerging trends lead to the conclusion that most of the member countries of SAARC are trying to reduce their trade relations with India. At the same time they are constantly trying to improve their trade links excluding India. It is ominous of the emerging patterns of economic cooperation within the SAARC region.

In the light of the proposals made at the Colombo summit for the SAARC Preferential Trade Area (SAPTA) it may be mentioned here that Bangladesh, Pakistan, Sri Lanka, and India were the signatories of the Bangkok agreement (Preferential Trade Agreement) signed in July 1975 under which each member country is expected to give certain preferential treatment to the co-signatories in the field of trade. This agreement was in fact signed under the auspices of Economic Commission for Asia and Pacific (ESCAP). But the impact of this agreement in expanding the intra-regional trade among the signatories (most of which belong to South Asia) has been very limited.[57] Mention may also be made of the recent wrangles over the matters of trade between India and Nepal. As mentioned elsewhere Nepal imposed heavy tariff barriers on Indian goods during the late 1980s despite its commitment to treat Indian goods preferentially under the bilateral agreements.

Thus, the evolution of SAARC did not actually have any favourable impact on the economic and trade relations among the countries of SAARC. This can be attributed to the political divergence of its member countries. However, it strengthens the need to create conducive atmosphere before embarking upon any specific measures for economic cooperations within the region.

It is clear from the foregoing discussion that the achievements of SAARC in the past seven years are quite modest. At the same time SAARC did not succeed in altering the intra-regional political relations of South Asia. Instead it was used as a vehicle for political polarization of the member States with India on one side and all other States on the other. It can also be discerned that contrary to any expectations SAARC could not create a salutary effect in the improvement of the intra-regional economic and trade relations among its member States. Thus the progress of SAARC in the direction of the fulfilment of its avowed objectives has been rather tardy if not dismal. That is, it is still struggling with the infantile disorders. It has yet to take off.

References

1. See SAARC Declaration adopted at Dhaka, 8 December 1985.
2. *Ibid.*
3. *Ibid.*
4. *Ibid.*
5. *Ibid.*
6. M. Mahmood, *Regional Integration in South Asia,* New Dellhi, 1987, p. 39.
7. Bimal Prasad (Ed.), *Regional Cooperation in South Asia Problems & Prospects* (Vikas, New Delhi, 1989) , p.6.
8. Bangalore Declaration para 11.
9. *Ibid.*
10. *Ibid.*
11. The Kathmandu Declaration (of SAARC), 4 November 1987.
12. *Indian Express,* 1 January 1989.
13. See the SAARC's Joint Communique issued at the end of the Islamabad Summit, 31 December 1988.
14. *Ibid.*
15. K.K. Bhargava, 'SAARC at Male: Retrospect and Prospect' *South Asia Journal,* 4 (3), January-March 1991, p. 263.

16. Male Declaration (Fifth Meeting of Heads of States or Governments), 23 November 1990, para 15.

17. *Ibid.*, para 10.

18. *Ibid.*, para 8.

19. *Ibid.*

20. *The Hindu*, 22 December 1991.

21. *Frontline*, 'Back in Colombo: The Summit at last' by T.S. Subramanian, January 17, 1992, pp.130-133, and Preeti, SAARC: A new economic thrust, *Link*, February 9, 1992, p.28.

22. K. Raman Pillai, 'Tensions with Regional Organizations: A Study of SAARC', *Indian Jourmal of Political Science*, Vol. 50, No.1, p. 25.

23 *Ibid.*, p. 25.

24. Pran Chopra, 'The Rising Salience of Politics in SAARC' in Satish Kumar (Ed.) *Yearbook on India's Foreign Policy 1985*, p . 99.

25 The stamp issued by Pakistan showed the state of Jammu and Kashmir as a separate territory and the Maldives stamp showed Sikkim as a separate entity. Raman Pillai, *op.cit.*, p. 25.

26. Narayan Khadka, 'SAARC A Nepalese Perspective', '*The Round Table* (309), 1989, p. 69.

27. Raman Pillai, *op.cit.*, p.23.

28. *Ibid.*, p. 23.

29. *Ibid.*, p. 24.

30. S.D. Muni, 'SAARC Summit Perspectives', *Mainstream*, November 7, 1987, p. 6.

31. *The Hindu*, 4 November 1991.

32. *The Hindu*, 8 November 1991.

33. *The Hindu*, 7 and 8 November 1991.

34. *The Hindu*, 7 November 1991.

35. Report by the Secretary-General on the Activities of the Association and the Secretariat — November 1990. IIA Resume of Intergrated Programme of Action, para on Agriculture.

36. *Ibid.*

37. *Ibid.*, see para on Education.

38. *Ibid.*

39. *Ibid.*, para on Health and Population Activities.

40. *Ibid.*

41. *Ibid.*

42. Report on the Meeting of the Council of Ministers, 7th Session, Islamabad, 8-9 November 1989, para 5.

43. Male Declaration, para 7.

44. Report of Secretary-General of SAARC, *op..cit.*

45. *Ibid.*

46. *Ibid.*

47. *Ibid.*

48. See Male Declaration, para 11.

49. Joint Communique issued after the Male Summit, 23 November 1990, paras 15 to 18.

50. K.K. Bhargava, *op.cit.*, p. 67.

51. Bimal Prasad, *op.cit.*, p. 11.

52. *The Hindu*, July 3, 1991.

53. The letter writeen by one N.N. Pandey in response to an article written by S.D. Muni goes as follows: "In Nepal the law and order situation is bad, prices are rising like never before, the Prime Minister has not been able to get ratified by Parliament the agreements signed with India, he has put his relatives in top administrative posts and even in the cabinet, the communists have got yet another anti-India slogan for the coming local elections and the people have already begun to say that the Panchayat days were better" , *Frontline*, April 24, 1992, p.112.

54 K.K. Bhargava, *op.cit.*, p. 266.

55. B. Mohanan, "Community Formation in SAARC 's External Relations: Lessons from ASEAN", *Indian Journal of Political Science*, Vol.41, No. 1 Jan.-March 1990, p.127.

56. B. Satyanarayanan, "Regional Economic Cooperation in South Asia: Scope and Prospects" in M.D. Dharmadasani (Ed.), *op.cit.*, p. 79.

57. Masroor Ahmed Beg, "Intra-SARRC Trade: A Dwindling Feature" , *India Quarterly*, Vol. 46, No.1, Jan.-March, 1990. p.47.

CHAPTER VII

SAARC — AN OVERVIEW — SUMMARY AND CONCLUSIONS

With the objective of gaining a meaningful understanding of the SAARC as a phenomenon, the present study attempted to inquire into various aspects of regional cooperation in South Asia in the preceding chapters. This study started with the basic conceptual discussion on regions, South Asia as a viable region and proceeded to study the evolution of SAARC as a regional organization of South Asia. The socio-economic and political dimensions of the States of the region, their internal problems, their interrelationships, the role and importance of the region in international relations and the impact of the global powers on the regional organization of South Asia have been discussed in detail. An evaluation of the functioning of SAARC and the progress made by it during the past seven years has also been undertaken.

We have started with a conceptual discussion and arrived at a working definition of 'region', which indicates that there were strong uniting factors in South Asia, like the geographical contiguity, proximity, historical background, commonalities in the social and cultural aspects and economic background. But there were also strong centrifugal forces working in the region. In spite of this, it was generally agreed that *prima facie* South Asia could be regarded as a coherent and viable region for the purposes of regional cooperation. In fact the present study considers this fact as a *fait accompli* as the evolution of SAARC has settled this question conclusively.

The genesis of SAARC has also been discussed. The origin of SAARC in its present form could be traced to the proposals mooted by the late President Zia-ur-Rahman of Bangladesh in 1980 followed by the circulation of a Working Paper on South Asian Regional Cooperation in November 1980. The formal discussions for the establishment of an institutional mechanism for regional cooperation in South Asia started with the Colombo meeting of the Foreign Secretaries of the seven States of South Asian region, i.e. Bangladesh , Bhutan, India, Maldives, Nepal, Pakistan and Sri Lanka in April 1981.

The evolution of regional organization in South Asia has indeed been very late in comparison to various other regions of the world, including other Asian regions. The reasons generally cited were differences among the States of the region, the most important among them being India and Pakistan. True to this background the major States of South Asia exercised caution in the talks held at Colombo in April 1981 and the subsequent meetings of Foreign Secretaries of the participating countries at Kathmandu in November 1981 and Islamabad in August 1982.

The turning point in the evolution of regional cooperation in South Asia as the study indicates was the New Delhi Meeting of Foreign Ministers in August 1983 where an embryonic form of regional cooperation viz., South Asian Regional Cooperation (SARC) was launched. After a few more meetings at the Foreign Ministers level the formal launching of SAARC in its present form took place at Dhaka in December 1985. The Dhaka Summit of the SAARC Heads of States or Governments adopted the Charter of the SAARC and marked the beginning of the regional cooperation amidst a lot of fanfare and publicity.

The SAARC Charter reaffirmed the conviction of the member States about the necessity and desirability of regional cooperation and declared that SAARC was intended to 'promote the welfare of the people of South Asia and to improve their quality of life, to accelerate economic growth, social progress and cultural development in the region... and to promote and strengthen collective self-reliance among the countries of South Asia'. The Charter also enunciated that cooperation within the framework of SAARC should be based on 'respect for the principles of sovereign equality, territorial integrity, political independence, non-interference in internal affairs of other States and mutual benefit'. The principles of Non-Aligment and the UN were also affirmed as the guiding forces of SAARC.

However, the evolution of SAARC with its lofty principles and objectives at a time when the growing internal problems within the member States and increasing mutual differences among the States of South Asia by no means reflected the ambience of regional cooperation. The attitude of the major States was rather cryptic whereas the smaller States evinced more enthusiasm.

As regards the institutional framework of the SAARC, a four-tier institutional set up is envisaged and became operational for SAARC. At the apex level is the summit meeting which takes place once every year. The second tier of the structure is the Council of Ministers, consisting of foreign ministers of the member States. The thrid one in the ladder is the Standing Committee consisting of foreign secretaries of member countries and the bottom line consists of Technical Committees on various subjects of cooperation consisting of representatives of the member States.

The SAARC Secretariat came into existence in February 1987 with headquarters at Kathmandu. It is headed by a Secretary-General and also consists of seven directors, one each from the member countries.

SAARC, though a late comer on the international scene, has been quite ahead of other regional organizations, like ASEAN in matters of institutional framework. But the institutional mechanism established by SAARC is rather modest compared to similar other organizations.

While comparing SAARC with other regional organizations it is found that in most of the cases political, social and ideological convergence facilitated their evolution. In the case of SAARC in spite of the existence of social, cultural and ethnic commonalities, the strategic, ideological divergence stemming from religious divergence and antagonistic political postures are found to be causing most of the damage to the unity of the region. However, the evolution of SAARC indicates the desire of the countries of South Asia to bring about a unity to realise the regional cooperation.

It is also observed that SAARC is different from the NAM and the UN in its size, area of operation, composition, structure and functions. But the objectives of SAARC, NAM and the UN coincide to a large extent. As such there is no incompatibility between SAARC and NAM or the UN. In its place SAARC is a welcome development in bringing about peace, cooperation, friendship and prosperity in the world at large and in South Asia in particular.

The enquiry has also sought to bring out the inherent convergent and divergent factors of the South Asian region. In the process it has also discussed the political systems, the ideological foundations and foreign policy postures of the countries of the region.

The study indicates that the South Asian States barring Maldives and to some extent Bhutan, have a common social, cultural, ethnic and historical background. India, Pakistan and Bangladesh too had a common historical background until their evolution as independent States.

Historically the Indian sub-continent boasted of a single social entity with cultural, religious, ethnic and geographical factors contributing towards this end. It does not mean, however, that the society of the sub-continent was politically, socially and culturally monolithic. But the centripetal force worked in evolving an identity of Indian sub-continent, have at the same time relegated the points of divergence to a level of insignificance.

The division in the political homogeneity of India occurred at the end of the freedom struggle. The British took political advantage in dividing the Indian nationalist movement on religious lines. Eventually this led to the emergence of the 'two-nation theory', and the ultimate division of India into two separate political entities, viz., India and Pakistan. The two States adopted divergent political, ideological and external postures. Thus there emerged two antagonistic States which have eventually become the two major States of South Asia.

The partition fall-out based on the religion-oriented 'two-nation theory' raked up controversial territorial claims and the two States entered into a conflict over the State of Kashmir. Though Kashmir become an integral part of India, Pakistan still disputes the status of Kashmir and this became a perpetual source of strain between the two States.

Bangladesh which emerged out of a chequered history also has a strong religion-based political and social system. Though India played a crucial role in liberating Bangladesh from the repressive control of West Pakistan within a short span of time she has developed antagonism towards India.

Sri Lanka geographically separated by the Indian Ocean from the Indian sub-continent developed a distinct historical background for itself. However, it has very close religious, social, cultural and ethnic affiliations with India. But the desire to come out of the shadow of the giant neighbour coupled with a religious diversity veered Sri Lanka away from the social and cultural influence of India.

Bhutan and Nepal, though have some commonalities with India in social, cultural and religious aspects, have more or less independent historical background. Maldives, an archipelago in the Indian Ocean is separated from other South Asian States by more than thousand miles. It has a very distinct historical, social, cultural, ethnic and political background.

The political systems of South Asia are more or less traditional and diverse. India adopted a secular and democratic system from the very beginning and Sri Lanka also followed a similar path except its non-secular approach. Pakistan and Bangladesh traversed a zig-zag path, witnessing experiments at democratic and elective systems as well as autocratic military regimes. As on today, both of them boast democratically and elected governments but their political systems cannot be said to have attained a fair degree of stability. Nepal in its past four decades witnessed a near absolute monarchy. However, there has been a change in its political system from monarchy to constitutional monarchy recently. Bhutan is a monarchy dominated by religion and traditional polity.

The study also indicates that the countries of South Asia are characterized by eternal internal turmoils and problems of political stability and national integration. All the States of the region have been facing this problem during the past few decades. Moreover the social, cultural, ethnic and religious affiliations of the people of the region transcending national boundaries created a crisis of mutual confidence and distrust. It is a common feature of the region that each of the States accuses its neighbour State for its internal troubles. Thus the political diversity and antagonism developed in the evolution of the major States of the region is further aggravated by the internal problems faced by the States of the region.

Another divergent factor is the religious composition of these States. While India and Nepal are predominantly Hindi States (though India is secular in its political system and social ethos), Pakistan, Bangladesh and Maldives are Islamic States with strong fundamentalist bias and Sri Lanka and Bhutan have Buddhismas their main religions. The role of religion in most of these States adds a new dimension to the mutual distrust and antagonism of the States of South Asia.

Naturally, it is found the divergent character of the political systems of the region results in a varied approach in their external relations. It also follows that their ideological postures, strategic perceptions and attitudes to the global issues are also born out by a characteristic difference.

However the South Asian States are one in their economic backwardness. All of them are predominantly agricultural (primary product) economies and heavily rely on the developed countries for their economic survival. The dependence of the South Asian States on the developed world is vindicated by the pattern of their external trade, balance of trade and payments position and their evergrowing external debt.

Further, the present study examined the Indo-centric nature of the South Asian region. Most of the States of the region over the past four decades developed an adversary relationship with India. The basis for this is partly the bilateral problems they have with India and partly it is psychological. This adverse relationship of the States of South Asia with India is characterized as Indophobia. Indophodia is a much publicized concept, generally aimed at tarnishing the image of India. In order to get to the basic realities of the concept the bilateral relations of India with each of the other South Asian States are also studied and finally an impression about the reality or otherwise of the phenomenon is presented.

India-Pakistan bilateral relations occupy the centre-stage of the South Asian relations. Pakistan, a creation of the partition of India on the basis of the two-nation theory sought to create a threat perception against India from the very beginning. Moreover, she has disputed accession of Kashmir to India and ever since made it a bone of contention between herself and India. Though Kashmir became an integral part of India, Pakistan tries to rake up the Kashmir issue time and again and even fought three wars with India on this question.

Based on religious rivalry and territorial claims Pakistan maintained adverserial relations with India throughout the past four and a half decades. The India-Pakistan relations all these years were characterized by a chilling no-war-no-peace syndrome. Both the neighbours have been engaged in an unending arms race neglecting their major problem of economic development. Each one wanted to gain a military superiority over the other. Of late the arms race has assumed new dimensions with Pakistan acquiring the nuclear capability.

Another feature of India-Pakistan bilateral relationship is the mutual accusation about the interference in each others internal affairs. Particularly Pakistan's interference in the Punjab and Kashmir crises during the part few years has been a source of irritation. Pakistan also accuses India of fanning the secessionist movements in Sind. But Pakistan's involvement in Kashmir assumed alarming proportions of late and even brought both the countries to the brink of war.

India and Sri Lanka bilateral relations witnessed some irritants in the early periods, i.e., in 1950s and 1960s over the question of repatriation of the plantation Tamils. Sri Lanka maintained distance from India during the 1960s and 1970s because of differences over ideological, strategic and political issues and because of the apprehensions about domination by India. The feeling of distrust nursed by Sri Lanka was mostly due to psychological reasons. Dispute over Kachchativu island and the demarcation of maritime boundaries also caused some irritants in their bilateral relations. They were, however, resolved in the mid-1970s during the regimes of Indira Gandhi in India and Sirimao Bandarnaike in Sri Lanka. The most serious problems between the two countries causing severe strains in their relations has been the Tamil separatist movement in the northern and eastern provinces of Sri Lanka. The problem still remained unresolved and India-Sri Lanka relations also remain in state of serious disenchantment.

India-Bangladesh relations were very cordial in the first five years after the emergence of Bangladesh as an independent State. This was mainly due to the role played by India in the liberation of Bangladesh. But the labours of love were lost soon and Bangladesh developed and maintained consistently anti-India postures during the past one and a half decades. Significantly, rise of Islam as the State religion of Bagladesh and the growth of anti-India postures went hand in hand in Bangladesh. There were however some issues like the sharing of Ganga waters, ownership of the New Moore island, Chakma refugees and the Tin Bigha corridor etc. which caused estrangement of India and Bangladesh relations.

India-Nepal relations also have been witnessing strains over the issue of trade and transit treaties between the two countries. Besides, the Nepalese resented the influence of India over the political turbulence rising time and again in Nepal. Nepal also resented the basic reality that its dependence on India was heavy and crucial to its very existence. Hence Nepal considered it necessary to reduce its dependence on India for its independence and survival. India-Nepal relations suffered severe setback during the late 1980s over the issue of trade and transit treaties and also over the Chinese arms sales to Nepal. However, India-Nepal relations improved and became quite cordial during the past few years because of the changes that have taken place in the political system of Nepal.

India-Bhutan and India-Maldives relations are quite cordial and are free from tensions. Maldives did not have any close relations with India until recently, however, it is now in a very cordial relationship with India. This is particularly so since the Indian assistance extended to Maldives in thwarting the attempted coup by some mercenaries of Sri Lankan origin. India-Bhutan relations are also marked by cordiality. Bhutan depends heavily on India for its economic survival and external relations. Recently Bhutan has been trying to diversify its external relations and also assert its identity as an independent State.

Most of the problems that caused tensions in the bilateral relations of India and her neighbours are not the making of India. They are not the main source of the much talked of Indophodia either. The major source of discord and distrust in the psychological fears that blow out the disparities in size and strength out of proportions. The problems also lie in the religionbased arch-rivalry between India and Pakistan. The tenacity shown by Pakistan in countering the pre-eminent position of India in South Asia strengthened the desire of the smaller neighbours of India to assert their identity in spite of their dependence on India. In fact the smaller States of South Asia achieved significant political (and material) gains by playing the bogey of Indian hegemonism.

India was an easy prey to the talk of Indophobia because of its giant size in relation to its neighbours and also because of her ambitious foreign policy postures. But India always tried to dispel doubts of Indian hegemony raised by her neighbours. India, in the process, had to give a lot of concessions to her smaller neighbours. India's insistence of keeping South Asia from the influence of outside powers was also construed as her desire for hegemony. In the ultimate analysis Indophobia was a convenient ruse for the smaller States of South Asia to tame their giant neighbour and wrest concessions from her. The evolution of SAARC further satisfied the quest of the smaller States of the region to gain identity and equal status with the major States of the region, India and Pakistan. Thus Indophobia turns out to be a propaganda stuff rather than a reality.

Another main theme is the influence of the major external powers, i.e., the United States, Soviet Union and China, on the intra-regional relations of South Asia and the prospects of regional cooperation. It has been attempted to analyse in historical perspective the relations between India, the core of South Asian region and her neighbours, particularly Pakistan, Nepal, Sri Lanka and Bangladesh and the way they have been affected adversely by the involvement of these major powers in this region.

The most important influence on South Asian relations and the prospects of regional cooperation in South Asia has been that of the United States of America. Considering South Asia as a strategically important region in the context of the cold-war politics at the global level the US wanted to befriend either of the major States of South Asia, India or Pakistan, to counter the spread of communism. Though initially the US was interested in India, India did not fall in line with the US thinking as she advocated the policy of non-alignment (keeping away from the super-power rivalries) from its early years of independence. US, then turned towards Pakistan which was quite enthusiastic about the idea, as it served her interest of countering the power and influence of India in South Asia. The US and Pakistan entered into formal alliance in 1955 and Pakistan joined willingly all collective security arrangements sponsored by the US. Then onwards US and Pakistan remained close allies except for small intervals of lukewarm relationship.

The US involvement in South Asia, particularly making friendship with Pakistan and offering her military assistance consistently strengthened the hostile postures of Pakistan. It has also encouraged her to resort to military adventure against India. In fact the US involvement in South Asia came at a time when India and Pakistan were trying to patch up their differences in the mid-1950s. However, this involvement eventually led to the Indo-Pak War of 1965 on the issue of Kashmir. The massive aid extended to Pakistan during the Afghan crisis triggered an alarming arms race between the two neighbours taking a severe toll of their bilateral relations as well as draining their meagre resources. Even today the US is seeking to intervene in the India-Pakistan relationship to keep alive Pakistan's aggressive designs against. India to check the growing power and influence of India. This is openly spelt out in the controversial Pentagon document.

The Soviet involvement in South Asia was more to counter the US involvement in the region. The Soviet Union could not get any patronage in South Asia except in India. Soviet Union and India became close friends only after the mid-1960s. The Soviet Union entered into a Treaty of Friendship and Cooperation with India in 1971, popularly known as the Indo-Soviet Treaty. During the war of Bangladesh liberation in 1971 the Indian subcontinent was brought to the brink of conflict between the two superpowers. This is due to commitment made by the Soviet Union in the Indo-Soviet Treaty because of which it countered the military threat posed by the US against India. The Indo-Soviet Treaty was also denounced by the neighbours of India, other than Pakistan.

The major havoc wrought by the Soviet Union in South Asia was by its military intervention in Afghanistan. It had a severe negative influence on India-Pakistan relations.

The major power which had interest in South Asia and actively involved and influenced the intra-regional relations of South Asia was China. China because of its own ambitions designs of being the only major power of Asia and its desire to curtail the growing power and prestige of India sought to befriend India's neighbours and systematically veered them away from the influence of India. The smaller neighbours of India, particularly Pakistan, Nepal, and Sri Lanka became more recalcitrant towards India with the support of China. The basic motive China had for this was the border disputes with India, apart from her power rivalries.

China entered into a close relationship with Pakistan in the early 1960s. Gradually both the countries became close allies. Their ties included political, military, technical and economic cooperation. The main convergent point between Pakistan and

China has been their animosity with India. China helped Pakistan in challenging the political and military power of India. Pakistan received military aid from China. China is also said to have helped Pakistan in achieving the nuclear capability.

China also helped Nepal in gaining a psychological strength to challenge the political power of India. Recently Chinese arms sale to Nepal caused misunderstandings between India and Nepal. China's relations with Sri Lanka since the early 1950s also came in the way of the friendly relations between Sril Lanka and India. Sri Lanka still maintains cordial relations with China.

Thus it was sought to drive home the point that the involvement of the major powers in the South Asian region invariably affected the cordial intra-regional relations. The major powers have helped in sowing the seeds of discords between India and her neighbours. This in turn marred the political atmosphere of the entire region. Regional cooperation in South Asia, in spite of the existence of the regional organization, SAARC could not make any headway, as the smaller States saw in it a forum to counter India with the political and military support of the external powers.

Finally, we have made an evaluation of the actual functioning of SAARC in the light of the divergent attitudes of the member States and various other influences. Mainly the politics of summitry were discussed taking into consideration both the reassertion of the basic principles of SAARC , the need for regional cooperation and the undercurrent of discord and the desire to score diplomatically over political adversaries. The discussions at the summits were generally confined to the non-contentious issues in strict adherence to the proscription laid down in the charter that discussion of bilateral and contentious issues should be avoided. But in informal meetings and press conferences etc. bilateral problems and contentious issues were invariably raked up. Almost at every summit the political atmosphere was vitiated by attempts made by the smaller States of the region and Pakistan to alienate and accuse India over bilateral and contentious issues. The summit diplomacy of SAARC could not help in clearing the feelings of mutual apprehensions and distrust. However, all the summits held so far have been marked by a show of pomp and pageantry. The ritualist conduct of SAARC summits at an extravagant scale reminds one of the 'Perantams'[1] in South Indian families.

It is found that the major decisions taken at various summits of SAARC Heads of States or Governments were generally confined to innocuous areas like introducing SAARC travel document, conducting of cultural festivals, observation of various calendar years to highlight certain issues of general interest etc. Whatever few important decisions were taken were normally neglected when it came to their actual implementation. The SAARC Convention on Suppression of Terrorism which was signed at Kathmandu and the Convention on Narcotic Drugs and Psychotropic Substances signed at Male still await either for meaningful implementation or even for ratification by the member States.

The Integrated Programme of Action and the areas of cooperation covered by it are also discussed in this context. It is discernible from the past record that most of the areas of cooperation covered by it are either peripheral or less important or whenever the matter is of some significance the *modus operandi* of its implementation did not touch any useful level of cooperation. Most of the activities undertaken under the IPA in various areas of cooperation were confined to seminars, conferences, workshops, meetings of experts or exchange of imformation. Decisions regarding the establishment of SAARC Documentation Centre in India and SAARC Centre for Tuberculosis in Nepal were taken quite sometime back but they have not materialized even till today.

The general impact of SAARC on the intra-regional political, social, cultural and economic relations has also been far from satisfactory. SAARC could not bring any salutary effect on the general ambience of the region. There has been further deterioration in the relations between India and the other member States of SAARC except Bhutan and Maldives. SAARC seems to have brought about a political polarization in South Asia. The recent developments indicate that India is more or less isolated in the region whereas all other States have shown more inclination to come closer as a group.

An attempt has been made to bring out the facts that the SAARC has not yet geared itself to the role it had envisaged itself in the Charter. The general principles enshrined in the Charter and reaffirmed time and again, viz., sovereign equality, territorial integrity, non-interference in internal affairs of other States and mutual benefit and the desire for promoting peace, stability, amity and progress in the region remained as pious precepts confined to pieces of paper and slogans. Basically it is found that sincerity of commitment is lacking in the members of SAARC. In spite of all this the member countries still express their faith in SAARC. Thus SAARC is in an evolutionary stage unable to come out of the dichotomy of the quest of the smaller States for their independent identity and the protection of their national interests *vis-a-vis* the general desire for achieving collective self-reliance. Thus SAARC, from a pragmatic point of view, is yet to reach the take-off stage.

The above brief summary of inquiry into various internal and external factors of intra-regional relations of South Asia and SAARC *per se* provides answers to the questions raised at the beginning of the study. Specific mention of those questions and brief answers thereto would be in order in our endeavour to articulate the findings of our study.

The first question relates to the concept of South Asia as a region and how far SAARC fits into the general framework of regionalism. It was questioned as to how far SAARC fits the framework of NAM.

Our findings do not discern any difficulties in identifying South Asia as a viable region nor is there any problem about the general framework of regionalism as far as SAARC is concerned. SAARC is quite in order as a regional organization of South Asia. In fact its need was felt for quite a long time and its actual emergence took longer time than other similar regional organizations. SAARC with its noble objectives is quite compatible with the ideals and objectives of the United Nations and the Non-Aligned Movement.

The second question was about the commitment of the members of SAARC to its avowed objectives of cooperation, peace, progress, prosperity and stability of the region.

Based on the information and evidence available it is very difficult to answer this question in affirmative. Every event that has taken place or has been taking place points to the grim reality of the operation of negative forces in this direction. The past seven years record since the evolution of SAARC does not by any standards provide reasons for complacence. During the last seven years the talk of cooperation received quite a bit of significance though as a facade, but peace, progress and stability of the region have been more elusive than ever. The events mentioned in our study and the happenings going on indicate how the mutual rivalries between the major partners of SAARC, India and Pakistan have taken serious turn endangering the peace in the sub-continent.

The third question is related to the mutual suspicions among the member States of SAARC. Especially it was asked how far Indian hegemonism in South Asia is real and how does it affect.

It is generally observed that the basic reality of the size and strength of India in relation to her neighbours gave scope for this kind of suspicions in the bilateral relations between India and her neighbours. The mutual suspicions in the bilateral relations have their roots in the social, cultural, religious, ethnic and political factors. The suspicions were rather psychological and by no means insurmountable. Once they are removed there will be closer interaction between India and her neighbours both at the State level and or at the people's level.

The talk of Indian hegemonism or Indophobia has its roots in the bilateral problems between India and her neighbours. India's ambitious foreign policy postures and her insistence of bilateralism in her dealings with her smaller neighbours is construed as hegemonic aspirations.[2] But the fact is that India is generally keen in maintaining good neighbourly relations with all her smaller neighbours. In fact India has been more interested in economic relations with her smaller neighbours. Indophobia is the imaginary problem fostered by Pakistan for obvious reasons and actively supported by the external powers, particularly the USA and China. The talk of Indophobia is in a way assertion of identity by the smaller States of South Asia. This way they were more or less successful in wresting quite a few concessions from India apart from isolating her both within the region as well as in SAARC.

It is very difficult to provide an answer to the fourth question relating to perception of the members of SAARC about their role in the organization. A dispassionate analysis of the events, policies, postures and deeds of the members of SAARC during the past seven years reveals that each of them has been more keen to promote her own political, strategic and economic self-interest than to strengthen regional cooperation. In a bid to project their problems and interests most of the time some members of SAARC have even did not bother about the possible rifts in the regional body.

The conduct of bilateral relations by most of the members since the establishment of SAARC does not indicate any desire in creating conducive atmosphere for the success of regional cooperation.[3] Even in the case of decisions taken under the purview of SAARC the lack of enthusiasm for their effective implementation explains about the sense of responsibility shown by most of the member States of SAARC.

The answer to the fifth question about the influence of outside powers on SAARC as per the analysis of the available facts points towards an affirmative. The major powers of the world, US, Soviet Union (now non-existent) and China did have a definite influence on the intra-regional relations of South Asia and *ipso-facto* on the functioning and the inner dynamics of SAARC.

US and China particularly contributed to the growing turbulence in the South Asian region during the past three or four decades. The US by entering into strategic alliance with Pakistan helped in perpetuating the India-Pakistan rivalries. The US also gave credence to the talk of Indian hegemony and Indophobia in South Asian region. China also maintained close relations with Pakistan, Sri Lanka, Nepal and Bangladesh. She played a key role in reinforcing the India-Pakistan rivalries by extending active assistance to Pakistan. China's policy in South Asia motivated by her ambitions of unrivalled leadership in Asia was mainly directed towards isolating India in South Asia. This also strengthened the anti-India postures of smaller States of South Asia.

The influence of major powers on South Asia and thereby on SAARC is likely to continue in future also. The US policy in South Asia spelt out in the Pentagon Document recently is a clear indication that its negative role in South Asia is going to continue in the coming years also. There is a lot of uncertainty about China's future policy towards South Asia but there is a reason to hope for the better in the wake of the recent positive developments in Sino-Indian relations.

The above summary of the present study and the answers derived out of it to the questions raised earlier indeed give us a comprehensive understanding of problems faced by SAARC and the reasons for its lacklustre performance. We can however filter down the whole thing and focus on the crucial problems that ultimately influence the progress of SAARC. In fact our intention in focussing the crucial problems is that it is in the resolution of these problems alone there lies the future of SAARC. In other words, the following are basic conditions necessary for the successful functioning of SAARC in future.

The Problems and Prospects of SAARC

The crucial or major problems of SAARC can be divided on the basis of the present study into three categories broadly; i.e., (i) the intra-regional politics, (ii) the external interference, and (iii) the structural problems of SAARC *per se.*

(i) *Intra-regional politics*

The problems fall within this category are:

(a) the bilateral relations between the member States,

(b) their internal problems,

(c) religious diversities,

(d) Indophobia or the general anti-Indian attitude of the South Asian States, and

(e) India-Pakistan rivalries.

These are the issues of fundamental nature governing the intra-regional relations on which the internal harmony in South Asia mainly depends. Naturally their resolution will provide a basic impetus to the success of SAARC.

It can be said that the bilateral relations among the South Asian States do not pose any insurmountable problems. Generally bilateral relations among States of this region connote relations between India and the other States of the region which are her neighbours. Except for India-Pakistan bilateral relations in all other cases, there are no real problems which defy solution. Even the India-Pakistan problems are the fall-out of partition only which are perpetuated on the basis of religious divide. As on today, the bilateral relations between India and Nepal, India and Bangladesh are showing signs of positive development.[4] India has cordial relations with Bhutan and Maldives. The irritants that exist in the Indo-Sri Lankan relations are rather psychological as they are rooted in the misconceptions and distrust than any concrete differences.

An objective and open-minded approach will clear the misunderstandings and mutual distrust in the bilateral relations among India and other South Asian States. A strong political will and a spirit of accommodation based on give and take will not only solve all the bilateral problems among these States but also will pave way for the progress of regional cooperation.

The internal problems or turmoils in various States of South Asia is a major factor in fomenting troubles in the bilateral relations of these countries. Most of the internal problems are systemic oriented and they can be solved by introducing necessary changes. The case of Nepal holds out as a striking example. Bangladesh is also on the road to stability following the changes that have taken place during the past one year. The Sri Lankan ethnic problem also could have been resolved had it been tackled in a proper perspective.

Generally autocratic, centralized and oppressive systems breed internal problems and conversely thoroughly democratic and decentralized systems will be less prone to internal instabilities. Multi-racial and multi-religious States such as the South Asian States need to introduce more participatory systems and the legitimacy of the systems should be traced to a well-established system of accountability.

Another important feature of the internal troubles is based on ethnic diversities. The ethnic differences erupting in the form of protest movements or separatist movements can be traced to the systemic weaknesses or imbalances in the process of development. However, the ethnic separatist movements once escalated breed terrorism, drug trafficking and import arms supplies from other countries.[5] These troubles foment mutual suspicions among the neighbours. This is what is happening in South Asia. The ethnic relations of these countries cutting across their boundaries are easily giving scope for mutual accusations. A collective approach to the resolution of the problems of this nature coupled with preventive measures like the Suppression of Terrorism and Drug Trafficking across the borders would be useful not only in resolving them but also in removing mutual suspicions.

South Asia, the bulk of which is the Indian sub-continent has been cradle of one civilization in which people of different religions, races and languages lived together in perfect harmony since times immemorial. Emerged as independent States in the recent past the States of the Indian sub-continent inculcated a characteristic hatred of 'Dayadulu' (Coheirs).[6] It is this hatred which gave way to the evolution of centrifugal tendencies in the region resulting in most of the smaller states looking for outside alliances. However, the people, cultures, ethnic affinities in the region and their psychological needs demand a cooperative approach to realize the goals of peace, prosperity and progress. To desire such an approach of ethnic and cultural cooperation may appear to be visionary, but it would bring a lasting peace in the region of South Asia and economic cooperation will follows as a naturally corollary.

It is clear that religious diversities play a key role in causing rifts among the South Asian States. India-Pakistan, India-Bangladesh, Pakistan-Bangladesh relations are particularly influenced by the religious factors. Even Nepal, Bhutan, Sri Lanka, Maldives are not immune to the baneful influence of religion. India is the only country in South Asia which professes and practices secular politics both internally and externally to a reasonable extent.

A change in the attitudes of the States and people towards religion and a secular approach to intra-regional relations in South Asia will go a long way in bringing the people of the region together and in improving the prospect of regional cooperation significantly. However, no dramatic change in this regard be expected from the ruling elites of various States of South Asia, atleast going by the track record of the past four decades. Yet, that is what is needed to boost up the regional cooperation in South Asia.

As the experts of foreign policy assert the linkage between domestic factors and foreign policy, any change in the intra-regional relations in South Asia on secular lines will be impossible without any changes on similar lines in domestic politics. Expecting such changes in the political systems of the region internally also appears to be a difficult dream to realise. However, it does not mean that such changes are impossible in the States of the region and in the intra-regional relations. For this, the people's involvement with a strong political will is the minimum requirement.

Another factor that has been influencing the progress of SAARC and is likely to affect its future prospects adversely is the deep-rooted suspicion among the States of South Asia against India, i.e., Indophobia. Something has to be done by all the member States of SAARC to remove this dubious phenomenon which has created a lot of bad blood in the intra-regional politics of South Asia. As the problem is centred round India, India needs to do a bit of back-bending for the sake of improved regional cooperation. In fact India has been doing it during the past few decades and the recent trends in her bilateral relations with the South Asian neighbours also indicate this attitude.[7]

On the part of the smaller States of South Asia also there should not be any reason worthwhile to harp on this much maligned aspect. The very establishment of SAARC has brought about a sovereign equality among all the States of the region irrespective of their size or strength. Hence, there is on scope for identity problem of the smaller States. Thus the smaller States of South Asia have to adjust to the reality of the core status of India in the region. Mutual trust and confidence among the smaller States on the one hand and India on the other, is the only way out of the this peculiar ailment of SAARC.

The problem of Indophobia among the States of South Asia is rather a psychological one and its remedy lies in the political will of the ruling elites of these States. Indophobia has been a convenient scapegoat for the problems of instability and domestic crises of the smaller States. It in fact is a part of the political culture and the problem of legitimacy of the government in these States. Thus some sort of democratic systems with a fair degree of accountability will be useful in removing the ubiquitous big-brother accusation by the smaller States of South Asia.

Thus Indophobia is not only a problem of wide disparities, in sizes and strengths of India and her neighbours, nor is it a mere manifestation of the quests for international exposure and identity but it is a problem of the basic nature of the political systems of the region. As long as the internal problems of the smaller States based on religious, social, ethnic, linguistic and cultural diversities remain unresolved through democratic means the political leadership in these States will always find India as an easy scapegoat.

The final solution to this malady affecting the future prospects of SAARC lies, therefore, in the political transformation of the States of South Asia from archaic autocratic systems to responsible democratic systems not only in letter but in spirit too.

The prospects in the near future for the SAARC on this point are neither too bleak nor too bright. Certainly South Asian States have been experiencing a lot of turmoils and changes in the recent past. One may expect that things might change for better in the region and particularly for the regional cooperation.

India-Pakistan Relations

As has often been mentioned by scholars and politicians alike the Indo-Pak ties are pivotal to the future success of SAARC. The future of SAARC is thus directly related to the future of the Indo-Pak relations. Any improvement in this regard will be advantageous to SAARC and any deterioration will affect it adversely.

The Indo-Pak relations, as has been mentioned in one of the previous chapters, is characterized by a '"no-war-no-peace syndrome" . Several times in the past hopes were raised about possible cessation of rivalries ushering in an era of peace, cooperation and development. But every time invariably the hopes were belied.

The recent happenings in Islamabad[8] and Karachi in which the Indian diplomats were subjected to torture and harassment by Pakistani authorities are ominous of the future prospects of Indo-Pak relations.

While India seems to have shown keen interest in bringing about harmony in Indo-Pak relations, Pakistan has been consistently trying to vitiate the chances of rapprochement.[9] Pakistan continues to harp on the Kashmir issue and makes it a basic precondition for the Indo-Pak normalization, while India considers Kashmir as an integral part of India and the issue is closed.

The fact that in spite of the signing and ratification of SAARC convention on Suppression of Terrorism by all the members of the SAARC including India and Pakistan, there have been continuous complaints about Pakistan's interference in Kashmir and of late alleged India's interference in Sind, speaks of the grim prospects of the future Indo-Pak relations. It certainly portends grim prospects for regional cooperation under SAARC.

The past and present pattern of Indo-Pak relations do not indicate any dramatic improvement in the near future. However, one can hope that saner counsel will prevail in the ruling elites of both the States, especially in Pakistan so that a permanent peace could dawn on the Indian sub-continent heralding a bright future of economic prosperity and social and cultural harmony.

The External Interference

As has been brought out in out study in an earlier Chapter· the role of major powers in affecting the regional cooperation in South Asia either positively or negatively is quite significant. With the dissolution and disintegration of the USSR, the major powers that are likely to affect the South Asian relations are only the US. and China. The success of SAARC, therefore, depends on the future policies of these two major powers towards South Asia.

The major powers are likely to show keen interest in South Asia in future also both for power, political and economic compulsions. But the countries of South Asia if they are interested in making SAARC a success have to keep themselves away from the influence of both the US and China. Already the US has made its intentions about the New World Order clear and it certainly does not hold any bright prospects for South Asia if India and Pakistan, particularly Pakistan continue the same external postures.

The need of the hour in South Asia is to make SAARC a model of South-South Cooperation so that the South Asian States achieve collective economic self-reliance and progress. It may be suggested that their relations with the developed countries and particularly with the US and China may be readjusted to suit this objective. We may also suggest a delinking of South Asia from the global system. That is, the States of South Asia by reducing their dependence on the major powers for military and economic aid could attain some sort of autonomy from the dominant international system. However, the States of South Asia can continue their trade with the developed countries but not at the political and economic cost of regional cooperation. More emphasis on South-South Cooperation will be more helpful for promoting regional cooperation in South Asia.

Structural Changes in SAARC

The decision-making process of SAARC has been a matter of controversy. It has been so formulated by the founders of the SAARC only to avoid political problems within the newly evolved organization. Now with the SAARC having completed seven years of its existence and completed the first round of annual summits hosted almost by all the member States (with only Bhutan expressing its inability to hold a summit at present) there is a need for review of SAARC's institutional mechanism and its performance and decision-making process.

The exclusion of contentious and bilateral issues from the purview of the SAARC deliberations has not only made it a non-starter but also brought in a situation of a *status-quo* in the conflict-ridden relations among the South Asian States. The members of SAARC may now think in terms of extending its area of operation to all issues and activities including those issues which may prove to be contentious. But SAARC should consider introducing a mechanism of checks and balances within its system to avoid misunderstandings and controversies. Differences may surface from time to time but escaping from the reality is not going to help in strengthening regional cooperation. In fact it is naive to expect SAARC to achieve regional cooperation, peace and properity in South Asia without trying to remove the bilateral differences among the member States. In this connection it may be worthwhile to establish a regional conciliation committee or arbitration mechanism *a la* the OAU[10] to sort out the bilateral problems among the member countries.

The unanimity principle in decision-making is also going to cause irritants in the regional organization in future. This may be substituted with a requirement of definite quota of votes in favour and the right of negative vote (Veto) may also be given to all members. This will ensure a check on hasty and controversial decisions, at the same time making it possible to take quick decisions whenever needed.

Conclusion

In the light of our study the above mentioned conditions, measures and changes in SAARC and its political environment will go a long way in strengthening peace, prosperity and harmony in South Asia.

It is a fact that SAARC is a right step in this direction. The very survival and existence of SAARC during the past few turbulent years in South Asia is itself a positive indication. But it is also a fact that SAARC remained only a white elephant and its achievements were rather insignificant and pale in comparison to its lofty objectives. SAARC has been used only as a platform to promote the identity of the smaller States of the region and also as a counter balance to the growing power and prestige of India. Parochialism, mutual suspicions and mere anti-India propaganda did hinder the progress of SAARC during past years. The member States of SAARC need a political will to promote SAARC as a true vehicle of regional cooperation in which their own economic and social progress is also involved.

In the end, it can be said that only political will and commitment to peace and progress on the part of the member States is the ultimate way for the future success of SAARC. Several studies have pointed out that there is ample scope for regional cooperation in all fields especially in the field of trade, commerce and industry. In fact voluntary organizations like the Marga Institute of Colombo and the Indian Council for South Asian Cooperation in New Delhi have been doing pioneering work to identify the areas of possible collaboration and to promote regional cooperation by undertaking and publishing studies in this area. Now it is only left to the political sagacity of the member States to make regional cooperation a reality. To put it allegorically, like individuals living in a society, States also have to compromise their differences and adopt a spirit of give and take. This is basic dictum to be followed by the States of South Asia to realize the objectives of peace, prosperity and progress through SAARC.

References

1. *Perantam* is the name given to functions in Hindu families of Andhra Pradesh where the relatives and friends of the organizer get together over a lunch or dinner. Both the organizer of the 'perantam' and the guests try to establish their identity at the function: the organizer to score a point by the show of pomp and the guests by showing their good neighbourliness in honouring the invitation. The internal discords are generally hidden but still politicking goes on. When the gathering is dispersed everybody evaluates the function in terms of his own interests. This is exclusively a celebration of womanfolks consisting of housewives, widows are not generally given any part in the celebration.

2. Leo E. Rose, 'India's Regional Policy: Non-military Dimensions', in Stephen P. Cohen, *The Security of South Asia* (Vistear, New Delhi, 1987), p.4.

3. The former Secretary, General of SAARC, K.K. Bhargava indirectly says that there is a lack of commitment and SAARC spirit in the member states and their foreign policies. K.K.Bhargava, 'SAARC at Male: Retrospect and Prospect', *South Asia Journal* Vol. 4, No.3, Jan-March 1991, p. 267.

4. The recent visit of Begum Khaleda Zia, Prime Minister of Bangladesh heralds a brighter future in bilateral relations of India and Bangladesh. Though most of the bilateral problems remain to be solved but the decks are cleared to resolve them in the near future.

5. Urmila Phadnis, 'Ethnic Dynamics in South Asian States' , *South Asia Journal*, Vol.3, No. 3, Jan-March 1990, p. 272.

6. 'Dayadulu' is a Telugu term used to denote coheirs in perpetual struggle for the distribution of ancestral property among themselves. In the process each one of them alienates himself from each other only to go into the fold of outsiders seeking help with a view to secure more than his due. The rivalry gets rooted into their minds and it gradually becomes a perpetual phenomenon.

7. Particularly India spared no efforts in improving her relations with Nepal, Bangladesh and Sri Lanka. The agreement reached between India and Nepal on trade and transit issues and the agreement signed between India and Bangladesh on the transfer of Tin Bhigha to Bangladesh on a perpetual lease is a pointer in this case.

8. The abduction and torture of Rajesh Mittal a Senior Diplomat in Indian Embassy in Islamabad in May, 1992 has not only hurt the sentiments of the Indian people but also jeopardised the on-going process of Indo-Pak negotiations for normalization of relations.

9. The Prime Minister of India, P.V. Narasimha Rao in a press conference on 30th June, 1992 lamented that 'Pakistan's response to India's efforts to improve Indo-Pak relations continues to be disappointing'. *Indian Express*, 1st July 1992.

10. Anirudha Gupta, ' SAARC and regional cooperative', *Mainstream*, 21 March 1992, p.15.

CHAPTER VIII

POSTSCRIPT

The events that occurred in the Indian subcontinent during the past few months are too important to be ignored. They have not only affected India and her neighbours but also had a serious impact on the very structure and survival of SAARC. The year 1992 witnessed some of the most unexpected and horrendous developments both in the politics of South Asia as well as in the realm of international relations. While the most unexpected and shocking event has been the demolition of Babri Masjid at Ayodhya, the failure of the Gulf war hero George Bush in securing re-election as President of the USA and the surprise election of Bill Clinton in his place, the political turmoils in Pakistan, the heinous assassination of President Premadasa and his political rival Lalith Athulathmudali that have jolted the politics of Sri Lanka, the blatant reassertion of the US as the international bully, the controversy over the NPT, the problems over the cryogenic rocket deal between India and Russia, the turbulence in the domestic politics of Nepal and Bangladesh and of course the successful conclusion of Dhaka Summit (of SAARC of Heads of state and government) though after two postponements are some of the important happenings that deserve a special mention. Each one of the above incidents has exerted a definite influence on the political equations in the South Asian region and *ipso facto* has affected the prospects of regional cooperation under SAARC.

The most shocking incident whose consequences proved to be far-reaching was the demolition of Babri-Masjid at the Ramjanambhoomi-Babri Masjid complex in Ayodhya on 6 December, 1992 by Hindu fundamentalist elements. It was so unexpected that the whole country was caught unawares and alarming consequences followed it. It was unexpected to take place, of all places, in India. It has stirred violently the communal chords in the entire country and at the same time seriously questioned the secular credentials of India.

Why and how did it happen and who were responsible for it is a complex and debatable question. But its very occurrence severely jolted the political and social fabric of not only India but the entire region of South Asia. The latent problem of religious divergence among the major countries of the region has suddenly came to the fore and brought forth a communal divide in the region. Not unexpectedly, the Pakistani and Bangladeshi official response was highly critical of the incident and the Indian Government. This in turn raked up the communal sentiments of the people in those countries. It has, thus, led to a violent and massive vandalist backlash against the Hindus and their religious places in Pakistan and Bangladesh. Several thousands of big and small temples were allegedly destroyed in those countries by communal vandals.

For the first time in the history of South Asia, religion has proved itself as a sensitive and divisive factor with the potential of creating socio-political strains in the entire region. Suddenly there was a new tension in the relations between India and her neighbours, particularly Pakistan and Bangladesh. The anti-Indian hawks in those countries got a golden opportunity to cry hoarse that Muslims in India were insecure.

The incident, however, did not result in any strains between India and Maldives (which is also an Islamic country) and understandably between India and Nepal or Bhutan or Sri Lanka. In fact, the Sri Lankan, Nepali or Maldivian or Bhutanese leadership has shown a remarkable equanimity and restraint. There were no communal backlashes in those countries.

The Ayodhya incident, has, however, had its impact on the activities of SAARC. Naturally the 7th Summit of the Heads of

State and Government of SAARC countries, which was to take place in the same month at Dhaka was postponed to January 1993. But because of the recurrence of the riots in some parts of India and the backlashes that took place in Bangladesh, the host country, the Summit had to be postponed indefinitely. The Summit was, eventually, held in April 1993.

Another incident which jolted Indian socio-political fabric and which has caused severe strains in Indo-Pak relations was the series of bomb blasts that occurred in Bombay on 12 March 1993 resulting in the loss of many lives and hundred of crores of rupees worth of property. The investigations into the Bombay blasts have resulted in evidence which pointed towards the role of Pakistani intelligence agency, ISI. Obviously, this resulted in severe strains in the relations of India and Pakistan.

India and Her Neighbours

Indo-Pak relations, one of the areas which has a considerable bearing on the successful functioning of regional cooperation, have not shown any improvement, rather there were quite a few moments of serious strains leading to further deterioration.

Already on the issues of Jammu and Kashmir and Punjab movements Pakistan's continued involvement caused serious concern to India. Particularly over the issue of Jammu and Kashmir, Pakistan has been trying to precipitate matters. There has been no let up in the abetment of insurgent activity. On the other hand, Pakistan has also been trying to rake up the issue in international circles. At the OIC meetings, at the UN, at the Non-Aligned meetings at Jakarta and during the International Human Rights Conference at Vienna, Pakistan left no stone unturned to rake up the issue.

The most opportune moment for Pakistan to carry on its propaganda-war against India was the demolition of the Babri Masjid. The incident has drawn a spontaneous response from the Pakistani government. There were widespread riots in Pakistan against minorities, particularly the Hindus. The Indian establishments there were particularly targetted in the riots which had an implicit section of the Government. The Government itself in a latent move, which is tantamount to interference in the internal affairs of India, sponsored a nationwide strike on 9 December 1992 to condemn the happenings at Ayodhya. Pakistan, further, took the opportunity to mobilize support against India among the Gulf and other islamic countries. Interestingly, while Pakistan's attempts to mobilize to GCC to condemn the incident was a partial success, the reaction of the Islamic countries of the Gulf, North Africa and South East Asia was more or less balanced and restrained. However, for sometime, it was a good alibi for the Pak rulers to divert the public attention from the domestic problems.

The strains in the bilateral relations between the two major powers of South Asia did not subside in the aftermath of the Ayodhya incidents, new problems have cropped up again and again and the tempo of deteriorating relations has been kept up, particularly with the overt and covert initiatives taken by Pakistan. The first salvo in the series of retributive acts was fired by Pakistan by asking India to curtail the staff strength at the Indian Consulate in Karachi. India, after trying unsuccessfully to reason with the Pakistan Government, took retaliatory measure ordering curtailment of Pakistani staff strength in their Bombay Consulate. The mutual apprehensions and tensions kept on making the diplomats the victims of reprisals on both sides. The last of the series is the expelling of a Pakistani diplomat from New Delhi as he was allegedly caught red-handed while engaging in an act of espionage, to which Pakistan declared another Indian embassy staff member as *persona non grata* without mentioning any specific reason.

The most important reason that has caused severe strains in Indo-Pak relations was the involvement of Pakistan in the bomb blasts which occurred in Bombay's key business centres in March 1993. It has been found by the investigating agencies that the whole episode was planned and executed by Pakistan's ISI with the help of some underworld elements of Bombay. The alleged culprits in the said incidents, the Memon brothers, escaped to Pakistan and have gone underground with the undeclared protection given by the Pakistani Government. India lodged serious protests with the Pakistani authorities and demanded to hand over the accused persons, who were taking shelter in Pakistan, to India. Pakistan refused to concede the Indian demand and continued to evade the issue while the culprits remained untraced.

The issue figured at the bilateral talks held between the Prime Ministers of India and Pakistan at Dhaka during the 7th SAARC Summit. The issue remains unresolved even now.

The tensions and continuing notes of discord in Indo-Pak relations not only vitiated the atmosphere of peace, goodwill and friendship in South Asia, thus hindering the prospects of regional cooperation in general, but have also placed hurdles in the progress of the SAARC activities. The case in point is the reservations expressed by Pakistan over the South Asia Preferential Trade Agreement (SAPTA) at the Dhaka Summit.

There is not much change in India's relations with the other South Asian Countries, at the same time there is no cause for worry. India's relations with Bhutan and Maldives continued to be cordial. The Indo-Napalese relations have improved considerably after the visit of the Prime Minister G.P. Koirala of Nepal. But the political turmoil that has started in the post-democratic revolution in Nepal have been taking anti-India overtones. However, at the official level, India-Nepal still maintain cordial and friendly relations and if there are no changes at the political level in Nepal, there is scope for continued cordiality if not further improvement in the relations of both states.

Indo-Bangladesh relations which have received a morale booster after the visit of Begum Khaleda Zia, Prime Minister of Bangladesh, have taken a downward turn in the aftermath of the Ayodhya incident. There were widespread violent reactions in Bangladesh against the Ayodhya happenings and the official reaction was also highly critical of the incident as well as the Government of India. The problems that have come up in implementing the agreement signed by the two countries on the return of Chakmas has also been a cause of worry. However, there is no reason to believe that there will be further deterioration in Indo-Bangla relations in the coming days.

Similarly, Indo-Sri Lankan ties have been stabilized on a cordial footing. The banning of the LTTE by the Government of India has been one of the important measures in removing the irritants between the two neighbours. Economically both the states have been following a liberalization programme and they have been trying to improve mutual economic cooperation. The tragic assassination of President Premadasa on 1 May 1993 has touched the sentimental chords in the Indo-Sri Lankan relations (India also faced a similar predicament when former Prime Minister Rajiv Gandhi was assassinated in May, the previous year). The changes that have taken place in the post-Premadasa period in Sri Lanka have not affected the cordial relations between the two countries. On the other hand, there is every reason to believe that there will be much more meaningful cooperation between the two countries both at the political and economic levels. The way the combination of President D.B. Wijetunga and Prime Minister Rani Wickramasinghe have been conducting their foreign affairs the above expressed optimism seems to be vindicated.

Dhaka Revisited

Following the precedent of the Colombo Summit the Seventh Summit of the SAARC Heads of State and Government has also undergone two postponements before actually taking place at Dhaka in April 1993. Postponement of the Summit originally scheduled to be held in December 1992 due to the Ayodhya happenings has brought to the fore the vulnerability of SAARC members, particularly Pakistan and Bangladesh, to the influence and sentiments of religion. The sharp and emotional reactions of the Government of Bangladesh and the Statements made by its leaders and official spokesmen in and out of Parliament have not only caused uncertainty about the holding of the SAARC Summit but also created tensions in the Indo-Bangladesh relations. Sri Lanka, Nepal, Bhutan and Maldives, however, have exercised considerable restraint in their reaction to the incident. Nevertheless the tentions at the venue of the summit, Dhaka, have necessitated the postponement initially by one month and subsequently for four months. In fact, the sustained efforts made by the Islamic fundamentalist groups in Bangladesh have caused anxiety to the organisers and the participants of the Summit till the last moment. Attempts were actually made by some of those elements to prevent the Indian Prime Minister P.V. Narsimha Rao from attending the Summit, which were, however, thwarted. Thus, the run up to the Dhaka Summit on 11 and 12 April 1993 was turbulent and there were many moments of uncertainty, tension and anxiety. At last, after passing another calendar year without a Summit, SAARC witnessed the seven Heads of State or Government come together for the seventh time to give another push to the cause of regional cooperation.

The Dhaka Summit had many important issues before it to consider and decide upon. The South Asia Development Fund, the containment of terrorism in the region, Child Welfare Programme and the much publicised proposals for the signing of the South Asian Preferential Trade Agreement (SAPTA) which was supposed to provide an economic content to the activities of SAARC for the first time. On the Poverty Alleviation Programme, the report of the Poverty Alleviation Commission, set up at the Colombo Summit, was ready for the consideration of the Summiteers. The report pointed out that between 30 and 40 per cent of the total population of the 1.1 billion of South Asia was below the poverty line.

The Summit, convened under the shadow of the bilateral tensions, did not initially evoke much expectations. However, as the date of the Summit approached most of the member States exuded confidence and enthusiasm. The exception, however, was Pakistan, which did not show much interest in the main issues under focus at the summit.

The leaders who have participated in the Summit have reiterated the importance of SAARC and emphasised the need for increased cooperation among the members in an atmosphere of peace, friendship and goodwill. There seemed to be complacence about the past achievements of the organization. The Indian Prime Minister P.V. Narasimha Rao and the Sri Lankan President R. Premadasa, however, have sounded more realistic and stressed the need for more serious involvement. Mr. Rao said, "Introspection leads me to conclude that the content and cooperation within the region has been slower than what we wanted for".[1] President Premadasa was rather more forth-right in saying, "what is the point of just makig lovely speeches and going away? Let us mean what we say and let us work to get results, let us not bring forth our differences so that regional development suffers".[2] The host Prime Minister Begum Khaleda Zia renewed the call for unity as the new Chairperson of SAARC. She said,"we should not allow any gap in bilateral relations to come in the way of cooperation, we are meeting at a vital time in world history and let us all push forward the cooperative arrangement we have. We should not be deterred, we should move ahead."[3]

However, amidst the desire for renewed efforts to forge unity and promote goodwill and cooperation, bitterness also crept in when Pakistan's Prime Minister Nawaz Sharif made a reference to Kashmir and his country's differences with India without naming them. He also made sharp references to the Babri Masjid incident terming it as "menace of religious fanaticism and intolerance."[4]

It was left to Premadasa, the outgoing Chairman and President of Sri Lanka, to discard the prepared speech and appeal to the members saying "Let us not discuss bilateral issues here and let not bilateral problems inhibit regional cooperation. Let us achieve something and take a message back to our people. Let the world not think we cannot even agree on development".[5] The same opinion was expressed by the Indian Prime Minister Rao and the Bangladesh Prime Minister Begum Khaleda Zia. The shadow of bilateral tensions between India and Pakistan, India and Bangladesh and Nepal and Bhutan has definitely made the comment of Nawaz Sharif, Prime Minister of Pakistan, more or less realistic when he said, "so long as bilateral problems persisted among member states, it would be difficult for SAARC to realise its full potential."

The Summit has dealt with all the major issues placed before it and arrived at some important decisions. The Heads of State and Government have accepted the report of the Poverty Alleviation Commission and pledged to stamp out poverty in the region by the year 2002. They have committed themselves to the eradication of poverty by implementing pro-poor development strategies at the micro and macro levels. An agenda of Action has been taken up which spelt out the strategy on various issues related to poverty alleviation and to evolve a policy to support it with adequate financial resources. The SAARC leaders also realized the link between the national efforts and external factors for the success of the poverty alleviation programmes and hence they urged all major actors on the world economic scene to create an atmosphere supportive of the poverty alleviation programmes of South Asia.[6] The Dhaka Declaration mentioned about the national level pro-poor plans to be prepared by each one of the members.

The recommendation of the South Asian Development Fund, set up at the Colombo Summit, were accepted by the Summit and it was decided to set up an Inter-Governmental Group (IGG) of SADF on an ad-hoc basis.[7] The Dhaka Summit also endorsed the Colombo resolution on Child Welfare and urged the member states to implement programmes appropriate in the national context. The Dhaka declaration expressed particular concern for the problem of terrorism and its adverse consequences. It was also reminded that some of the members have yet to take enabling measures to give effect to the SAARC Convention on Suppression of Terrorism. In fact, till today Pakistan and Bangladesh have yet to pass appropriate measures regarding the implementation of both the SAARC Convention on Suppression of Terrorism and Convention on Prevention of Traficking in Narcotics and Psychopathic Drugs. This indicates the seriousness of commitment time and again reiterated by the SAARC members in regional cooperation. It is also ominous of the fate of the new measures being approved and to be approved by the SAARC.

Signing of the South Asian Preferential Trade Agreement (SAPTA) by the SAARC Foreign Ministers is by far the most significant achievement of the Dhaka SAARC Summit 1993. The finalization of the draft and signing of the agreement was not altogether a smooth affair. It involved a lot of diplomatic activity and also the pragmatism of the member states. Pakistan has been less enthusiastic about the idea right from the beginning and has tried to express reservations at various levels and on various occasions. Even during the preparatory meetings on the eve of and during the Summit its approach was sceptic and lukewarm. It seems the unanimous approval by all other members with a lot of enthusiasm has prompted Pakistan to toe the majority line in finally signing the agreement. Still Pakistan wanted to dilute the plan of even the product-to-product agreement. It sought to extend the scope of Article 11 of the draft agreement which related to non-application of the provisions of the agreement particularly to situations where preference has already been granted to other states outside the framework of this agreement and to third countries under bilateral, multilateral agreements.[8] Considering the trends of trade relations Pakistan had with India during the past two decades (despite being partners in Asian Currency Union

Pakistan's trade with India has been dwindling constantly)[9] its main intention was to exclude the trade concessions to India. However, the fact the SAPTA was signed at Dhaka was itself a major step forward in furthering regional cooperation in South Asia. In fact the SAARC members have tried to follow the line of other regional organization like the EC, ASEAN, NAFTA, etc.

The sense of pragmatism and vision shown by SAARC leaders in signing the SAPTA has received all round appreciation throughout the region. However, while an umbrella agreement was signed which provided that the "liberalization of trade should be done in such a manner that all countries in the region could share the benefits of trade expansion equally", there was no unanimity on the time limit for making the SAPTA operational. In the absence of a clear-cut time frame it is likely that the completion of the schedules at bilateral and at the regional level may take more time and the actual launching of the preferential trade might be pushed further indefinitely.

The Dhaka Summit also witnessed some sort of friction between India and Pakistan. The usual bilateral meeting between the two Prime Ministers was not scheduled at all. But after some pursuation from other leaders of SAARC both the leaders agreed to meet briefly. However, the meeting lasted only a few minutes where the Indian Prime Minister said to have insisted that there won't be any dialogue between the two countries unless and until the Bombay blasts' case suspects were not handed over to India. Thus the gloom of the Indo-Pak tensions also left its mark at Dhaka.

Unipolar World and South Asia

The Clinton Administration in the US has picked the threads from where the previous Bush administration left while dealing with its foreign policy. The self-styled role of global policeman so blatantly assumed by the US has dispelled all doubts about the newly emerged unipolar system. The arrogance and impunity with which the US sought to exercise control over the global politics left no hopes of the democratization of the international politics and the United Nations. Thus the chances of improved North-South relations and of liberalization of international trade and finance have also become remote. It therefore becomes more imperative for the developing countries to increase cooperation among themselves and try to achieve collective self-reliance. Thus, the need for regional cooperation also increases in this context.

It is, however, more relevant here to examine the implications for South Asia of the newly emerged unipolar world. How does the US, the only superpower of the world look at the politics of South Asia? How far does it contribute to the cessation of hostilities among the major states of the region?

The attitude of the Americans towards South Asia did not seem to have undergone any major change, despite the drastic changes that have occurred in the international system. Obviously the US administration has been trying to keep its traditional support to Pakistan in tact at the same time trying to coax India into toeing its line on the question of nuclear non-proliferation. The issue that has been receiving the upper-most consideration by the US, is making India, some-way-or-other, accept the NPT or some other regional arrangement similar to it. India's persistant denial to enter into any such arrangement and her more vocal reactions to the international economic issues like the Dunkel proposals, etc. have hardened the attitude of the US. Still the US in her self-styled role of the peace-keeper of the world and the leader of the free-world made every effort to allay the fears of India. The ambivalent posture, however, did not help her in any way in convincing India. The US attitude did not help in improving the intra-regional relations of South Asia.

However, the United States has been showing some realistic approach towards India and the Indo-Pak relations. While India's liberalized economic policies found favour with it, the US has been more forthcoming in entering into some meaningful cooperation with India. The joint naval exercises conducted by India and US recently are an evidence of this trend. This does not mean that the US has any intention of entering into any strategic relationship with India on a large scale. In fact, it was made clear by Mr. Mallott during his visit to India and Pakistan during May 1993.[10] American interest in South Asian region remained mainly on containing proliferation of nuclear weapons. The Clinton administration's policy envisaged the signing of NPT by India and Pakistan as a long-term goal, while its immediate efforts were to "cap and then over time reduce and finally eliminate possession of mass destruction weapons and their means of delivery".[11] Consistent with this policy, the recent ban imposed by the US on ISRO of India and the Glavkosmos of Russia regarding the supply of cryogenic rocket engines and its technology to India.

India maintained that she needed the cryogenic engines for the development of GSLV to launch its INSAT II communication satellites. The ISRO Chairman Prof. U.R. Rao during his visit to Washington has categorically stated that the cryogenic technology sought to be acquired by India did not have any military implications. The Russians too have resented the American action. Perhaps to show that its policy is even-handed the US administration has imposed sanctions against and Pakistan also (against China for supplying M-11 missiles in violation of the MTCR guidelines and against Pakistan for importing them). All this, does not, however, absolve the US of double standards, as it is the major exporter of arms to the Third World. The sanctions imposed on China and Pakistan in connection with the transfer of M-11 missiles served the dual purpose of sending signals to India about its balanced approach as well as warning to China not to take the US for granted particularly in maintaining its monopolistic control over South Asia.

Coming to the Kashmir issue, the Clinton administration's stand does not indicate any major shift from the previous administration's policy. The emphasis on the Shimla Agreement as the basis of a solution, the stand on the plebiscite and the concern for the alleged human rights violations in Kashmir remain the same. But the language and the accent has undergone a perceptible change. Washington seems to have assumed the role of an honest broker in finding a peaceful solution to the Kashmir issue, only with the consent of both India and Pakistan. In this regard, it has not created any favourable impression on India. However, the US has been consistently trying to pressure India and Pakistan to enter into a dialogue. In the same vein it has time and again exerted pressure on Pakistan to contain sponsoring of terrorism against India. Though it is intended to mollify the sentiments of India, the US action of asking Pakistan not to encourage terrorism in Kashmir, is a realisation of the fact that it is also likely to hurt its own national interests.

The Indian diplomacy tried to capitalize on the seemingly realistic US perceptions on South Asia and sought to pursuade the US to place Pakistan on the list of states sponsoring terrorism. However, India's persistent efforts did not succeed. The evidence shown by India of Pakistan's involvement in the Bombay blasts of 12 March, 1993 has not convinced the Americans. Obviously, the interests of the US are involved only when an American is killed or its own economic interests are jeopardised or its close allies are affected. Naturally, the US decision not to put Pakistan on the list of terrorist states has caused a serious disappointment in India and has given a morale booster to the Pakistan's government.

The American postures towards the intra-regional politics of South Asia in general and the India-Pakistan dispute over Kashmir in particular have been more of a vindication of its intentions as the sole superpower in the newly emerged unipolar world. The American dominated new international system is ordained only to serve its own economic, military, strategic and political interests as an unchallenged power rather than to seek peace and development in the Third World. With the challenge posed by the developed countries of the Western Europe and Japan on the economic front and the possible competition from countries like India in the fields of trade and science and technology, the US is likely to assume more aggressive postures in the coming years. The collapse of the Soviet Union, the taking of an economically battered and politically chaotic Russia, the softened attitude of China and debt-burdened countries of the South have created a conducive political ambience for the hegemonic ambitions of America.

The way US could successfully force Russia to renege on its agreement with India on the supply of cryogenic rocket engines and the related technology and the manner in which Russia buckled under the pressure is an indication of the unrivalled political supremacy of the US over the international system. Similarly, the sanctions imposed on the Chinese firms for supplying M-11 missiles to Pakistan also shows the assertion of American domination. The monopolistic control and leverage enjoyed by the US is further indicated by the efforts made by India and Pakistan to draw the American support against each other.

It is obvious that the interests of the South Asian states on the resolution of their mutual problems do not appeal to the US as long as it does not affect its own national interests. Thus the change in the international power structure from the previous bipolar system to the present American dominated system did not in any way alter the future prospects of South Asia.

In present politico-economic and strategic ambience the states of South Asia, in their over-enthusiasm to reap the benefits of open-door economic policies, are more likely to fall in line with America rather than entering into a mutually beneficial economic and political relationship and promote regional cooperation. Hence, the rhetoric of regional cooperation in South Asia needs than lip-sympathy, which most of the states of the region give generously, to become a reality.

References

1. April 11, 1993, *The Hindu*.
2. Kalyan Chaudhuri, "Summit at Last - in the shadow of bilateral tensions", *Frontline*, May 7, 1993, p. 37.
3. *Ibid.*
4. April 11, 1993, *The Hindu*.
5. *Frontline, op. cit.*, n.2, p. 39.
6. *Ibid.*
7. April 13, 1993, *The Hindu*.
8. April 12, 1993, *The Hindu*.
9. See Chapter VI, *Supra.*
10. Frontline, June 18, 1993, pp. 41-42.
11. *Ibid.*, p. 41.

SELECT BIBLIOGRAPHY

DOCUMENTS:

Treaty of Friendship between India and Bhutan, 8 August, 1949.

Treaty of Friendship between India and Nepal, 31 July, 1950.

Treaty of Peace, Friendship and Cooperation between India and USSR, 9 August 1871.

Treaty of Friendship, Cooperation and Peace between India and Bangladesh, 19 March 1972.

Agreement on Bilateral Relations between India and Pakistan (Simla Agreement), 3 July, 1972.

India-Sri Lanka Agreement on the Tamil Ethnic Problem, 29 July 1987.

Joint Communique of the First Meeting of Foreign Secretaries of South Asian Countries, Colombo, 21-23 August 1981.

Report of the Committee of the Whole, Colombo, 31 August 2 September 1981.

Joint Communique of the Third Meeting of Foreign Secretaries of South Asian Countries, Islamabad, 7-9 August 1982.

Joint Communique of the Fourth Meeting of Foreign Secretaries of South Asian Countries, Dhaka, 28-30 March 1983.

SARC Declaration, 2 August 1983.

Report of the Standing Committee, First Session, New Delhi, 27- 29 February 1984.

Report of the Standing Committee, Second Session, Male, 7-8 July 1984.

Speech of Mrs. Indira Gandhi, Prime Minister of India at New Delhi inaugurating the First Meeting of Foreign Ministers, 1 August 1983.

Speech delivered by Mr. P.V. Narasimha Rao at the First Session of SARC Standing Committee, New Delhi, 27 February 1984.

Joint Communique, First Meeting of Foreign Ministers, 1-2 August 1983.

Charter of the SAARC, Adopted at Dhaka, 8 December 1985.

SAARC Summit Declaration, Dhaka, 8 December 1985.

Declaration adopted at the Second Summit of the Heads of State, Government, of SAARC, Bangalore, 17 November, 1986 (Bangalore Declaration).

Joint Communique issues at the end of the Fourth Summit of SAARC Heads of States/Government, Islamabad, 30 December 1988.

Declaration adopted at the end of the First Meeting of the Heads of States/Government, Male, 23 November 1990.

Report by the Secretary-General (SAARC) on the activities of the Association and the Secretariat, November 1990.

India-Nepal Joint Communique issued at the end of the visit of Nepal's Prime Minister Mr. K.P. Bhattarai to India, New Delhi, 10 June 1990.

American Foreign Policy Documents, Department of State, Government of United States of America, 1987.

BOOKS:

A. Appadorai and M.S. Rajan *(India's Foreign Policy)* South Asia Publications, New Delhi, 1988).

A.G. Noorani, *India and Superpowers and the Neighbour's Essays in Foreign Policy* (South Asia Publications New Delhi, 1985).

Amitava Mukherjee, *India's Policy Towards Pakistan,* Allied, New Delhi, 1983).

A.G. Noorani, *Aspects of India's Foreign Policy*, (Jaico, Bombay, 1969).

Asghar Ali Engineer, *Ethnic Conflicts in South Asia* (Sage, New Delhi, 1988).

Atiur Rahman, *Political Economy of SARC* Sterling, New Delhi, 1986).

Baljit Singh, *Indian Foreign Policy: An Analysis*, (Asia Publishers Bombay, 1975).

Barry Buzan, Gowher Rizvi *et al.*, *South Asia Insecurity and Great Powers*. (MacMillan, London, 1987).

Benazir Bhutto, *Daughter of the East.*

Betty B. Burch and Alle B. Cole (Eds.), *Asian Political Systems: Readings on China, (Japan, India and Pakistan,* Van Nostrand, USA, 1968).

Bhabani Sengupta, *Fulcrum of Asia: Relations Among China, India, Pakistan and USSR* (Konark, New Delhi 1988).

________*(Ed.), Regional Cooperation and Development in South Asia,* Vols. I and II (South Asia Publication, New Delhi, 1986.

Bhabani Sengupta, *South Asian Perspectives: Seven Nations in Conflict and Cooperation* (BRPC, Delhi, 1988).

________*,Soviet Perspectives of Contemporary Asia.*

Bimal Prasad (Ed.), *Regional Cooperation in South Asia.*

Problems and Prospects (Vikas, New Delhi, 1989).

B.K. Madan, *Towards Monetary Cooperation in South Asia* (Concept, New Delhi,1986).

B.M. Jain, *South Asia, India and the United States* (RBSA, Jaipur, 1987).

Bruce Russet, *International Regions and the International System* (Rand McNally, Chicago, 1967).

Charanjit Chanana (Ed.), *South Asia : The Changing Environment* (MERB Book Shelf, New Delhi, 1979).

Craig Baxter, Y. Malik *et al., Government and Politics in South Asia* (Vangaurd, Lahore, 1988).

________*,Bangladesh, A new nation in an old setting* (West-view Press, London, 1984).

Darshan Singh, *Soviet Foreign Policy Documents* (New Delhi, 1988).

David Seddon, *Nepal - A State of Poverty* (Vikas, New Delhi, 1987).

Denis Wright, *Bangladesh, The Indian Ocean Relations* (1971-75).

Dieter Braun, *Indian Ocean - Region of Conflict or Zone of Peace,* (Oxford University Press, Delhi, 1983).

D.P. Kumar, *Nepal : Year of Decison* (National, New Delhi, 1980).

Emajuddin Ahmed (Ed.), *Foreign Policy of Bangladesh : A Small State's Imperative* (Dhaka University Press, Dhaka, 1984).

Gopal Krishna (Ed.), *Contributions to South Asian Studies* (Oxford University Press, New Delhi, 1982).

Hassan Gardezi and Jamil Rashid (Eds.), *Pakistan : The Roots of Dictatorship,* (Oxford University Press, New Delhi, 1983).

H.N. Mishra, *Bhutan - Problems and Politics* (Heritage, New Delhi, 1982).

Henry A. Kissinger, *Years of Upheaval* (Vikas, New Delhi, 1982).

Kalim Bahadur (Ed.), *South Asia in Transition : Conflict and Tensions* (Patriot, New Delhi, 1986).

K.L. Kamal and Prabha Arun, *Pakistan : Democracy at the Crossroads* (Yuvraj Publishers, Jaipur, 1988).

K.P. Mishra *et al.*, *South Asia - Pacific Perspectives and Strategies* (Continental, New Delhi, 1988).

K.P. Mishra and V.D. Chopra, *South Asia Pacific Region - Emerging Trends* (International Institute for South Asia - Pacific Studies, New Delhi, 1988).

K.R. Singh, *Indian Ocean : The Big Power Presence and the Local Response* (Manohar, New Delhi, 1977).

K. Satyamurthy (Ed.), *South Asian Regional Cooperation* (Institute of Asian Studies, Hyderabad, 1982).

Larry Diamond, Juan J. Linz and S.M. Lipset (Eds.), *Democracy in Asia* (Vistaar Publications, New Delhi, 1989).

Leo E. Rose, *The Politics of Bhutan* (Cornhell University Press, Ithaca, 1977).

Lok Raj Baral, *The Politics of Balanced Interdependence : Nepal and SAARC* (Sterling, New Delhi, 1988).

Lois J. Cantori and Steven L Spiegel (Eds.), *International Politics Region : A Comparative Approach* (Prentice Hall, New Jersy, 1970).

M. Mahmood, *Regional Integration in South Asia : Perspectives and Prospects* (S. Chand and Co., New Delhi, 1987).

M.A. Zafar Shah, *India and the Superpowers* (Vikas, New Delhi, 1983).

M.D. Dharamdasni (Ed.), *South Asian Regional Cooperation* (Shalimar, Varanasi, 1985).

________, *Contemporary South Asia* (Shalimar, Delhi, 1985).

M.J. Akabar, *India : The Seige Within* (Penguin, Bombay, 1985).

————————, *Nehru : The Making of India* (Viking, Delhi, 1988).

M.S. Agwani *et al.* (Eds.), *South Asia : Stability and Regional Cooperation* (CRRID, Chandigarh, 1983).

Pandav Nayak (Ed.), *Pakistan - Dilemma of a Developing State* (Aalekh, Jaipur, 1985).

________ (Ed.) *Pakistan - Society and Political* (South Asia Publications, New Delhi, 1989).

Partha S. Ghosh, Cooperation *and Conflict in South Asia* (Manohar, New Delhi, 1989).

P.C. Mathur (E.d.), *Government and Politics in South Asia*, Vol. I and II (S.A.P., Jaipur, 1985).

P.K. Mishra, *Dhaka Summit and SAARC* (K.P. Bhagchi and Co., Calcutta, 1986).

P. Ramaswamy, *New Delhi and Sri Lanka* (Allied, New Delhi, 1987).

Ponna Wignaraja and Akmal Hussain (Eds.), *The Challenge in South Asia : Development, Democracy and Regional Cooperation* (Sage, New Delhi, 1989).

Pradeep Bhargava, *Political Economy of Sri Lanka* (Navrang, New Delhi, 1987).

Pran Chopra, *Contemporary Pakistan* (Vikas, New Delhi, 1983).

P. Sharan, *Government and Politics of Sri Lanka* (MPBC, New Delhi, 1986).

Rakesh Gupta, *India : Security Problems in the Nineties* (Patroit, New Delhi, 1989).

Rajendra Sareen, *Pakistan : The India Factor* (Allied, New Delhi, 1986).

Ram Rahul, *Royal Bhutan* (ABC, New Delhi, 1983).

Ramakant (Ed.), *China and South Asia* (South Asia Publications, New Delhi, 1988).

Ratna Tikoo, *Indo-Pak Relations - Politics Divergence and Convergence* (National, New Delhi, 1987).

Ronald Y. Yalem, *Regionalism and World Order* (Public Affairs Press, Washington D.C., 1965).

Roy S. Cline, James Arnold and Roger, E. Kanet, *Asia in Soviet Global Strategy* (Westview Press, London, 1987).

Richard A. Falk and Saul H. Mendlovitz (Eds.), *Regional Politics and World Order* (W.H. Freeman, San Fransisco, 1973).

Susanne H. Rudolf and L. Rudolf, *In Pursuit of Lakshmi* (Orient Longman, Bombay, 1987).

Sajjad Hyder, *Foreign Policy of Pakistan*, (Vangaurd, Lahore, 1987).

Satish Kumar (Ed.), *Yearbook of India's Foreign Policy*.

S.D. Muni, *Foreign Policy of Nepal* (National, New Delhi, 1973).

————, *Nepal : An Assertive Monarchy* (Chetna, New Delhi, 1977).

————, Nand Anuradha Muni, *Regional Cooperation in South Asia* (National, New Delhi, 1984).

Srikanth Paranjpe, *India and South Asia Since 1971* (Radiant, New Delhi, 1986).

Sisir Gupta, *Kashmir—A Study in India-Pakistan Relations* (Asia Publishing House, Bombay, 1966).

S.S. Bindra, *Determinants of Pakistan's Foreign Policy* (Deep and Deep, New Delhi, 1988).

————, *India and Her Neighbours : A Study of Political, Economic and Cultural Relations and Interactions* (Deep and Deep, New Delhi, 1985).

————, *India - Bangladesh Relations* (Deep and Deep, New Delhi, 1982).

Stanely Wolpert, *Boots of Confrontation in South Asia* (Oxford University Press, New York, 1982).

Shelton U. Kodikara, *South Asian Strategic Issues : Sri Lankan Perspectives (Sage, New Delhi, 1990).*

Stephen P. Cohen, *The Security of South Asia : American and Asian Perspectives* (Vistaar, New Delhi, 1987).

Sudarshan Chawla, *Changing Patterns of Security and Stability in Asia* (Praeger, New York, 1980).

Surjit Mansingh, *India's Search for Power : Indira Gandhi's Foreign Policy (1966-82)*, (Sage, Berverly Hills, Ca., 1984).

Theodore A. Couloumbis and James H. Wolfe, *Introduction to International Relations: Power and Justice* (Delhi, 1982).

T.V. Kunhi Krishnan, *The Unfriendly Friends : India and America* (New Delhi, 1974).

T. Nirmala Devi, *Regional Economic Cooperation in South Asia* (Chugh Publications, Allahabad, 1989).

T.N. Kaul, *India and Asia* (Lancer International, New Delhi, 1989).

Urmila Phadnis, S.D. Muni *et al.* (Eds.), *Domestic Conflicts in South Asia*, Vol. I, New Delhi, 1986).

Urmila Phadnis and E.D. Luithui, *Maldives - Winds of Change in Atoll State* (South Asia Publications, New Delhi, 1985).

V.B. Kulkarni, *Pakistan - Its Origins and Relations with India* (Sterling, New Delhi, 1988).

V.D. Chopra (Ed.), *Pakistan and Asian Peace* (Patriot, New Delhi, 1985).

———— (Ed.), *Studies in Indo-Pak Relations* (Patriot, New Delhi, 1984).

V.P. Dutt, *India's Foreign Policy* (Vani Educational Books, New Delhi, 1984).

Vijay Kumar, *India and Sri Lanka - China Relations (1948-84)*, (New Delhi, 1986).

Virendra Narain and B.S. Upreti (Eds.), *SAARC : A Study of Perspectives and Politics* (South Asia Publications, New Delhi, 1991).

ARTICLES :

Abul Ahsan, 'New Horizons for SARC', *Mainstream*. Annual, 1987.

A.B. Vajpayee, 'India and the Changing International Order', *Indian and Foreign Review*, Vol. 15, No.9, 15 February 1978.

A.B. Noorani, 'The Neighbourhood', *Seminar* (317), Annual, January 1986.

A.G. Naidu, 'Bhutan Looks outwards'. Its search for identity, *The Indian Journal of Political Science*, Vol. 47, No.4, Oct-Dec. 1986.

Amit Gupta, Pakistan's Arms Acquistions and Its implications for India', *IDSA Journal*, Vol. 16, No.2, 1986.

Anirudha Gupta, 'SAARC and Regional Cooperation', *Mainstream* Vol. 29, No.22, March 21, 1992.

A.R. Bhuyan, 'Intra-Regional Trade Expansion in South Asia.' Trends, Abstacles and Prospects, *South Asia Journal*, Vol. 4., No.1, July-Sept. 1990.

Asmi Raza, 'Patch up with Nepal.' *The third concept*, Vol.4, No.49, March 1991.

Arif A. Waquif, 'Exploring Potential areas of Industrial Cooperation in South Asia *South Asia Journal*, Vol.1, No.1, October-Dec., 1987.

Bhabani 'Sengupta, Pakistan; Towards an Understanding,' *Economic and Political Weekly*, Vol. 26, No. 49, 7 December 1991.

________,Heat in the Himalayas, *Monthly Public Opinion Surveys*, April 1989.

Bharat Wariawala, 'Timid Search for Status', *Seminar* (256) December, 1980.

________, 'New World Order Abarted ?' *Seminar* (389) Annual, January 1992.

Bibek Debroy, 'South-South Cooperation', *Foreign Trade Review*, October-December, 1988.

B. Mohanan, 'Community Formation in SAARC's External Relations: Lessons from ASEAN, '*The Indian Journal of Political Science*, Vol. 51, No. 1, January-March, 1990.

Bruce Mathews, 'Sri Lanka in 1988 : Seeds of Accord', *Asian Survey*, Vol. 29, No.2, February 1989.

Byran Pfaffenberger, 'The Cultural Dimensions of Tamil Separatism in Sri Lanka', *Asian Survey*, Vol.21, No.1, November 1981.

C.A. Perumal, 'South Asian Relations : Problems and Prospects', *The Indian Journal of Polotical Science*, Vol. 49, No. 1, Jan. - March 1988.

________ and R. Thandavan, 'Ethnic Violence in Sri Lanka : Causes and Consequences', *Indian Journal of Political Science*, Vol. 50, No. 1, January - March 1989.

Craig Baxter, 'Bangladesh in 1990', *Asian Survey*, Vol. 31, No. 2, February 1991.

________and Syedur Rahiman, 'Bangladesh Votes - 1991: Building Democracy Internally', *Asian Survey*, Vol. 31, No. 8, August 1991.

C. Raja Mohan, 'Indian Strategic Environment in the 1990s', *Monthly Public Opinion Surveys*, Feb., March, April 1990.

Devin T. Hagetry, 'India's Regional Security Doctrine', *Asian Survey*, Vol. 31, No. 4, April 1991.

Dhruba Kumar, 'Managing Nepal's India Policy', *Asian Survey*, Vol. 30, No. 7, July 1990.

Dar Bahadur Bishta, 'Nepal in 1988 - Many losses, Some gains', *Asian Survey*, Vol. 29, No. 2, February 1989.

Emajuddin Ahmed and D.R.J.A. Nazneen, 'Islam in Bangladesh', Revivalism and Power Politics, *Asian Survey*, Vol. 30, No. 8, August 1990.

Gamani Corea, 'Regional Cooperation in South Asia : Perspective and Prospects', *South Asia Journal*, Vol. 1, No. 3, July - September, 1987.

Gurcharan Singh Dhanjal, 'SAARC : A Summit Fiasco', *Mainstream*, 14 December, 1991.

__________'SAARC on the Move?', *Mainstream*, 11 January, 1992.

Howard Wiggins, 'US-Soviet Relations Across the Arc of Rimland Asia', *Asian Survey*, Vol. 23, No. 8, Aug. 1980.

Imtiaz H. Bokhari, 'South Asian Regional Cooperation : Progress, Problems, Potential and Prospects', *Asian Survey*, Vol. 25, No. 4, April 1985.

Ishtihaq Hussain, 'Bangladesh - India Relations : Problems and Prospects', *Asian Survey*, Vol. 28, No. 11, November, 1988.

Jay W. Scrybe, 'Demand for Carving of Bhutan Unjustified', *Link*, 12 January, 1992.

Jivogin Jagic, 'Non-Alignment and Asia', *India Quarterly*, Vol. 44, No. 1 & 2, Jan. - June 1988.

J. Laxminarsimha Rao, 'China and India's Security', *ISDA Journal*, Vol. 1, No. 1, October - December 1991.

John W. Garver, 'China - India Rivalry in Nepal: The Clash over Arms Sales', *Asian Survey*, Vol. 31, No. 10, October 1991.

J.P. Anand, 'India's Indian Ocean Neighbours', *Monthly Public Opinion Surveys*, Vol. 34, No. 8, May 1989.

Jyothirmoy Banerjee, 'Hot and Cold Diplomacy in Indo-Pak Relations', *Asian Survey*, Vol. 23, No. 3, March 1983.

Kamal Hussain, 'Bangladesh's Sovereignty and an Independent Non-aligned Foreign Policy', *Man and Development*, Vol. 7, No. 4, December 1985.

Kamaljeet Singh, 'Bhutan Facing Troubles', *World Focus*, November - December 1990.

K.D. Kapur, 'Nuclear non-proliferation Regime and the US', *India Quarterly*, Vol. 44, No. 3 & 4, July - Dec. 1988.

K.K. Bhargava, 'SAARC at Male : Retrospect and Prospect', *South Asia Journal*, Vol. 4, No. 3, Jan. - March 1991.

K.P.Bhanumathi, 'Bhutan's Crisis Boies over', *World Focus*, Nov. - Dec. 1990.

K.P. Mishra, 'Regional Peace and Security : Coalescence and Clash in Indo-Pak Relations', *India Quarterly*, Vol. 40, No. 3 & 4, July - December 1984.

K. Subramaniyan, 'India and the Security of the Subcontinent', *India Quarterly*, Vol. 36, No. 3, July - Sept. 1980.

Leo E. Rose, 'The Himalayan Border States : "Buffers" in transition' *Asian Survey*, Vol. 3, No. 2, Feb, 1963.

L.P. Singh, 'Regional Power and Global Power in Arms Control - India and America and Nuclear Affairs', *India Quarterly*, Vol. 35, No. 3, July - Sept. 1978.

Lok Raj Baral, 'Nepal in 1986 - Problem of Political Management', *Asian Survey*, Vol. 27, No. 3, Feburary 1987.

__________India and the South Asian Security : A Nepali Perspective', *South Asia Journal*, Vol. 4, No. 4, April 1991.

Leszek Buszynaki, 'ASEAN : A Changing Regional Role', *Asian Survey*, Vol. 27, No. 7, July 1987.

Manorama Kohli, 'Indian Foreign Policy : A Geopolitical Perspective', *India Quarterly*, Vol. 46, No. 4, Oct. - Dec. 1990.

__________'Bhutan's Changing Strategic Perceptions,' *India Quarterly*, Vol. 42, No. 2, April - June 1986.

Marshall R. Singer, 'Sri Lanka in 1990', *Asian Survey*, Vol. 31, No. 2, February 1991.

__________'New Realities in Sri Lankan Politics', *Asian Survey*, Vol. 30, No. 4, April 1990.

Martin Walker, 'George Bush's New World Order', *Mainstream*, 16 February, 1991.

Masroor Ahmed Beg, 'Intra-SAARC Trade : A Dwindling Feature', *India Quarterly*, Vol. 46, No. 1, Jan. - March 1990.

Maya Chaddha, 'Reagan's Strategy in South Asia', *India Quarterly*, Vol. 38, No. 3 & 4, July - December 1982.

Mehrunnisa Ali, 'Soviet-Pak ties : Soviet Union in the Afghan Crisis', *Asian Survey*, Vol. 23, No. 9, Sept. 1983.

M.G. Kabir, 'Religion, Language and Nationalism in Bangladesh', *Journal of Contemporary Asia*, Vol. 17, No. 4, 1987.

Michael Brecher, 'International Relations and Asian Studies : The Subordinate State System of Southern Asia', *World Politics*, Vol. 15, No. 2. 1967.

Mohammad Ayoob, 'India-Pakistan and Superpower Rivalry', *World Today* (London), Vol. 38, No. 5, May 1982.

__________'The Primacy of Political', *Asian Survey*, Vol. 25, No. 4, April 1985.

M.S. Prabhakara, 'Bangladesh : Fears of "Big Brother" and Goodwill', *Strategic Digest*, December 1984.

M.S. Rajan, 'A Unipolar World Calls for Demaratization', *Mainstream*, 22 June 1991.

M.V. Bratersky and S.I. Lunov, 'India at the end of the Century : Transformation into a Regional Power', *Asian Survey*, Vol. 30, No. 10, October 1990.

N.A. Sharma, 'South Asia and the World Economy : The Emerging Perspectives', *South Asia Journal*, Vol. 4, No. 2, October - December, 1990.

Nalini Kanth Jha, 'Cultural and Philosophical roots of India's Foreign Policy', *International Studies*, Vol. 26, No. 1, January - March 1986.

Narayan Khadka, 'South Asian Association for Regional Cooperation : A Nepalese Perspective', *The Round Table* (309), 1989.

__________'Nepal's Stagnant Economy—The Panchyat Legacy', *Asian Survey*, Vol. 31. No. 8, August 1991.

Narotham Gaan, 'Superpower Involvement in India-Pak Relations', *India Quarterly*, Vol. 46, No. 4, October - December 1990.

N.C., 'Foreign Policy : New Challenges', *Mainstream*, 22 June 1991.

Niranjan Khilnani, 'India's Political and Economic Policies Towards her Neighbours', *The Round Table*, (301), 1987.

N.P. Banskota, 'Nepal : Towards Regional Economic Cooperation in South Asia *Asian Survey*, Vol. 21, No. 3, March 1981.

Pan Tongven, 'New World Order - According to Mr. Bush', *Mainstream*, 30 November 1991.

Parmanand, 'Nepal Today', *World Focus*, November - December, 1990.

Parminder S. Bhogal, 'Pakistan's India Policy from Zia to Benazir', *India Quarterly*, Vol. 45, No. 1, Janurary - March 1989.

Partha S. Ghosh, 'Terrorism and SAARC', *India Quarterly*, Vol. 43, No. 2, April - June 1987.

Peter J. Betrocci, 'Bangladesh in early 1980s : Practarian Politics in an Intermediate Region', *Asian Survey*, Vol. 22, No. 10, October 1982.

P.K. Srivastava and Rajni Kothari, 'SAARC', *Seminar* (324), August 1986.

Pramod Kumar Mishra, 'Determinants of Intra-regional Relations in South Asia', *India Quarterly*, Vol. 36, No. 1, January - March 1980.

__________'Towards a framework of South Asian Regional Cooperation : Colombo to Kattonandu', *Foreign Affairs Reports*, Vol. 31, No. 12, December 1982.

__________'South-South Cooperation and SAARC', *Monthly Public Opinion Surveys* July - August, 1989.

P.S. Jayaramu, 'Foreign Policy Behaviour of India, Afghanistan, and the Himalayan Kingdoms, A Balance of Power Interpretation', *The Indian Journal of Political Sciences*, Vol. 50, No. 4, October - December 1989.

Purshotham Bhattacharya, 'Foreign Policy Coordination in the European Community', *India Quarterly*, Vol. 46, No. 1, January - March 1990.

Rahiman Sobhan, 'Political Economy of South Asian Cooperation', *South Asia Journal*, Vol. 1, No. 3, January - March 1988.

Rai Singh, 'ASEAN : Comparison with SAARC', *World Focus*, Vol. 8, No. 1, January 1987.

Raj Kumar, 'Regional organizations and Third World Countries', *India Quarterly*, Vol. 47, No. 1-2, January - June 1991.

Rajendra Prasad, 'Revising South Asian Security', *ISDA Journal*, Vol. 1, No. 1, October - December 1991.

Rajiv Kumar, 'Coordination of Economic Policies in South Asia : Prospects and Problems and Modalities', *South Asia Journal*, Vol. 1, No. 3, July - September 1988.

Resul B. Rais, 'An Appraisal of US Strategies in the Indian Ocean', *Asian Survey*, Vol. 23, No. 9, September, 1983.

__________'Pakistan in 1988', *Asian Survey*, Vol. 29, No. 2, February 1989.

__________'Pakistan in Regional and Global Power Struction', *Asian Survey*, Vol. 31, No. 4, April, 1991.

Rathinam Indurthy, 'Fragility of Democracy in Pakistan : The Military as the Root Cause', *Indian Journal of Political Science*, Vol. 52, No. 3, July - September 1991.

Ravinder Kumar, 'India, Pakistan and Bangladesh : An Overview, 1990.

Riaz Hassan, 'Religion, Society and the State of Pakistan : Pirs and Politics', *Asian Survey*, Vol. 27, No. 5, May 1987.

Rohiteshwar Dubey, 'Indophobia as the Oilment of SAARC', *The Indian Journal of Political Science*, Vol. 49, No. 1, January - March 1988.

R.S. Jadav, 'Regimes in International Politics : A Study of the Indian Ocean', *India Quarterly*, Vol. 47, No. 1-2, January - June 1991.

R.V.R. Chandrasekhar Rao, 'Regional Cooperation in South Asia', *The Round Table* (293), 1985.

Salahuddin Ahimed, 'The identity of the sub-continent', India, *International Centre Quarterly*, Summer, 1980.

Satish Kumar, 'A Note on Pakistan and Regional Security', *India Quarterly*, Vol. 36, No. 4, July - September 1980.

S.D. Muni, 'Beneficial Dilateratism in South Asia', *India Quarterly,* Vol. 35, No. 4, October - December 1979.

__________'India and Regionalism in South Asia : A Political Perspective', *International Studies,* Vol. 17, 1978.

__________'Building Regionalism from below', *Asian Survey,* Vol. 25, No. 4, April 1985.

__________'Sino-Bhutanese Boundary and Implications for *India', Mainstream,* 14 June 1986.

__________'Reaganis South Asia Policy : Strategic Dimensions', *IDSA Journal,* Vol. 16, No. 2, 1986.

__________'South-South Cooperation in Southern Asia', *Man and Development,* September 1990.

__________'India and Post Cold-War Order - Opportunities and Challenges', *Asian Survey,* Vol. 31, No. 9, September 1991.

Shah Alam, 'State Religion in Bangladesh : A Critique of the Eighth Amendment to the Constitution', *South Asia Journal,* Vol. 4, No. 3, January - March 1991.

Shamshul Haq, 'Beyond Bangalore', *South Asia Journal,* Vol.1, No. 1, October - December 1989.

Shanta K. Hennayaka, 'The Peace Accord and the Tamils in Sri Lanka', *Asian Survey,* Vol. 29, No. 4, April 1989.

Shelton U. Kodikara, 'Continuity and Change in Sri Lankan Foreign Policy', *Asian Survey,* Vol. 20, No. 9, September 1980.

__________'The Changing Crisis in Sri Lanka : The J.V.P., The Indian Troops and Tamil Politics', *Asian Survey,* Vol. 29, No. 7, July 1989.

__________'The International Environment and Indo-Pak Power Struggle in 1990s : A View from Sri Lanka', *South Asia Journal,* Vol. 4, No. 2, October - December 1990.

Sisir Gupta, 'Issues for the Indo-Pak Summit', *India Quarterly,* Vol. 28, No. 2, April, 1972.

Sivananda Patnaik, 'Sri Lanka and South Asian Subsystem : A Study of Submacro International Politics, *India Quarterly,* Vol. 36, No. 2, April 1980.

S.M. Muztaba Razvi, 'Conflict and Cooperation in South Asia', *The Round Table* (299), 1986.

__________'India and the security of the Indian Ocean, South Asian States', *The Round Table* (311), 1989.

S. Nanjundan, 'A New World Order?' *Economic and Political Weekly,* June, 1-8, 1991.

S. Nihal Singh, 'Can the US and India be real friends?' *Asian Survey*, Vol. 23, No. 9, September 1983.

S. Nihal Singh, 'Why India goes to Moscow for Arms?' *Asian Survey*, Vol. 24, No. 7, July 1984.

________'SAARC and Indo-Pak ties,' *Monthly Public Opinion Surveys*, January 1989.

S.N. Kohli, 'Indian Ocean : Area of Tension' *India Quarterly*, Vol. 42, No. 2, April - June 1986.

Sridhar K. Khatri, 'South Asian Regional Cooperation : Its Implications for Nepal', *Asian Survey*, Vol. 25, No. 4, April 1985.

Srikanth Paranjpe, 'Gorbachev, Asian Pacific Security', *India Quarterly*, Vol. 46, No. 2 & 3, April - September 1990.

Sukhdev Shah, 'Bhutan's Economy', *Asian Survey*, Vol. 29, No. 8, August 1989.

Sukhamoy Chakravarthy, 'Vision of South Asian Region : A medium text perspective', *South Asia Journal*, Vol. 3, No. 4, April - June 1990.

Syed Azizul Ahisan and Bhumitra Chakma, 'Problems of National Integration in Bangladesh', *Asian Survey*, Vol. 29, No. 10, October 1989.

Syed Nazrul Islam, 'The Chittagong Hill Tracts in Bangladesh : Integrational Crisis between Centre and Periphery', *Asian Survey*, Vol. 21, No. 12, December 1987.

Syedur Rahman, 'Issues and Agenda for South Asian Regional Cooperation : A Bangladeshi Perspective', *Asian Survey*, Vol. 25, No. 4, April 1985.

Stephen P. Cohen, 'Security Issue in South Asia', *Asian Survey*, Vol. 13, No. 3, March 1975.

________'India within the Region', *Seminar*, July 1983.

Thomas Abraham, 'Sri Lanka and India : The Past and the Present,' *Man and Development*, Vol. 8, No. 3, September 1986.

T.K. Oommen, 'State and Religion in Multi-religions Nation States : The case of South Asia', *South Asia Journal*, Vol. 4, No. 1, July - September 1990.

T.N. Kaul, 'Panchasheel in Asia - Role of India', *India Quarterly*, Vol. 44, No. 1-2, January - June 1986.

Uma Singh, 'Erosion of Ruling Alliance in Pakistan', *Link*, 12 January, 1992.

Umashankar Phandis, 'Maldives Making Progress', *World Focus*, November - December 1990.

Urmila Phandis, 'Role of State in Sri Lanka's Ethnic Conflict', *Mainstream*, 24 November 1990.

__________'Ethnic Dynamics in South Asian States', *South Asia Journal*, Vol. 3, No. 3, January - March 1980.

V.N. Vishvanathan, 'Indo-Sri Lankan Relations towards confidence building', *India Quarterly*, Vol. 46, No. 1, January - March 1990.

V.P. Dutt, 'Relations with Neighbours', *World Focus*, Nos. 23-24, November - December 1981.

V.R. Panchamukhi, 'Cooperation in Industrial Development in the SAARC Region: Some Reflections', *South Asia Journal*, Vol. 4, No. 1, July - September 1990.

V. Suryanarayan, 'India's Sri Lanka Policy, A Need for Reappraisal', *South Asia Journal*, Vol. 4, No. 4, April - June, 1991.

__________'A Policy for Peace : On India-Sri Lanka Relations', *Frontline*, 11 October 1991.

William J. Barnds, 'India and America at odds', *International Affairs*, Vol. 49, No. 3, July 1973.

Yogendra K. Malik, 'The Rise of Hindu Militancy : India's Secular Democracy at Risk', *Asian Survey*, Vol. 29, No. 3, March 1989.

Y.S. Khanal, 'Political Economy of South Asian Cooperation', *South Asia Journal*, Vol. 3, No. 3, January - March 1990.

Zalmay Khalizad, 'Pakistan : The Making of a Nuclear Power', *Asian Survey*, Vol. 16, No. 6, June, 1976.

Zillur Rahman, 'Islam and Bengali Nationalism', *Asian Survey*, Vol. 25, No. 8, August 1985.

INDEX